Whitestein Series in Software Agent Technologies

Series Editors:
Marius Walliser
Stefan Brantschen
Monique Calisti
Thomas Hempfling

This series reports new developments in agent-based software technologies and agent-oriented software engineering methodologies, with particular emphasis on applications in various scientific and industrial areas. It includes research level monographs, polished notes arising from research and industrial projects, outstanding PhD theses, and proceedings of focused meetings and conferences. The series aims at promoting advanced research as well as at facilitating know-how transfer to industrial use.

About Whitestein Technologies

Whitestein Technologies AG was founded in 1999 with the mission to become a leading provider of advanced software agent technologies, products, solutions, and services for various applications and industries. Whitestein Technologies strongly believes that software agent technologies, in combination with other leading-edge technologies like web services and mobile wireless computing, will enable attractive opportunities for the design and the implementation of a new generation of distributed information systems and network infrastructures.

www.whitestein.com

Applications of Software Agent Technology in the Health Care Domain

Antonio Moreno
John L. Nealon
Editors

Birkhäuser Verlag
Basel · Boston · Berlin

Editors' addresses:

Antonio Moreno
Computer Science and Mathematics Department
University Rovira i Virgili
ETSE, Av. dels Països Catalans, 26
43007 Tarragona
Spain
e-mail: amoreno@etse.urv.es

John L. Nealon
Department of Computing
Oxford Brookes University
Wheatley Campus
Wheatley
Oxford OX33 1HX, UK
e-mail: johnnealon@brookes.ac.uk

2000 Mathematical Subject Classification 68T35, 68U35, 94A99

A CIP catalogue record for this book is available from the
Library of Congress, Washington D.C., USA

Bibliographic information published by Die Deutsche Bibliothek
Die Deutsche Bibliothek lists this publication in the Deutsche Nationalbibliografie;
detailed bibliographic data is available in the Internet at <http://dnb.ddb.de>.

ISBN 3-7643-2662-X Birkhäuser Verlag, Basel – Boston – Berlin

© 2003 Birkhäuser Verlag, P.O. Box 133, CH-4010 Basel, Switzerland
Part of Springer Science+Business Media
Cover design: Micha Lotrovsky, CH-4106 Therwil, Switzerland
Printed on acid-free paper produced from chlorine-free pulp. TCF ∞
Printed in Germany
ISBN 3-7643-2662-X

9 8 7 6 5 4 3 2 1   www.birkhauser.ch

Contents

Introduction: Agents in Health Care

John Fox

Agent technology has become a leading area of research in AI and computer science and the focus of a number of major initiatives. One of these is the AgentCities project funded by the European Union 5th Framework research programme (http://www.agentcities.org/). AgentCities is a federation of specialist communities with a common interest in agents, one of which is concerned with health care. In this book, John Nealon and Toni Moreno have brought together an interesting set of papers that discuss the many practical issues that arise in trying to build agent applications in medicine. The papers are not simply focused on the health care domain however: they also succeed in raising a number of theoretical issues of wide relevance to the general field of agent research.

In their introductory paper the editors identify two categories of agent systems: *individual agents* that are capable of carrying out cognitive functions autonomously (such as reasoning, decision-making and planning) and *distributed, multi-agent systems* which are "collections of autonomous agents that communicate between themselves to coordinate their activities in order to be able to solve collectively a problem that could not be tackled by any agent individually". Individual agent technologies offer platforms for building advanced expert systems to assist individual clinicians in their decision-making and workflow while distributed multi-agent systems have the potential to improve the operation of health care organizations, where failures of communication and coordination are known to be important sources of error.

To my knowledge, the first example of an agent system being used in a health care application was the AADCARE system developed by Jun Huang ([1], [2]) as part of the research activities carried out in another EU project, DILEMMA. The main aims of DILEMMA (see http://www.ehto.org/aim/volume2/dilemma.html) were to develop tools, methodologies and architectures with which to construct clinical decision support and workflow systems, and to build applications in general medical practice, hospital-based cancer care, and shared care of cancer and cardiology patients. The latter activity involved primary care physicians, nurses, and paramedics outside the hospital in consultation with hospital-based specialists. In order to develop a model for shared care, Huang took the DILEMMA decision support technology and put a "wrapper" around it to enable it to support simple conversations between individual DILEMMA agents. In this way, they could carry out such tasks as placing requests for information and services, and acknowledging and managing those requests.

Nealon and Moreno note that "the usual properties of intelligent agents match quite precisely with … needs in [the health care] field (basically autonomous, intelligent, proactive, collaborative and distributed)". Huang's work was an early indicator of this promise - and this is confirmed by the present collection of papers. The range of application domains, from organ transplantation to clinical trials; from hospital and nursing care to care in the community, and from the management of diabetes to the treatment of wounds and infections, is impressive.

Nealon and Moreno go on to say that the reason for this match is that medical care is characterised by a "vast open environment, characterised by shared and distributed decision making and management... requiring the communication of complex and diverse forms of information between a variety of clinical and other settings, as well as the coordination between groups of health care professionals with very different skills and roles". On the face of it, their belief is again corroborated by the range of individual and multi-agent functions that are exercised in this set of papers. Huang's agent was limited to *reasoning* and *decision-making,* but while these remain prominent requirements for the agents described in this collection we also find health care agents that *monitor, schedule, plan, teach* and *negotiate.*

In contrast to this substantial growth in cognitive functionality, I was surprised to see that there has been relatively little extension of Huang's communication scheme. The FIPA Agent Communication Language (ACL) provides the standard communication scheme for most of the multi-agent applications described in this collection. I expected that the need for precise and complex communication in Medicine, which must also be succinct and timely in safety-critical situations, would demand far more conversational expressiveness than the FIPA set currently offers.

On the other hand our formal understanding of agent communication languages is considerably greater than it was a decade ago. Unlike Huang's set of performatives the FIPA ACL has a clear compositional semantics, so the compositional semantics of the FIPA performatives might satisfy all the communicational requirements of the clinical workplace. However our knowledge of medical communications is probably too limited to be sure of this – a research question to be addressed perhaps?

This is just one interesting question raised by this timely and varied book, which is a valuable showcase for a range of projects, and a persuasive demonstration of the kinds of potential applications and services that agent systems can implement. The AgentCities consortium has done a great service in facilitating the creation of this research community, and Nealon and Moreno are to be thanked for editing the papers into such a stimulating volume. I suspect it marks the "end of the first phase" of research in this field and I think that the book should find an audience well beyond the specialist health care community

References

[1] Huang, J., Jennings, N.R., Fox, J., "Cooperation in distributed medical care" in *Proc. 2nd International Conference on Cooperative Information Systems*, 255-263, Toronto: Toronto University Press, 1994.
[2] Huang, J., Jennings, N.R., Fox, J., "Agent based approach to health care management" *Applied Artificial Intelligence*, 9, 401-420, 1995.

Advanced Computation Laboratory. Cancer Research UK. 44 Lincoln's Inn Fields. London WC2A 3PX.
E-mail address: jf@acl.icnet.uk

Agent-Based Applications in Health Care

John Nealon and Antonio Moreno

Abstract. In this paper we introduce the main issues related to the deployment of agent-based systems in health care. First, we comment on the characteristics of health care problems and we argue that multi-agent systems are a good choice to tackle problems with these features. This belief is supported with a number of exemplar applications of agent-based systems in medical domains. We also discuss several lines of research that have to be covered before multi-agent systems can be successfully deployed in real health care settings. We conclude that multi-agent systems do have an increasingly important role to play in health care domains, because they significantly enhance our ability to model, design and build complex, distributed health care software systems.

1. Introduction

Health care at all levels - local, regional, national and international - is a vast open environment characterized by shared and distributed decision making and management of care, requiring the communication of complex and diverse forms of information between a variety of clinical and other settings, as well as the coordination between groups of health care professionals with very different skills and roles. It is the aim of health care software systems to operate effectively in this environment, in order to meet the information needs of patients and health care providers. Practitioners in health care environments, in particular, require that the information is both timely and error-free, such that recommendations or decisions offered by the software systems are secure and trustworthy [1].

There is a growing interest in the application of agent-based techniques [2], [3] to problems in the medical domain1. In this paper we explain which are the characteristics of the problems in this area, and we argue that multi-agent systems are indeed an interesting tool to solve them, since the usual properties of intelligent agents match quite precisely with our needs in this field (basically with the requirement of having autonomous intelligent proactive collaborative entities in a distributed environment). This volume is another empirical confirmation of this claim, since it presents an extensive list of agent-based systems that are being developed across Europe to solve a wide range of problems in health care (from the management of organ and tissue transplants to the provision of personalised access to medical information to diabetic patients). All these systems are being developed by the members of the AgentCities.NET Working Group on Health Care Applications [7].

Despite the adequacy of multi-agent systems in the building of health care systems, it must be stressed that there are still many research topics that have to be thoroughly studied before multi-agent systems may be successfully deployed in real health care settings. Section 3 offers a summary of the main current research and development topics relevant to the application of agents to health care.

2. Agent-Based Systems in Health Care

2.1. Agents and Multi-Agent Systems

An agent is a software entity that applies Artificial Intelligence techniques to choose the best set of actions to perform in order to reach a goal specified by the user. It is normally assumed that they have the following properties:

- They can react timely and flexibly to the dynamic and unexpected changes in their environment.
- They have an autonomous and independent behaviour, which is not controlled by any external entity.
- They can take the initiative and perform proactively actions that may help them to reach their goals.
- They can communicate with users or other agents. Thus, they can exchange information, engage in complex negotiations, and coordinate their activities to cooperate in the joint resolution of a problem.
- Agents usually have reasoning, planning and learning capabilities that allow them to display an intelligent behaviour.

A multi-agent system [2], [3] might be defined as a collection of autonomous agents that communicate between themselves to coordinate their activities in order to be able to solve collectively a problem that could not be tackled by any agent individually. In recent years it has been argued that multi-agent systems may be considered as the latest software engineering paradigm [8], [9]. This kind of system may be used in domains with the following features:

- The knowledge required to solve the problem is spatially distributed in different locations.
- Several entities, while keeping their autonomous behaviour, have to join their problem-solving abilities to be able to solve a complex problem.
- The problems in the domain may be decomposed in different sub-problems, even if they have some kind of inter-dependencies.

2.2. Characteristics of Problems in the Health Care Domain

It is interesting to note that many problems that appear in health care share a number of similarities. Noting these similarities is a good first step towards finding a framework that may be used to approach most of these problems. Among the most important characteristics of problems in the medical field we can cite the following:

- It is very usual that the knowledge required to solve a problem is spatially distributed in different locations. For instance, the problem of patient scheduling [10, 11, 12] consists in scheduling the different tasks to be performed on a hospitalised patient (e.g. a number of different analysis and tests). Normally, each unit of the hospital keeps its own information about the patients hospitalised in that unit and about the schedule of the activities with the unit's equipment. There are units that provide services to all the other units of the hospital, such as X-rays or blood tests. It is not trivial to coordinate the schedule of different tests to be performed in different units, especially if, apart from the temporal restrictions derived from the separate location of different units, there are also medical restrictions among the tests (e.g. one test has to be performed at least two hours after another test).

- The solution of a problem involves the coordination of the effort of different individuals with different skills and functions, usually without the supervision of a single centralised coordinator. The provision of health care typically involves a number of individuals - inpatients, outpatients, physicians, nurses, carers, social workers, managers, receptionists, etc. - located in many different places. Patients could be at home, at work, in hospital, or on vacation, while the health care providers are often at a number of institutions or locations within institutions, providing services such as diagnosis, treatment, surgery, laboratory testing, radiography, and so on. All these people must coordinate their activities to provide the best possible treatment to the patient.

- Health care problems are quite complex, and finding standard software engineering solutions for them is not straightforward. For instance, coordinating the process of organ transplant in a country is not an easy task [13]. When a new organ is available, it is necessary to find very quickly the most appropriate receptor of the organ, which may be located in a medical centre hundreds of miles away from the donor's location. Furthermore, as commented above, each hospital keeps the data of the patients of that hospital who are in the waiting list for a certain type of organ. It would be quite difficult to design and implement a centralised complex system (e.g. a standard decision aid expert system) to solve this coordination problem.

- In the last few years there has been a shift in health care practice towards health care promotion, shared patient-provider decision-making and managed care, creating an increased demand for information and online services [14, 15]. The shared decisions and actions of all concerned need to be coordinated to make sure that the care is efficient and effective. To facilitate this decision-making task, and to ensure the communication and coordination processes run smoothly, software systems are needed that will reduce errors in diagnosis and treatment, deliver health care to remote locations, improve medical training and education, and make health care information more accessible to patients, their families and carers, alike. To meet these needs the software systems must be proactive in anticipating the information and knowledge needs of users and deliver it in a timely manner, support synchronous and asynchronous communication, and facilitate collaborative decision making between the various individuals involved in the process of managing and delivering health care services.

- There is a great amount of medical knowledge available on the Internet. It is necessary to provide ways of accessing the most relevant information as easily, flexibly and timely as possible. This access to medical information is necessary both for medical practitioners and for patients. In the former case, they have to be aware of all the new medicines, techniques and treatments appearing in their field of expertise; however, most practitioners lack the time to search for all this information and filter the one they need exactly. In the latter, citizens demand a more active role in the management of their care, and they want to find relevant information as easily as possible (but they usually lack the skills to search for the most adequate knowledge relevant to their specific personal needs). In both cases it is important to receive appropriate information from useful and reliable sources in a proactive way, without having to devote time and effort to look for, analyse, evaluate and filter it.

2.3. Adequacy of Agent-Based Systems to Health Care Problems

We would like to argue in this paper that multi-agent systems offer an appropriate tool to tackle this kind of problems. Some reasons to support this claim are the following:

- The components of a multi-agent system may be running in different machines, located in many different places. Each of the agents may keep part of the knowledge required to solve the problem, such as patient records held in different departments within a hospital or in several hospitals, clinics and surgeries, in an insurance company, or in government organisations. Therefore, multi-agent systems offer a natural way of attacking inherently distributed problems.

- One of the main properties of an intelligent agent is sociability. Agents are able to communicate between themselves, using some kind of agent communication language, in order to exchange any kind of information. In that way they can engage in complex dialogues, in which they can negotiate, coordinate their actions and collaborate in the solution of a problem (e.g. different units of a hospital may collaborate in the process of patient scheduling [10, 11, 12].

- When a problem is too complex to be solved in a single system, it is usual to decompose it in subproblems (which will probably not be totally independent of each other). In multi-agent systems there are techniques of distributed problem solving [16], in which a group of agents may dynamically discuss how to partition a problem, how to distribute the different subtasks to be solved among them, how to exchange information to solve possible dependences between partial solutions, and how to combine the partial results into the solution of the original problem. Thus, multi-agent systems can handle the complexity of solutions through decomposition, modelling and organising the interrelationships between components.

- Agents can also be used to provide information to doctors and patients. There are information agents (also called Internet agents, [17], that are specialised in retrieving information from different sources, analysing the obtained data, selecting the information in which a user is especially interested, filtering redundant or irrelevant information, and presenting it to the user with an interface adapted to the user's preferences.

- Another important property of agents is their proactivity; their ability to perform tasks that may be beneficial for the user, even if he/she has not explicitly demanded those tasks to be executed. Using this property they may find relevant information and show it to the user before he/she has to request it. For instance, if it knows that the user has had heart problems in the past and might need this information urgently, a personal agent that also knows that the user is about to travel abroad could look for information about the medical centres in the towns to be visited that have a cardiology department.

- The basic characteristic of an intelligent agent is its autonomy. Each agent takes its own decisions, based on its internal state and the information that it receives from the environment. Therefore, agents offer an ideal paradigm to implement systems in which each component models the behaviour of a separate entity, that wants to keep its autonomy and independence from the rest of the system (e.g. each unit of the hospital may keep its private data, or each hospital may use a different policy to rank the patients that are waiting for an organ transplant).

Thus, we think that the basic properties of intelligent agents (autonomy, proactivity, social ability) and the features of multi-agent systems (management of distributed information, communication and coordination between separate autonomous entities) suggest that they offer a good option to consider when trying to solve problems in health care domains.

2.4. Fields of Application within Health Care

Intelligent agents have already been proposed to deal with many different kinds of problems in the health care domain (see [4], [5], [6], [7] and the rest of the chapters of this volume). Just to give a short list of examples, some of the fields in which they are already being applied are the following:

- Patient scheduling: in patient appointment scheduling, where medical procedures have become more complex and their tests and treatments more interrelated, manual and traditional software solutions have been shown to be inadequate while a multi-agent solution gave significantly improved results [10, 11, 12]. The complexities of medical appointment scheduling have been successfully formalised and implemented in an agent framework [18].
- Organ and tissue transplant management: the agent-based coordination of tissue or organ transplants across a hospital [19, 20, 21] could provide significant improvements in the time required to pull together the resources required for a transplant operation. This approach could also be feasible at a regional level where each hospital has a list of waiting patients, and when an organ is available somewhere in the region, the hospital transplant coordinators must get in touch and quickly find the most appropriate recipient [13].
- Community care: coordinating all the activities that have to be performed in order to provide an efficient health care to the citizens of a community (especially older or disabled citizens). Agents can provide remote care monitoring and information for such groups as the elderly and chronically ill. There is an elderly care management system [22] in which one agent is associated with each elderly person that is responsible for receiving medical data, giving reminders to the person, and alerting the medical centre if something is wrong.
- Information access: the deluge of medical information available on the Internet has led to the development of information agents to collect and organise this information, such as the Multi-Agent Retrieval Vagabond on Information Networks (MARVIN) [23], developed by the Health On the Net Foundation and the Swiss Institute of

Bioinformatics, or a multi-agent system that helps to manage the UK National Electronic Library for Communicable Diseases [24]. An information agent, based on a user profile, has proactively performed the role of locating, assessing, retrieving, filtering and presenting information from many distributed sources on a periodic basis [25]. An intelligent user interface to adapt to a clinicians requirements, specialism and the characteristics of diabetic patients whose records are being accessed uses a multi-agent framework to coordinate these possibly conflicting requirements [26]. It has also been implemented a multi-agent system that provides mobile users with information about the medical centres or the doctors available in a particular town, and that lets the user access his/her medical record or book a visit to be examined by a doctor [27].

- Decision support systems: A distributed decision support system based on the multi-agent paradigm can monitor the status of a hospitalised patient and help to diagnose the state of the patient [28], or support co-operative medical decision- making [29], [30].
- Training: agents can help to improve medical training and education in distance-learning tutoring systems [31].
- Internal hospital tasks: Patient information retrieval and workflow management using agent communication techniques and medical ontologies is being applied to the management of patients suffering from stroke [32, 33]. A cooperative multi- agent framework can support the heterogeneous transaction workflow process among the people involved in patient care management [34]. Multi-agent systems have also been suggested for monitoring the application of medical protocols [35], or controlling the usage of restricted use antibiotics [36].
- Senior citizen care: a group of special interest for the application of agent-based systems are the senior and the disabled citizens, to whom this technology could be useful to help to increase their ability to lead an independent life. Those agent systems have to be devised to provide aid in carrying out activities of daily living, and health care maintenance. In addition, they will provide links to the outside world, including entertainment and information, and will facilitate communication with family and the environment. Their functions may include standardised behavioural assessments useful in medical monitoring. These kinds of tools may be used to facilitate the health care and social interaction of senior citizens person, and may delay their institutionalisation by prolonging the period of relative independence [37]. A European IST project, TeleCARE, aims to design and develop a configurable agent-based framework for virtual communities focused on supporting assistance to elderly people employing tele-supervision and tele- assistance [38].

3. Research and Development Challenges

There are several issues that must be addressed if multi-agent systems are to be successfully deployed in real world health care applications. A discussion of the most significant of these follows.

3.1. Communication standards

Health care systems are complex, diverse and dispersed. Consequently, the development, dissemination and utilization of common communication standards, vocabularies and ontologies are and will be central to the development of multi-agent systems in health care. In the main, communication standards (sometimes called specifications or protocols) already exist. For some time the EU and US standardization bodies for health care information and communications technology have been overseeing the development of communications standards. The EUs CEN/TC 251 [39] aim is to achieve compatibility and interoperability between independent systems, to support clinical and administrative procedures, technical methods to support interoperable systems as well as requirements regarding safety, security and quality. The two most well known US standardization bodies, the American Society for Testing and Materials Committee on Healthcare Informatics (ASTM E31) [40] and Health Level Seven (HL7) [41], are involved in similar work. ASTM E31 is developing standards related to the architecture, content, storage, security, confidentiality, functionality, and communication of information. HL7 is mainly concerned with protocol specifications for application level communications among health data acquisition, processing, and handling systems. Its scope is wide in that it attempts meet the communication requirements of entire health care organisations, while most other efforts focus on the requirements of a particular department, whereas most standards organisations produce standards for a particular healthcare domain such as pharmacy, medical devices, imaging or insurance (claims processing) transactions. HL7s domain is clinical and administrative data. "Level Seven" refers to the highest level of the International Standards Organisation's communications model for Open Systems Interconnection. HL7 defines the data to be exchanged, the timing of the interchange, and the communication of certain errors to the application. The seventh level supports such functions as security checks, participant identification, availability checks, exchange mechanism negotiations and, most importantly, data exchange structuring.

3.2. Ontologies

Ontologies are being developed specifically for health care applications. The best known examples are GALEN [42], the Unified Medical Language System (UMLS) [43], Systematized Nomenclature of Human and Veterinary Medicine (SNOMED) [44]. The aim of GALEN is to produce a computer-based multilingual coding system for medicine. The GALEN Programme is developing a clinical terminology - the GALEN Common Reference Model for medical concepts. The medical concepts represented can be represented using a scheme that can both be manipulated by computers and accessible to health care professionals. The representation scheme that is being used to build the GALEN Common Reference Model is known as GRAIL - the GALEN Representation And Integration Language. It is intended for use by clinical application builders, both when developing clinical applications, and as a run- time resource when those applications are in service. The U.S. National Library of Medicine (NLM)'s UMLS project develops and distributes multi-purpose, electronic "Knowledge Sources" and associated lexical programs, for use in the development of systems concerned with patient records, digital libraries, Web and bibliographic retrieval, natural language processing, and decision support. The UMLS project is a long-term NLM research and development effort designed to facilitate the retrieval and integration of information from multiple machine-readable biomedical information sources. Major barriers to effective retrieval and integration of information from these sources include the variety of vocabularies and classifications used in different sources and by different users and the sheer number and wide distribution of potentially relevant information sources. These barriers deter health care professionals and researchers from using available machine-readable information and also hamper the development of effective search interfaces that might assist these users. The UMLS is a relational database connecting by concept over 60 vocabularies, thesauri, medical problem lists, etc. Its purpose is to make it easy for health professionals, medical librarians, and researchers to retrieve and integrate information from different machine-readable sources as computer-based patient records, databanks, bibliographic and full text databases, and expert systems. SNOMED's design is based on the premise that a detailed and specific nomenclature is essential to accurately reflect, in computer readable format, the complexity and diversity of information found in a patient record. SNOMED is designed for applications such as telemedicine, population-based outcomes analysis, cost-effectiveness studies, practice guidelines and the integration of electronic medical record information into a single data structure. Nevertheless, the story on ontologies is not as clear as that on communication standards. Although bioinformatics and health care informatics are fields that have active communities developing ontologies, as we have seen with GALEN, UMLS and SNOMED, their use has lagged behind their potential, despite the huge drive by health care professionals to bring health care information into clinical workstations and onto the Internet. Why is this? GALEN provides a common terminology that is currently of limited scope, while UMLS lacks a strong organisational structure, and SNOMED provides only diagnosis nomenclature and codification. Those who are building health care applications are using ontologies that have been or are being developed to meet specific needs, each with its own representation of the world, suitable to the purpose it has been developed for. There is as yet no common ontology. The experience of system developers [45] strongly suggests that the development of a single or a small number of ontologies for the health care domains is non-productive since no single domain requires such an ontology, and the overlap between ontologies is often minimal. Perhaps, this challenge will eventually be taken up in the mould of CYC [46], but that is not likely in the immediate future. Alternatively, machine learning techniques for the automatic construction of ontologies are being developed [47, 48, 49, 50]. In the meantime, researchers working in related areas are sharing and extending existing ontologies.

3.3. Security and privacy issues

Security is concerned with the protection of information from unauthorised access while stored and communicated, and privacy protection with the avoidance of unnecessary identification. The increasing dependence on information and communication technologies in health care organisations in order to collect, transmit, store, and assess data has brought the dual issues of security and privacy to the fore. It is accepted that medical data, such as genome information, medical records and other personal information must be treated with the greatest respect with regard to privacy and privacy [51]. The European Union has been enforcing the protection of medical data of individuals since 1995 [52], and in many countries, such as in Spain, these recommendations are among the most modern state laws that address the specific protection of this kind of data. Recently a US law that regulates the treatment of medical data was passed [53]. This law establishes which rules must be followed by the software business in this field, and the fines that will be applied to those that do not comply with the regulations. This text, however, does not force any specific standard for storing or transmitting data. The usual properties of confidentiality, integrity and non-repudiation should be guaranteed in any agent-based health-care system. The use of cryptographic methods is also important to protect the access to data while it is being transmitted between agents (some issues related to secure communication are discussed in [54]. Frameworks that help to construct multi-agent systems are beginning to address security issues. For instance, an authentication mechanism is being added to Jade [55, 56, 57]. A user will give a username and a password to enter the system; then the system will provide an identity certificate that may be used by the agents associated with that user. This certificate will include aspects such as the identities of the user and of the emitting entity, identification of the algorithms used to protect the certificate, and its validity period. It is also suggested in [58] that agents should also have authorization certificates that allow them controlled access to particular resources; these permissions could be obtained from the user at creation time or by delegation of other agents of the system. In summary, it is obvious that the research on secure access to data, such as authentication of users, delivery and use of certificates, cryptographic methods, or security in wireless communications, will be fundamental to ensure that agents may safely deal with medical data and only authorised users may access or update this kind of information.

3.4. Safety critical issues

Agent-based systems are increasingly being used to support decision making in health care, a domain intrinsically uncertain and hazardous. Clinicians are well aware of these risks, and a recurring theme in physicians' criticism of health care computer systems is one of doubts concerning reliability, and the associated acceptance criteria for reliability which are related to risk and safety considerations. Consequently, everyone working in this area should be aware that very small system errors or misunderstanding in the specification of systems can lead to catastrophic consequences [1]. There exist powerful theoretical models of agency [59, 60, 61], and techniques for the specification and formalisation of agent-based systems, and techniques to analyse and manipulate such specifications, utilising symbolic information to determine appropriate behaviour, are beginning to emerge, based on well-established research from AI [62, 63, 64]. For example, tableaux for multi-modal belief or knowledge logics [65], tableaux for multi-modal belief or knowledge logics with linear-time temporal logic [66], tableaux for belief-desire-intention logics with either linear or branching-time temporal logics [59], and resolution for knowledge logics with linear-time temporal logics [67].

3.5. Legal issues

The distributed aspect of multi-agent systems and the lack of electronic borders facilitate the construction of multi-agent systems in which agents are representing organisations and individuals from different countries. If a multi-agent system is used to enhance the provision of health care to citizens of a wide area, such as coordinating the management of organ transplants in different countries, one of the most difficult issues to consider is the fact that agents should conform to the local, national and international regulations in their area. The use of deontic logic would be appropriate to formalise and reason about the permissions and obligations of each agent in a system. A very promising research direction in this area is the definition of electronic institutions (see e.g. [68], [69]. An electronic institution includes a performative structure (a graph of scenes, where agent-agent interactions take place), a dialogical framework (which comprises an ontology, a set of illocutions and protocols to use them through conversation graphs) and a set of norms, which determine obligations that an agent may acquire through its actions. An e-institution prescribes the actions an agent may take and where, and imposes limits on the questions and answers which form the conversation between agents. Thus, an institution simplifies the task of preparing an agent for a negotiation task, since the range of the discourse is predefined in the dialogical framework and the rules which must be adhered to for the negotiation to complete satisfactorily are laid down in the performative structure.

3.6. Social acceptance

Citizens continuously demand more control over their medical information. They would like to have permanent access to it, such as via the Internet and digital TV, but they want to make sure that only those authorised to do so can have access to it, and only when appropriate. Individuals need to be confident that this information will not be disclosed, either on purpose or inadvertently, to third parties, such as government, employers, insurance companies, marketing companies, pharmaceutical companies, who may then use it for their own purposes. This feeling implies, aside from the security issues mentioned above, the need to build a relation of trust between citizens and agents that provide the access to sensitive information [54]. We consider that the AgentCities initiative may be a very important step in this direction; as it will promote the construction of platforms all around the world that will provide agent-based services, the human users of these systems will start to use them and gain confidence in the relegation of tasks to autonomous entities. Work on trust [70] provides an interesting analysis of relevant issues in this area.

3.7. Professional acceptance

In general, it has been observed that health care professionals are quite reluctant to accept and use new technologies. In the first place, they usually have a very busy schedule, so they lack the time to be aware of the latest advances in technologies and how they could be used to reduce their workload. They refuse to use new tools if they are not integrated smoothly into their daily workflow. They also often mention the lack of time and personnel to convert all the required medical data into an electronic format, so that it can be easily accessed and managed - medical records are usually hand written and distributed in different departments of a medical centre. Some doctors also mention the hype built around Artificial Intelligence and, especially, expert systems, twenty years ago, which did not live up to their expectations, and they may reasonably argue that the intelligent autonomous agent paradigm, so fashionable today, may also fail to deliver real world results. Security in the access to data is also a common concern for health care professionals. Agent systems have the potential to introduce many innovations in the way in which computer systems respond to clinicians. For example, they could identify the user by behaviour or even voice, adapt the user interface to their way of working, and document diagnoses and therapies.

3.8. General issues

There are also many technical problems associated with the development of multi- agent systems in any domain (not especially related to health care). These include user expectations and acceptance, the lack of universally accepted standard agent communication languages, protocols and architectures (although FIPA seems to be clearly leading these efforts and their suggestions are starting to become a de facto standard), how to describe the services offered by agents, how to discover the presence of agents that provide a given service, how to guarantee the identity of an agent that is making a certain request, security, safety and trust issues, how to implement agents that offer wireless access to services (e.g. from mobile phones or PDAs, which will probably be the key towards a massive use of agent technology in the near future), how to handle properly the interactions between software agents and humans, and integration with pre-existing health-care systems.

4. Conclusion

In this position paper we want to argue that multi-agent systems have a set of characteristics that make them appropriate to be used to improve the provision of health care to citizens:

- They may be integrated with existing applications, for example agents may access a database to obtain the information about the patients of a certain hospital [13].
- The agents in a multi-agent system may be running in different locations, for example there may be an agent associated to each department of a medical centre [27], or an agent associated to each person that is included in a health care program in a certain community [22].
- The standards provided by FIPA [71] and the FIPA-compliant frameworks of multi-agent system development are reaching a level of maturity that make it feasible to think in world wide applications that coordinate the activities of health care in different countries, for example coordinating the management of organ transplant with a whole European perspective, following ideas similar to the ones suggested in [13].
- The autonomy of each agent in a multi-agent system permits to maintain the independent views of each modelled actor, for example each agency involved in the provision of health care to a community, such as social workers, health care professionals or emergency services may have different private policies that determine their relationship with other agents and their individual decisions [22].
- Information agents may help both citizens and health care professionals to obtain up-to-date and relevant health care information from Internet, for example see [23].

- Agents may help to address the growing demand of patient-centred management of medical data, for example it is feasible to think about the possibility of having personal agents which are able to get in touch with agents at a medical centre to receive information about their medical record or to make an appointment to be visited by a doctor [27].

References

[1] Fox, J., Das, S. Safe and sound: Artificial Intelligence in hazardous applications. AAAI Press/MIT Press, 1st edition, (2000)

[2] Weiss, G. Multi-agent systems. A modern approach to Distributed Artificial Intelligence. M.I.T. Press, (1999)

[3] Wooldridge, M. An introduction to Multiagent systems. John Wiley, Chichester, (2002)

[4] Shankararaman, V. (ed.) Proceedings of the Workshop on Agents in Health Care, at the 4th International Conference on Autonomous Agents - AA 2000.. Barcelona, (2000)

[5] Cortés, U., Fox, F., Moreno, A. (eds.). Proceedings of the Workshop on Agent Applications in Health Care, at the 15th European Conference on Artificial Intelligence, ECAI 2002, Lyon, (2002). A revised and extended version of the best papers will appear in 2003 in a special issue of AI-Communications

[6] Moreno, A. and Garbay, C. (eds.), Special issue of Artificial Intelligence in Medicine devoted to Software Agents in Health Care. (2003) (in press)

[7] AgentCities Working Group on Health Care Applications. More information available at the web page http://wwwcms.brookes.ac.uk/hcwg

[8] Petrie, C. Agent-based software engineering. In: Agent-Oriented Software Engineering. Lecture Notes in Artificial Intelligence, Vol. 1957. Springer-Verlag, Berlin, (2001), 58-76

[9] Jennings, N. On agent-based software engineering. Artificial Intelligence 117, (2000), 277-296

[10] Decker, K., Li, J. Coordinated hospital patient scheduling. Proceedings of the 3rd International Conference on Multi-Agent Systems, ICMAS-98. Paris, France, (1998)

[11] Kumar, A.D., Kumar, A.R., Kekre, S., Prietula, M.J., Ow, P.S. Multi-agent systems and organizational structure: the support of hospital patient scheduling. In: Proceedings of the Leading Edge in Production and Operations Management, South Carolina, USA, (1989)

[12] Marinagi, C. et. al. Continual Planning and scheduling for managing patient tests in hospital laboratories, AIM 2000, (2000), 139-154.

[13] Aldea, A., Lpez, B., Moreno, A., Riao, D., Valls, A. A Multi-Agent System for Organ Transplant Co-ordination. In: Quaglini, S., Barahona, P., Andreassen, S. (eds.): Artificial Intelligence in Medicine. Lecture Notes in Computer Science, Vol. 2101, Springer-Verlag, Berlin, (2001), 413-416.

[14] Silverman, B.G., Andonyadis, C., Morales, A. Web-based health care agents; the case of reminders and todos, too (R2Do2), Artificial Intelligence in Medicine, 14(3), (1998), 295-316

[15] Shankararaman, V., Ambrosiadou, V., Robinson, B. Agents in Medical Informatics, IASTED International Conference on Applied Informatics, Austria, (2000)

[16] Durfee, D.H. Distributed problem solving and planning. In [2], 121-164.

[17] Klusch, M. Information agent technology for the Internet: a survey. Data and Knowledge Engineering, Vol. 36 (3), (2001), 337-372

[18] Hannebauer, M., Mller, S. Distributed Constraint Optimization for Medical Appointment Scheduling, 5th International Conference on Autonomous Agents (AGENTS 2001), Montreal, Canada, (2001)

[19] Vzquez-Salceda, J., Corts, U. Using Agent-Mediated Institutions for the distribution of Human Tissues among Hospitals. Advanced Course on Artificial Intelligence (ACAI-01), Prague, Czech Republic, (2001), 205-209

[20] Vzquez-Salceda, J., Padget, J.A., Corts, U., Lpez-Navidad, A., Caballero, F. Formalizing an electronic institution for the distribution of human tissues. To appear in [6]. March 2003 (in press)

[21] Moreno, A., Valls, A.. Bocio, J. Management of Hosipital Teams for Organ Transplants Using Multi-Agent Systems. In: Quaglini, S., Barahona, P., Andreassen, S. (eds.): Artificial Intelligence in Medicine. Lecture Notes in Computer Science, Vol. 2101, Springer-Verlag, Berlin, (2001), 413-416

[22] Beer, M.D., Huang, W., Sixsmith, A. Using agents to build a practical implementation of the INCA-Intelligent Community Alarm- system. In: Jain, L.C., Chen, Z. and Ichalkaranje, N. (eds.): Intelligent Agents and their applications. Studies in Fuzzinesa nd Soft Computing, Physica-Verlag, Berlin, (2002), 320-345

[23] Baujard, O., Baujard, V., Aurel, S., Boyer, C., Appel, R.D. MARVIN, a multi-agent softbot to retrieve multilingual medical information on the Web. Medical Informatics 23 (3), Taylor and Francis, London, (1998), 187-191

[24] Kostkova, P., Mani-Saada, J., Weinberg, J. Agent-based up-to-date data management in the National Electronic Library for Communicable Disease. In [5], 59-63.

[25] Lobato, E., Shankararaman, V. PIRA: A Personalised Information Retrieval Agent, IASTED International Conference on Artificial, Intelligence and Soft Computing, Honolulu, (1999)

[26] Marshall, P., Greenwood, S. The Use of Emergent Behaviour in a Multi-Agent System to Drive Self-Adaptation at the Interface, Joint Web Intelligence/Intelligent Agent Technology (2001 WI/IAT), Japan, (2001)

[27] Moreno, A., Isern, D. Accessing distributed health-care services through smart agents. Proceedings of the 4th IEEE International Workshop on Enterprise Networking and Computing in the Health Care Industry (HealthCom 2002), Nancy, France, (2002), 34-41

[28] Barro, S., Presedo, J., Castro, D., Fernndez Delgado, M., Fraga, S., Lama, M., Vila, J. Intelligent telemonitoring of critical-care patients. IEEE Engineering in Medicine and Biology Magazine, 18 (4), (1999), 80-88

[29] Lanzola, G., Gatti, L., Falasconi, S., Stefanelli, M. A Framework for Building Co- operative Software Agents in Medical Applications. Artificial Intelligence in Medicine, 16(3), (1999), 223-249

[30] Larsson, J.E., Hayes-Roth, B. Guardian: An Intelligent Autonomous Agent for Medical Monitoring and Diagnosis. IEEE Intelligent Systems, (1998), 58-64

[31] Farias, A., Arvanitis, T.N. Building Software Agents for Training Systems: A Case Study on Radiotherapy Treatment Planning. Knowledge-Based Systems, (10), (1997), 161-168

[32] Quaglini, S., Stefanelli, M., Cavallini, A., Micieli, G., Fassino, C., Mossa, C. Guidance- based Careflow Systems, Artificial Intelligence in Medicine, 20(1), (2000), 5-22

[33] Marchetti, D., Lanzola, G., Stefanelli, M. An AI-based Approach to Support Communication in Health care Organizations. In: Proc. 8th Conference on Artificial Intelligence in Medicine in Europe - AIME 2001, Cascais, Portugal, (2001)

[34] Huhns, M.N., Singh, M.P. Managing Heterogeneous Transaction Workflows with Co- operating Agents. In: Jennings, N.,Wooldridge, M. (eds): Agent Technology: Foundations, Applications and Markets. Springer-Verlag, Berlin, (1998)

[35] Alamillo, T., Alsinet, T., Bjar, R., Anstegui, C, Fernndez, C., Many, F. Automated monitoring of medical protocols: a secure and distributed architecture. To appear in [6], March 2003 (in press)

[36] Godo, L., Puyol-Gruart, J., Sabater, J., Torra, V. A multi-agent system approach for monitoring the prescription of restricted use antibiotics. To appear in [6], March 2003 (in press)

[37] Corts, U. et al. Assistive technologies for the disabled and for the new generation of senior citizens: the e-tools architecture. In [5], 18-22

[38] Camarinha-Matos, L.M., Afsarmanesh, H. Virtual Communities and Elderly Support, Advances in Automation, Multimedia and Video Systems, and Modern Computer Science, V.V. Kluev, C.E. DAttellis, N. E. Mastorakis (eds.), WSES, (2001), 279-284

[39] CEN/TC251 (European Committee for Standardization/TC251), http://www.centc251.org

[40] ASTM E31: http://www.astm.org/COMMIT/COMMITTEE/E31.htm

[41] HL7 (Health Level 7), http://hl7.org

[42] OpenGALEN: http://www.opengalen.org

[43] UMLS, http://www.nlm.nih.gov/research/umls

[44] SNOMED, http://www.snomed.org

[45] Agentcities Working Group on HealthCare meeting, Agentcities ID2, Lisbon, September (2002). More information available at the web page http://wwwcms.brookes.ac.uk/hcwg

[46] Cyc Knowledge Base, http://www.cyc.org

[47] A. Madche, S. Staab. Mining Ontologies from Text. In: Dieng, R., Corby, O. EKAW-2000 - 12th International Conference on Knowledge Engineering and Knowledge Management, Juan-les-Pins, France. Lecture Notes in AI. Springer-Verlag, Berlin (2000)

[48] A. Madche, S. Staab. Ontology Learning for the Semantic Web. IEEE Intelligent Systems. 16(2), (2001), 72-79

[49] Kietz, J-U., Maedche, A., Volz, R. A Method for Semi-Automatic Ontology Acquisition from a Corporate Intranet, In: Proc. of the EKAW'2000 Workshop Ontologies and Texts, (2000)

[50] Faure D., Nedellec, C. Knowledge Acquisition of Predicate-Argument Structures from technical Texts using Machine Learning. In: Proceedings of Current Developments in Knowledge Acquisition:. In: Fensel D., Studer, R. (eds.): EKAW-99. Springer-Verlag, Karlsruhe, (1999), 329-334

[51] de Moor, G. Privacy Issues and Grid Environments, HealthGRID 2003, Lyon (2003)

[52] Directive 95/46/EC of the European Parliament and of the Council of 24 October 1995 on the protection of individuals with regard to the processing of personal data and on the free movement of such data.

[53] US Department of Health and Human Services. Standards for Privacy and Individually Identifiable Health Information. Federal Register, v.65 (2000), 82461-82510.

[54] Wong, H., Sycara, K. Adding security and trust to multi-agent systems. In: Proceedings of Workshop on deception, fraud and trust in agent societies, Autonomous Agents, Seattle, (1999), 149-161

[55] Bellifemine, F., Poggi, A., Rimassa, G. Developing multi-agent systems with a FIPA compliant agent framework, Software Practice and Experience, 31, (2001), 103-128

[56] Bellifemine, F., Poggi, A., Rimassa, G. JADE- A FIPA compliant agent framework, Proceedings of Practical Applications of Intelligent Agents and Multi-Agents, London, (1999), 97-108

[57] Quaglini, S., Stefanelli, M., Cavallini, A., Micieli, G., Fassino, C., Mossa, C. Guidance- based Careflow Systems, Artificial Intelligence in Medicine, 20(1), (2000), 5-22

[58] A. Poggi, G. Rimassa and M. Tomaiuolo, Multi-user and security support for multi-agent systems. In: Proceedings of WOA 2001 (Dagli oggetti agli agenti), Omicini, A., Viroli, M. (eds.), (2001), 20-26

[59] Rao, A. S. Decision Procedures for Propositional Linear-Time Belief-Desire-Intention Logic. In Proc. ATAL'95. Lecture Notes in AI, Vol. 1037, Springer-Verlag, Berlin, (1996), 102-118

[60] Rao, A. S., Georgeff, M. P., Modeling Rational Agents within a BDI-Architecture. In: Proc. KR'91. Morgan Kaufmann (1991) 473-484

[61] Linder, B. van, Hoek, W. van der and Meyer, J-J.Ch. Formalising Abilities and Opportunities of Agents. In: Meyer, J-J.Ch. and Treur, J. (ed.): Agent-Based Defeasible Control in Dynamic Environments. Handbook of Defeasible Reasoning and Uncertainty Management Systems. Kluwer, Dordrecht, Boston, London, (2002) 253-307

[62] d'Inverno, M., Fisher, M., Lomuscio, A., Luck, M., de Rijke, M., Ryan, M. and Wooldridge, M. Formalisms for Multi-Agent Systems. In: The Knowldedge Engineering Review (1997) 12, 3

[63] Di Marzo Serugendo, G. A Formal Development and Validation Methodology Applied to Agent-Based Systems. Infrastructure for Agents, Multi-Agent Systems, and Scalable Multi-Agent Systems. (eds.) Wagner, T., Rana, O., Lecture Notes in AI, Vol. 1887, Springer-Verlag, Berlin, (2001), 214-226

[64] Ndumu, D. T. and Nwana, H. S., Research and Development Challenges for Agent-Based Systems. IEE Proc. Softw. Eng. 144 (1), (1997)

[65] Halpern, J. Y. and Moses, Y., A Guide to Completeness and Complexity for Modal Logics of Knowledge and Belief. Artif. Intell. Vol. 54, (1992), 319-379

[66] Wooldridge, M., Dixon, C., Fisher, M.A. Tableau-Based Proof Method for Temporal Logics of Knowledge and Belief. J. Appl. Non-Classical Logics 8 (3) (1998) 225-258

[67] Dixon, C., Fisher, M. and Wooldridge, M. Resolution for Temporal Logics of Knowledge. J. Logic Computat. 8 (3), (1998), 345-372

[68] Esteva, M., Rodriguez, J.A., Sierra, C., Garcia P., Arcos, J.L. On the formal specifications of electronic institutions, Agent-mediated electronic commerce. The European AgentLink Perspective, Lecture Notes in AI, Vol. 1991, Dignum, F., Sierra, C. (eds.), (2001), 126- 147

[69] Vzquez-Salceda. J., Corts, U. Using Agent-Mediated Institutions for the distribution of Human Tissues among Hospitals, Advanced Course on Artificial Intelligence, Praga (2001) 205-20

[70] Castelfranchi, C., Falcone, R. Principles of trust for MAS: Cognitive anatomy, social importance, and quantification. In: Proceedings of the International Conference on Multi Agent Systems, Los Alamitos, (1998), 72-79

[71] FIPA: Foundation for Intelligent Physical Agents, http://www.fipa.org

John Nealon, Department of Computing, Oxford Brookes University, Oxford OX33 1HX, UK
E-mail address: johnnealon@brookes.ac.uk

Antonio Moreno, Computer Science and Mathematics Department, Universitat Rovira i Virgili, ETSE Campus Sescelades, Av. dels Pasos Catalans 26, 43007-Tarragona, Spain
E-mail address: amoreno@etse.urv.es

Building an
Agent-Based Community Care Demonstrator
on a Worldwide Agent Platform

Martin Beer, Richard Hill, and Andrew Sixsmith

Abstract. This paper describes a project designed to show how a global multi-agent architecture can be used effectively to support care in the community. Services in this area are notoriously difficult to coordinate with the direct and indirect involvement of a large number of independent, autonomous agencies, each of which has its own priorities and aspirations. Also, by the very nature of the services provided the caring community is highly mobile and distributed making the collection and dissemination of information extremely difficult. The Integrated Community Care (INCA) project has been designed to show how multi-agent technology can be used effectively to address some of these issues in a timely and cost-effective manner. The flexibility provided by such architecture allows an integration of services based on a regularly updated Individual Care Plan in a way that has been very difficult to achieve in practice. This increased flexibility not only allows the better customization of the care to the current needs of the client but also provides an effective means of recovery when things go wrong.

1. Introduction

Recent years have seen a shift in focus in the services provided to older and chronically sick people from institutional care to care in the community. Community Care is typically provided by a range of independent organizations and agencies, each needing to meet its own targets and objectives and to integrate the service with their other responsibilities in a coherent and efficient manner. This often leads to serious service inefficiencies, as there are inadequate systems in place to share relevant information without compromising the security of the information held. Another factor is that a considerable amount of community support is provided by informal carers who are excluded from the general care management system because of difficulties in integrating them without breaching the official confidentiality requirements. The growth of an effective open agent network such as Agentcities [19] allows effective co-operation (information sharing and communication between autonomous information systems) to take place without compromising the security of the client and the agencies involved. Since each agent has complete autonomy it can respond according to the rules of the organization it represents, providing an effective and assured guardian that is totally under that organizations control.

In this paper we describe the principles behind a distributed Agent-Based Integrated Community Care (INCA) system. A demonstrator system, implemented using the ZEUS agent-building toolkit [15] is also described in order to demonstrate the feasibility of the approach and its potential practical benefits. This demonstrator shows that the technologies proposed allow effective communication without compromising integrity and privacy. In particular they allow an approach to be taken that allows minimum collection of information in that the Home service agent can be configured so that it only releases private or sensitive data in case of an emergency, when such information is of value.

The objective of the INCA Project is to investigate how community care can be developed in the internet age through the use of multi-agent technology. The motivation for this has been a consideration of the agent society's social abilities in:

- Promoting effective care systems that:
    - provide better services and resources to clients,
    - enhance social interaction between them, and with their carers
    - deliver more effective care
- Providing the high-abstraction level care management strategies by linking all relevant agencies into a single framework of accountability.
- Giving an in-depth understanding of the health information framework that underpins the delivery of high quality, effective community care, including the formularization of the links between the disparate agencies involved.
- Establishing a single Agent-Based care monitoring facility that can be used by all care professionals to assist in effective monitoring and diagnosis.
- Developing cooperative structures within the community structures to change service provision and care policies through the use of automated agent involvement in planning, scheduling, organizing (both formal and informal) care and even directing care service programs.
- Devolving care management and responsibility to those providing the care by providing shared supervision and teamwork and by separating the organizational from the social requirements, developing a much more responsive and client centered environment that adapts rapidly to changing needs.

Some of these objectives have already been investigated in the medical domain through the use of multi-agent system architectures. For example, the GUARDIAN system [10] considered patient monitoring in a Surgical Intensive Care Unit. Support is provided for collaboration among specialists, each an expert in a specific domain but fully committed to sharing information and knowledge among each other and the nurses that continuously monitor the patient in the physicians' care. A system devoted to diabetes care has been presented, where cooperation not only between the medical specialists, but also others, such as administrators is supported within the agent community [13]. An Agent-Based system has also been described that supports collaboration among general practitioners and specialists about patient healthcare [11].

A more general Agent-Based telemedicine framework has been reported [5] that can assist specialists in diagnosing difficult cases through information sharing, cooperation and negotiation. In this case each specialist has their own Tele-medicine-Oriented Medical ASsistant (TOMAS) agent that behaves as a medical assistant and has two generic functions:

- an agenda for managing appointments, and
- methods for access to patient records.

Support for tele-medicine is provided through the remote exchange of patient data, cooperative annotation of cases and negotiation of appointments. These approaches have been greatly assisted by moves to standardize medical information through the formalization of patient and other records [6]. Some of the flexibility offered by the mobile access to records and services is being demonstrated by the Ward-in-Hand project[1], but only in the relatively restricted environment of a conventional hospital ward.

The INCA project aims to take these forward from the purely medical domain and integrate them into the general community care environment, where the linkages are less formal and effective cooperation and negotiation is essential if appropriate care is to be delivered. A major difference is that it is rarely possible to share information as freely as within the purely medical domain because of the involvement of different agencies and individuals with widely differing requirements. The agent community therefore has to act as a coordinator and filter to ensure that appropriate and correct information is distributed to all concerned. Also, since help is likely to have to travel some distance it is often better to provide whatever assistance is readily available in a timely manner, rather than the optimal solution that may arrive too late.

2. The INCA Demonstrator

The demonstrator uses multi-agent technology to enhance the mechanisms for the systematic and widespread assessment of the health of the elderly out-side of a conventional clinical care regime. Enhanced assessment provides a valuable and timely source of information and knowledge that enables the optimization of care provision and management. Non-invasive assessment technology provides a source of health information that is well suited to identifying subtle, yet important, changes in an individual's condition. This can then be combined with appropriate knowledge sources available elsewhere on the agent network to trigger pre-emptive care and treatment. [9] Appropriate care is then be provided in an effective and timely manner.

The demonstrator explores the following three functional elements:

Within-home monitoring techniques: in which devices can be integrated into existing home environments. These may be passive such as movement monitors, etc. but can also be explicitly designed assistive technologies for communication, mobility and environmental control. The value of these is that the data generated is semantically richer and better suited to comparison between individuals. [8]

Automated Log Analysis: Usage is retrieved and automated analysis techniques are used to provide preliminary information on end-users activities.

Agent-Based knowledge management: The Agentcities network provides a general facility that can be used to review care for specific individuals and the community in general, improving the direction of care management and delivery.

3. The Care Environment

The delivery of community-based services presents a number of organizational, managerial and logistical problems that undermine the effectiveness and efficiency of services. While community care has typically involved limited use of information technology, recent developments have seen significant application development. Information technology within the community care environment currently involves a number of autonomous systems; home monitoring, community alarms, care management systems and emergency systems command and control systems. Each element of care is provided by different autonomous bodies, which maintain their own individual management information systems. The overall management of the care typically resides outside of these systems, protecting individual bodies from disclosing sensitive and irrelevant information. This is illustrated by the high-level activity model shown in Figure 1 Key to the development of a proper care regime for any client is the Individual Care Plan that provides the link between the client's needs and the means by which they should be met. This not only includes the Direct Care activities normally associated with community care and discussed elsewhere [3]. These need to be reviewed and updated continuously as the client's requirements change both by monitoring and analysis of information collected [8] and through negotiation between the agencies, as appropriate. Indeed McDonald [14] describes the Individual Care Plan as:

> 'not simply a 'basket of goods and services', it is a complex set of human relations, and the achievement and maintenance of which requires skills, both in the negotiation and management of change'
> [p61]

Its preparation is therefore a complex process that requires flexibility and support for contingencies so that the necessary services are provided in a timely and efficient manner. Figure 2 gives the basic components of this process.

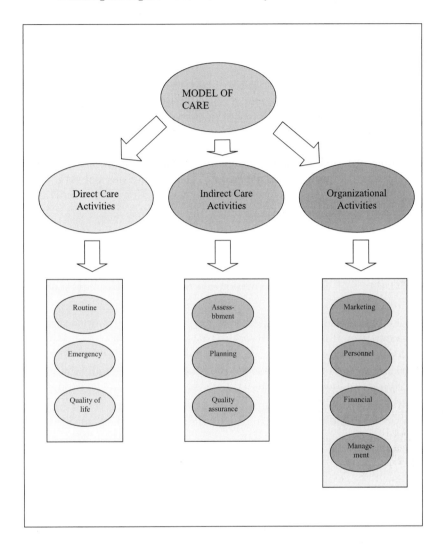

FIGURE 1. High Level Activity Model of Care

4. Designing the Multi-Agent System

Jennings et al. [12] in reviewing the ADEPT project interpreted organizations as distributed federated structures incorporating competition and coordination and proposed that agent architectures are highly suitable for mirroring this structure. This is basically the approach taken by INCA but care has to be taken not to take this analogy too far as for example when Symonds and Kelly [18] talk about the 'myth of the market' since in our case:

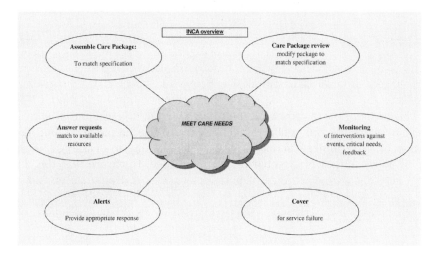

FIGURE 2. The Basic Components of the INCA Architecture

- the prime consumers (the *Clients* are not the actual purchasers)
- occupational regulation overrides market regulation
- legal obligation overrides market opportunities
- risk to others makes it a social issue rather than an individual matter.

All these are prime research issues for the agent community and need to be addressed if widespread deployment of any but the most basic trading agent-based solutions are to come about. In particular, the agent approach adopted can:

- Replace conventional technology, such as existing telephone-based services [7]
- Integrate specific functions into a single, comprehensive, framework for service delivery. The end users then have a single access point to services, rather than the piecemeal approach currently adopted.
- Enhance information sharing between all parties in a controlled and open manner through the interoperation and cooperation of different sets of agents from different communities.
- Develop new services, particularly those aimed at enhancing quality of life. These include more general services from other service providers and agent communities available on the network.
- Provide flexible, rather than dedicated, solutions, which are readily customizable to an individual's changing requirements.

5. Constructing the Agent Community

The adoption of an agent mediated approach has made it possible to integrate the existing care systems in a way that makes cooperation natural between highly heterogeneous agencies, since only the communication now has to be standardized. It allows the INCA system to interface directly to the wide range of existing databases, knowledge bases and control systems, already in place. The much broader care picture is therefore be monitored effectively, and is of great help to care managers in developing the most effective and efficient care programme for each individual, including the elimination of unnecessary duplication of resources.

This care regime is developed into an Individual Care Plan that acts as the master template, not only defining the regular care to be provided, but also the actions to be taken under different situations. These range from asking a neighbour to call if no movement is detected by a certain time, to ensure that the client is up and active, through a range of potential responses depending on individual circumstances to an immediate requirement to call the Fire Service if unusual heat levels are detected or the Police should unexpected movement be tected, for example when the client is out. Most of these interventions require action by independent Care Providers on the basis of pre-existing contracts that form the basis for negotiation as to who actually responds in any individual case. This requires multi-dimensional negotiation at a number of levels if acceptable levels of service are to be assured. The current arrangements have great difficulty with this as only limited information is available. It may for example be appropriate to notify an informal carer who can respond rapidly because they are close to the scene either in place of or in addition to a professional carer or the emergency services so that at least some assistance is available at the scene. This more sophisticated approach can only work effectively with full cooperation and information exchange between all parties involved.

The issue of timely intervention when delivery of the assistance promised fails can also be addressed in a similar way. The appropriate agent identifies the anticipated failure as soon as the problem becomes evident. It then attempts to renegotiate its commitment, either by finding another agent that will take it on, or by making a revised commitment. The form of this nwegotiation is defined by the requirements of the Individual Care Plan and the contracts between the Care Coordinator and the various Care Providers. The agent also develops a record of the reliability of the various agencies and builds this into its negotiating strategy. This approach follows that outlined by Beer et al. [2]

6. The Activities Supported

While community care covers a wide range of activities, four basic scenarios are considered in this paper, chosen to illustrate the effectiveness of the Agent-Based approach in developing a fully cooperative environment for providing the care required:

1. The development and updating of an Individual Care Plan. Care Planning is the specification of a *package* of care services according to an assessment of the needs of the individual.

2. The monitoring of the effectiveness of that Individual Care Plan
3. Responding to failure to deliver the specified care in a timely and effective manner
4. Reviewing the Individual Care Plan so that it continues to meet the objectives and desires of the client.

A number of organizations and individuals play a part in these activities. They can be grouped effectively into groups of actors, as shown in Table 1. The interactions between these actors can then be shown in the form of Use Case diagrams.

6.1. Developing an Individual Care Plan

Before care can be provided effectively, the care coordinator has to assess need, and develop an individual care plan that meets the clients requirements. This can be quite difficult, particularly with the severely disabled or those with dementia. If assessment is undertaken at an assessment centre it ignores the specific circumstances and problems that occur in the home environment. However observation of a person in their own home requires considerable resources if an effective result is to be achieved. The monitoring facilities of the INCA system provide an effective means by which this assessment can be made within the client's familiar environment, which can be further refined as additional information is collected.

A significant part of the assessment is determining what the overall objectives of the care regime are to be. These are likely to include enhancing the quality of life by for example maintaining or improving one or more of:

- physical health and wellbeing
- emotional or mental health
- peace of mind
- safety and security
- practical support
- personal care
- personal finances
- control over day-to-day life
- reduction of risk

as well as rehabilitation outcomes such as:

- regaining skills and capabilities
- improving confidence and morale
- improving the ability to go out
- reducing symptoms

This means that the care regime needs to be developed continually as the balance of these objectives changes. Also, the choice of carer depends not only on their own capabilities but also on the current set of objectives that the Care Coordinator wishes to achieve. This makes the choice of carer not just a simple resource allocation issue, but one where quite complex negotiations both with the client and the carers may be required.

TABLE 1. The Actors

NAME	DESCRIPTION
Care Coordinator	The agency responsible for providing the range of services necessary to ensure that the client is properly cared for. The Care Coordinator is responsible for preparing an Individual Care Plan and monitoring its effectiveness in meeting the needs of the client. This is often the Local Authority or some other official body with a legal duty to provide the necessary care.
Care Provider	The various agencies and individuals responsible for providing the care specified by the Individual Care Plan. This will include Social Workers, Health Care Professionals, Care Assistants, Emergency Services, Social Services etc. who can provide and extremely wide range of care services, if required.
Informal Carer	The various relatives, friends, neighbours etc. who provide some form of support and assistance in an informal way (i.e. outside the Individual Care Plan), but is often essential to allow the client to continue living at home. This is often flexible and responsive and can range from totally unstructured and so not recognized at all in the Individual Care Plan through to fully recognized and integrated with the efforts of the professional carers.
Client	The person who lives in their own dwelling (either an ordinary house or a sheltered home) and who receives a package of community care services. This package may range from minimal interventions, such as social alarm systems, through to an intensive mix of community support services.

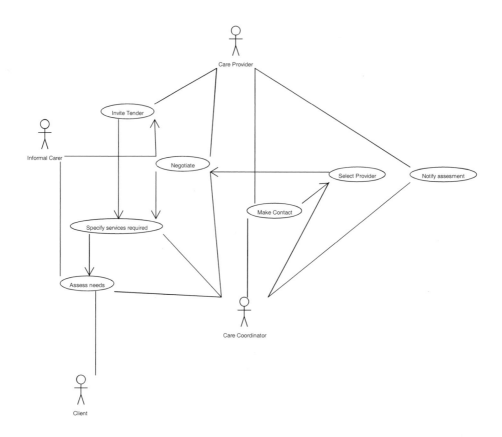

FIGURE 3. Individual Care Plan Development

The INCA architecture also allows informal carers to be recognized as an integral part of the care regime and for them to be properly informed at all stages. This is important as many of the objectives outlined above can be best achieved by close friends and family, but this must be recognized within the framework otherwise considerable duplication of resources will ensue. This is a major issue with current care systems, where they are often effectively ignored.

The stages in doing this are shown in Figure 3.

6.2. Monitoring the Care Plan

Once the care plan has been established it needs to be continuously monitored, and regularly reviewed, otherwise the care regime will rapidly drift away from meeting the real needs of the client. The INCA architecture provides for this by continuously monitoring both the client and the care interactions, and identifying when further intervention is required.

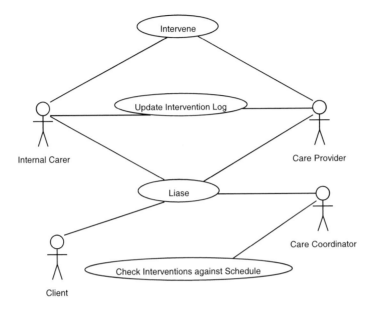

FIGURE 4. Monitoring the Individual Care Plan

Figure 4 shows the interactions involved in informing all concerned of the care required at any time.

6.3. Responding to Failure

In any system dependent on such a wide variety of autonomous individuals, there are inevitably occasions when the necessary level of care, as specified in the Individual Care Plan can not be delivered at the time specified. This can range from a particular carer being held up in traffic to serious problems that put the safety and wellbeing of the client in jeopardy. Contingency arrangements have therefore to be included, that are triggered as soon as the potential failure to meet the care obligations is identified. Agent architectures can be shown to perform well in this respect, without developing serious instabilities that would affect large numbers of other individuals. This is important both for maintaining the stability of care to all clients and for scalability reasons.

Figure 5 shows the interactions involved.

6.4. Reviewing the Care Plan

Finally we need to consider the processes required to review the Individual Care Plan as shown in Figure 6. Considerable volumes of information are being generated continuously about both the client and the operation of the care regime. When the safety and security of the client is assured, much of this information will simply stay in the Home Unit where it will be used to identify longer-term

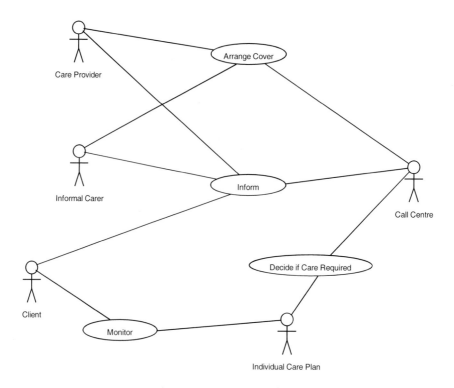

FIGURE 5. Responding to Failure

trends. When an issue arises, not only will an emergency response be triggered to deal with the immediate problem, but the distributed agent architecture also provides for the Individual Care Plan to be reviewed. Since different information is required for this purpose than for immediate response to the initial emergency the data filtering and knowledge synthesis capabilities of an Agent-Based information system come directly into play [16][17].

7. Using the Demonstrator

The current demonstrator deploys home agents across the Agentcities network. They then communicate with the rest of the agents on the main platform. Potential users can download the necessary code to deploy their home agent from the project web site. They then need to install this in their own version of the Zeus agent platform [15] and when the full set of local agents are started communication is established with the INCA server and a minimal Individual Care Plan is prepared. This deals solely with the handling of emergency alerts which are routed directly

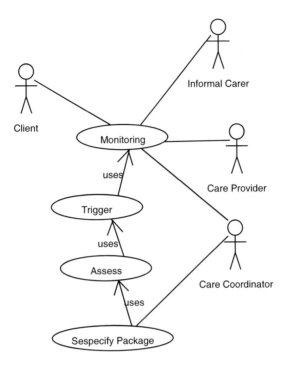

FIGURE 6. Reviewing the Care Plan

to the Emergency Services. The system is thus able to respond to basic requests for help immediately. Once this initial plan is entered in the database the user is able to access it through a web interface that allows it to be modified as required to meet individual need and the home unit agent can be used to assess the effectiveness of the INCA architecture to meet that need.

8. Further Work

There are a number of additional agents that could beneficially be deployed to demonstrate the capabilities and flexibility of the INCA architecture. These might include:

1. mobile agents that emulate wireless connected Personal Digital Assistants (PDAs) that can demonstrate the communication possibilities for the various care workers involved
2. a global monitor that shows the home agents connected and their status at any time. This is likely to be Web based and be

linked to the pages that allow modification of the Individual Care Plan.

3. customized help and information services based on information agents that know of the client's interests and requirements. This can have a considerable benefit in combating social isolation.

4. monitoring facilities not only for the home, but also for the carers so that the client knows when to expect them, and is kept fully informed of any necessary changes in plan.

5. differing configurations to deal with a range of circumstances. For example, the monitoring facilities could be used in burglar alarm mode when the property is unoccupied and carers could be informed as appropriate to avoid wasted journeys.

The mobile agents are already under development using the JADE/LEAP platform. These will deploy to PC hosted simulators for typical mobile devices in the first instance. Whether we shall be able to allow free deployment in the same way as the home unit agent will depend on the license restrictions imposed on us by the various software suppliers. Current intention is to allow free deployment of as many different types of agent as possible so that we gain a wide evaluation of the technology from as many potential users as possible.

The current demonstrator is concerned primarily with the delivery of a specified service level. It therefore deals with the communication and negotiation between the various interested parties rather than the detailed operation of the sensor networks in the home. There are other projects that are concerned more directly with this.[4][8]

9. Conclusions

The INCA project can now demonstrate the effective deployment of a set of agents designed to cooperate in the timely and effective delivery of community care across the Agentcities network. The cooperative activities are very different from the trading situations that have been studied extensively, and so this project gives very different insights into the design and construction of large-scale multi-agent networks. In particular we can study:

- the architectural consequences of using an open multi-agent system to support an application domain that requires high levels of reliability and security
- the interactions between the various autonomous information sources and the architectural requirements for their reliable interoperation with the various agents. This brings us into the area of Web Services and will allow us to inform the debate on how such services should be built and integrated.

- the use of mobile and static agents to deliver the necessary services and the implications for doing this on a global platform
- scalability issues as any realistic scenario for deploying INCA would require the linking of thousands of home units and hundreds of carers. We need to study the behaviour of networks of this size before we can even think of trying to deploy such agents.

The use of a general agent network architecture means that agents can be deployed on existing and future agent architecture without the necessity to construct independent architectural frameworks as has previously been the case. As more facilities and services become agent based they can be readily integrated into the INCA framework in a way that is just not possible with existing community care frameworks. The current demonstrator intentionally does not use security features that are becoming available on agent platforms, as it is intended as a test bed with which to investigate some of the issues discussed in this paper. The use of a standard agent architecture and a readily available agent development platform means that such features as this, and many others can be added very quickly when standards are agreed and they are added to the development environments.

10. Acknowledgements

The programming of the demonstrator has been undertaken by Iain Anderson, Wei Huang an Philip Doherty as part of the project work required within their degree studies. The project is also in receipt of an Agentcities Deployment Grant from the European Union Agentcities.rtd project (IST-2000-28385).

References

[1] M.Ancona, E.Coscia, G.Dodero, M.Earney, V.Gianuzzi, F.Minuto, S.Virtuoso (2001), "Ward-In-Hand: wireless access to clinical records for mobile healthcare professionals" Proc. TEHRE 2001 m-Health Conference, 1st Annual Conference on Mobile & Wireless Healthcare Applications, 11 - 14 November 2001, London, UK.

[2] Beer, M. D., Bench-Capon, T., & Sixsmith, A. (1999b), 'The Delivery of Effective Integrated Community Care with the aid of Agents', Proceedings of *ICSC99*, Hong Kong, December 1999. (Lecture Notes in Computer Science 1749, Springer-Verlag pp303-398)

[3] Beer, M. D, Huang W. & Sixsmith, A. (2002), "Using Agents to Build a Practical Implementation of the INCA (Intelligent Community Alarm) System", in L. C. Jain & Z. Chen, & N. Ichalkaranje, "Intelligent Agents & their Applications", Springer, pp320-345.

[4] Celler, B. G.,Earnshaw, E. W., Ilsar, E.D, Betbeder-Matibet, L., Harris, M. F., Clark, E. D., Hesketh, T. and Lovell, N. H. (1995), Remote monitoring of health status of the elderly at home: A Multidisciplinary Project on Ageing at the University of NSW, Int. Journal of Biomedical Computing, vol.40, pp147-155.

[5] Della Mea, V., (2001), "Agents acting and moving in healthcare scenario: a paradigm for telemedical collaboration", IEEE Transactions on Information Technology in Bioscience, **5**, 10-13.

[6] Department of Health (2001), Building the Information Core: Implementing the NHS Plan, January 2001.

[7] Fisk, M. (1989), *Alarm Systems and Elderly People*, Planning Exchange, London.

[8] Haigh, K. Z., Phelps, J. & Geib, C. W., (2002), "An Open Agent Architecture for Assisting Elder Independence", in The First International Joint Conference on Autonomous Agents and Multi-Agent Systems (AAMAS), pages 578- 586. July 2002.

[9] Haigh, K. Z. & Yanco, H., (2002), "Automation as Caregiver: A Survey of Issues and Technologies", in AAAI-02 Workshop on Automation as Caregiver: The Role of Intelligent Technology in Elder Care, pages 39-53. July 2002.

[10] Hays-Roth, B., and Larsson, J. E., (1996), "A domain specific architecture for a class of intelligent agent monitoring systems", *Journal of Experimental and Theoretical Artificial Intelligence*, **8**, 149-171.

[11] Huang, J., Jennings, J. R., and Fox, J. (1995), 'An Agent- Based Approach for Distributed Care Management', *Applied Artificial Intelligence: An International Journal*, vol. 9, no. 4, pp401-420.

[12] N. R. Jennings and T. J. Norman and P. Faratin (1998), 'ADEPT: An Agent-Based Approach to Business Process Management', *ACM SIGMOD Record*, **27:4**, 32-39.

[13] Lanzola, G., Falsconi, S, and Stefanellii, M., (1995), "Cooperative software agents for patient management", Lecture Notes in Artificial Intelligence, 934, 173-184.

[14] McDonald, A. (1999), 'Understanding Community Care', MacMillan Press Ltd., London, UK.

[15] Nwana, H., Ndumu, D., Lee, L., and Collis, J., (1999) 'ZEUS: A Tool-Kit for Building Distributed Multi-Agent Systems', *Applied Artificial Intelligence Journal*, vol. 13, no. 1 pp129- 186.

[16] Preece A. D., Hui, K-Y., Gray, W. A., Marti, P., Bench- Capon, T. J. M., Jones, D. M., and Cu, Z., (1999) 'The KRAFT Architecture for Knowledge Fusion and Transformation', 19th SGES International Conference on Knowledge-based Systems and Applied Artificial Intelligence (ES'99), Springer, Berlin.

[17] Sahuguet, A., and Azavant, F. (1998), W4F: the WysiWyg Web Wrapper Factory. Technical report, University of Pennsylvania, Department of Computer and Information Science. http://cheops.cis.upenn.edu/ sahuguet/WAPI/.

[18] Symonds, A. & Kelly, A. (eds) (1998), 'The Social Construction of Community Care', Macmillan Press Ltd., London, UK.

[19] Willmott, S. et al, (2002), "Agentcities Network Architecture", in *Proceedings of the first International Workshop on Challenges in Open Agent Systems*, July 2002

School of Computing & Management Sciences, Sheffield Hallam University, Sheffield, United Kingdom.
E-mail address: m.beer@shu.ac.uk & r.hill@shu.ac.uk

Department of Primary Care, University of Liverpool, Liverpool, United Kingdom.
E-mail address: sixsmith@liv.ac.uk

Agent-Based User Interface Adaptivity in a Medical Decision Support System

Sue Greenwood, John Nealon and Peter Marshall

Abstract. Previous work at Oxford Brookes University developed a system to advise on diabetes treatment that enabled data to be displayed according to the choices of each user. Due to the time critical nature of the problem, spending time searching through the data was not feasible. This reduced the usefulness of the system in the clinical setting for which it was designed. Thus a more automated approach was required. A multiagent system has been utilised to drive the adaptivity. A set of simple agents, each concerned with a single aspect of the system, communicate with each other and the suggested summary is a result of the emergent behaviour of the whole system. While emergent behaviour is used in other areas where agents have been applied, notably robotics, it is novel to use this approach in adaptive interfaces. This paper first considers the use of reactive agents to provide a context for the application of emergence in the area of self-adaptive interfaces. The field of adaptive interfaces is also considered to identify approaches that have been used in the past. An emergent multiagent system using a two-layer model is then described. This approach has been applied and tested to the problem of providing self-adaptivity at the interface to allow for decision support to be delivered in real-time for a clinician to employ.

1. Introduction

The work described in this paper is concerned with the provision of accurate dosage advice for diabetic patients. This project has produced a PDA-based system into which patients enter various details about their diet and physical condition and are given accurate dosage advice for the insulin that they require [1]. In collecting data from the user, this system is also a repository of information about the day-to-day condition of the patients.

As part of the project, a desktop computer based system was also developed to allow the data from the PDA to be made available to the clinician. This system provided the required data visualisations. However, the context in which it is used, that of a standard consultation, does not allow enough time for a clinician to access the data to find the salient information from a given dataset (a patient record) or browse the visualisations. The current project was undertaken to address this problem.

As the clinician did not have sufficient time to make use of a system that allowed them to analyse the data, it was decided instead to investigate the possibilities of developing a computer system that carried out the evaluation and allowed the medical professional to simply review what the system had produced. The constraints that had to be met were that the system should act in real time to find the interesting patterns in the data and then meet the individual requirements of each clinician. A prescriptive system that forced the user into a particular way of working would have been anathema to the work habits of clinicians, the intended users, so a system that could adapt itself to the work habits of the users was required. To this end, an adaptive interface was developed. This system needed to be capable of learning user preferences and relating them to the patterns in the data. The system was required also to provide a summary of the dataset in the form of a set of recommendations for data views. A multiagent system was developed to drive the adaptivity. A set of simple agents, each concerned with a single aspect of the system, communicate with each other and the suggested summary is a result of the emergent behaviour of the whole system.

2. Diabetes Mellitus

Diabetes mellitus is one of the most common acute diseases and affects a significant proportion of the population. The least severe form of the disease is known as impaired glucose tolerance. This may or may not develop into full-blown diabetes, which has two forms, type I diabetes and type II diabetes. Type II is less severe but more common, and is often treated by a strict diet and/or tablets. In some cases however, insulin replacement therapy may be required. In the case of type I diabetes, patients always requires insulin replacement therapy. Type I sufferers may experience some temporary remission during the early stages of the disease (known as the honeymoon period) but after this, they will require regular insulin replacement therapy for the rest of their lives.

Diabetes is a disease caused by the breakdown of one of the body's feedback mechanisms. Glucose (sugar) is the body's natural energy source. It is obtained from food and used throughout the body although primarily by the muscles and brain. While the liver plays a large part in the regulation and storage of blood glucose, it is insulin as produced by the pancreas that is the most important hormone.

As with all hormones, insulin is a messenger chemical that is secreted as and when needed by the body to create the feedback loop in a process. In this case it is concerned with the maintenance of the blood glucose level. When an excess of glucose is detected in the pancreas, insulin is secreted which promotes the transfer of glucose to cells. As the blood glucose level drops insulin production decreases and so the amounts of glucose present in the blood returns to normal. Another hormone glucagon performs the opposite task encouraging the release of glucose from cells when the level drops too low. This is normally a highly effective system with glucose concentrations kept at between 4 and 6 mmol/l.

In Type I diabetes, there is a major insulin deficiency and the level of blood glucose increases. The body attempts to remove some of this by excretion in urine. To attempt to compensate, the kidneys must work continuously to remove excess glucose and this produces the characteristic symptoms of increased urination and thirst. Eventually the body can no longer metabolise glucose and so must turn to another process to provide energy. This is achieved by the breaking down of fat cells. This highly inefficient process produces organic acids that provide an important alternative energy source for the brain when present in small amounts. In large concentrations, such as those observed in untreated Type I diabetes, these organic acids or ketone bodies accumulate in the blood stream and urine. They eventually reach a critical concentration and ketoacidosis occurs. This leads to coma and death.

By taking insulin, the diabetic patient can cause their blood glucose levels to reduce but if they take too much, the body's blood glucose level can drop too low again causing coma and death. Thus, keeping the blood glucose level at a safe level is a matter of maintaining a fine balance. Normally the body can modify its insulin and glucagon production as required to allow control at the level of relatively subtle shifts with the feedback systems in the body ensuring that this process can be carried out accurately. When insulin production is impaired and the patient must provide the necessary insulin themselves, it becomes more difficult to control the system as insulin will be taken at a few relatively fixed points in the day and feedback cannot be constantly provided and the first hint that the blood glucose level has moved out of range can be the onset of a hypoglycaemic reaction or 'hypo' when the body attempts to shut down.

Recent major studies have confirmed conclusively that the main aim of diabetes treatment should be to maintain the body's blood glucose level as near to the normal level as possible [2, 3].

In diabetic patients the body cannot produce its own insulin, so the patient is required to regularly take enough insulin to balance the blood glucose levels. This involves the patient in trying to determine how much insulin they will need based not only on the current blood glucose level but also considering various other factors. These include what, and how recently, the patient has eaten; to what intensity and how recently they have taken exercise; how they are generally feeling health wise; the time of day and whether their blood glucose has recently gone outside safe limits.

3.   Diabetes Treatment System

The multiagent system described in this paper is part of a research and technical development collaboration with the Diabetes Trials Unit of Oxford University. The objective of the partnership is to allow diabetic patients, clinicians, diabetic nurses and researchers to interact efficiently and effectively with a highly integrated diabetes treatment system. The system architecture includes several interacting elements. The two core elements are the handheld diabetic patient insulin dosage advisor and the diabetes clinic decision support system described in this paper.

The portable advisor, POIRO Mk2, is based on the POIRO system developed by the collaboration [1]. POIRO proved highly effective and user friendly, but was developed originally on a large and expensive hand-held computer, the Epson EHT-10. It was ported to the Apple Newton and subsequently to Palm OS® PDAs, incorporating significant improvements. The PDA system has recently completed a successful clinical study at the Radcliffe Infirmary in Oxford.

At a clinic visit the diabetic patient provides the doctor with details of their blood glucose levels, insulin taken, and 'hypos', recorded in a 'log-book'. However, these records even if completed in full - which is not universally the case - do not provide the clinician with information concerning the factors affecting the patient's metabolism when each glucose reading and corresponding insulin injection was taken. With the advent of the PDA based system, the diabetic patient now has an incentive to enter not only the data which the logbooks were designed to store but also background factors as these are needed to allow the system to make its recommendations. As part of its operation, the PDA-based system stores this information.

Diabetic Patients got on well with the PDA-based system in trials and when in use, the system amassed useful records not only of their glucose levels and insulin dosages but also collected data concerning some of the relevant environmental factors that influenced these. It was felt that if this information could be uploaded to a clinician's system, it could provide a great deal more information about the day-to-day condition of the patient than had previously been possible. To this end, a data visualisation package was created to allow healthcare professionals to view graphs and tables summarising the relevant points from the data.

One of the key features of a clinician/patient consultation is that it takes place over a very short time, perhaps between seven and fifteen minutes. As this is all the time available to the clinician with a patient to discuss how their health has been over the previous period of three to six months, there is insufficient time to allow for the use of the uploaded data, except for the more experienced clinicians. However, it is increasingly the case that diabetic patients are being treated by general practitioners or specialist nurses, who do not have the same level of experience and knowledge to interpret the data in the way that experienced clinicians are able to. Therefore, support in analysing the data was required.

It was considered necessary to automate the process of finding the relevant patterns in the data, so that the amount of time that was needed to make effective use of the system was reduced significantly. However, different clinicians work in different ways and might be interested in viewing the data in different ways too. They might even wish to view the data in differing ways for a patient different, which further complicates the issue. So while adding pattern finding functionality is a useful first step; because of the way that clinicians work and the very short time frame in which the interaction with each patient takes place, this in itself is not sufficient to make the system worthwhile. If time were not such an important factor, then simply producing a system that was customisable might be sufficient. The fact that a clinician does not have the time to spend customising a system means that any useful system had to be able to tailor itself to the clinician rather than relying on the clinician tailoring the system to their needs.

Our work investigates whether multiagent-based emergent adaptivity at the interface can produce useful and meaningful behaviour in the form of automatically adapting the system to the user. To achieve this, the system must be able to determine the interests of the user and any patterns in the data that are relevant to those interests. These interests could vary as each patient is considered, so a system with the ability initially to learn a clinician's interests and then dynamically change the areas of interest to be investigated with each new set of data is required.

An adaptive approach was chosen to allow for the fact that there *are* patterns in the interactions of the users, that are different for different users. The time constraints put on clinicians , the target users provided one of the main considerations. That is,. The clinician needed to access the factors relevant to them in the data, taking the minimum amount of time from the consultation.

The initial focus of the work was on the needs of clinicians. However,, since the management of diabetes is changing, moving from hospital based treatment to treatment centred in Health Centres it is entirely possible that in the future other health care professionals might come to need access to the data provided. The system developed was thus required to accommodate to the needs of potentially disparate classes of users in addition to the variation within the initially considered user class.

In reviewing the requirements of the system, they were:

- to learn over time to both tailor itself to the user and to make its pattern identification effective.
- to cope with the sometimes short time scale of operation.
- to correlate between user actions and data patterns.
- any system suggestions should be an adjunct to the main operation so that the user could use or ignore them as they saw fit.

The idea of allowing the system to carry out part of the work, to have, as Wooldridge [4] suggests, agents in certain circumstances take the initiative rather than wait for users to say exactly what they require of the system, is very appealing. This is especially the case when one considers the perennial issue of the time constraints that clinicians are under. As the goal in this project was to allow the system to do the initial filtering work for the clinician, the idea of an agent-based approach seemed an appropriate one to consider.

4.   An Agent-Based Approach

In his definition of intelligent agents, Muller [5] classifies agents into three main categories: reactive agents; deliberative agents and interacting agents. He then goes on to develop a taxonomy based on these three types and suggests the type of architecture that might be applicable for particular classes of problem. These classifications are worth a closer examination.

Reactive agents Muller defines as those that express reactivity and real time behaviour. Typically, these will have little if any explicit world model and will make decisions at run-time based on simple behaviour-action rules. Classically, this approach has been used in the field of robotics with Brooks subsumption architecture [6] being the ubiquitous example. This is a layered architecture where each individual entity is only concerned with a particular part of the task and it is through the combination of all the activity that the functionality of the whole system emerges. The idea of emergent behaviour is closely linked to this.

While an emergent behaviour approach is most closely associated with robotics research, it has had some application at the user interface. The work of Wavish and Graham [7] shows that reactive agents can produce interesting results in other areas. They have created systems with reactive agents as actors where the behaviour of the system emerges from the interactions of the 'actors'. This suggests that when it is possible to identify each important aspect in a system, agents concerned with each might be able to produce complex behaviour through their interaction.

This idea has been applied to the provision of an adaptive interface. Agent driven adaptive interfaces have been developed where the agents unobtrusively observe the user and make inferences based on the user's actions [8]. In our work, the idea of unobtrusively observing the user as a data source has been used but a community of simple agents has been employed where each is concerned with a particular facet of the interaction and the overall behaviour emerges

The classical approach to developing a system such as this is to develop explicit models of the various entities that the adaptive interface needs. Thus user models, task models and system models are developed. If such models were developed then it might seem logical to use a deliberative agent to control such a system, however, there are problems with this approach. The specification of the current system highlights two important issues. The first is that of speed. A large complex user model is less likely to be able to respond quickly to changes. In a system where the user's interaction with the system involves a series of short consultations, an unwieldy model is not the best choice. A more fundamental issue relates to the actual domain. As discussed above, the data that is now available and that this system is designed to display has not been available before. Thus while clinicians have a good idea about what is important, it is very possible that there are patterns and relations that can only be observed when the data now available is examined. Thus a system that can attempt to derive its own organisation for the data is going to be more useful than one where the relationships have to be explicitly described at design time as is the case with a high level model. For these reasons, it was decided to employ a system of reactive agents

5.   The Multiagent System in Action

At the interface, there is a series of agents each concerned with a particular aspect of the functionality. Being simple reactive agents they are able to rapidly respond to changes. As noted above however, such simple reactive agents do not usually express complex behaviour. In this work, the agents are provided with the facility to adapt their reaction thresholds over time and by interacting extensively with other agents, produce through emergence a more complex system. From the point of view of the data, by using a series of reactive agents that are each responsible for a particular facet of the data (statistic derived from the data), such as means, upper and lower quartiles, and allowing them to build up relationships with other data agents, the system is able to self organise itself in such a way that it models the patterns in the data.

When attempting to work at a low level and provide adaptivity by carrying out observation at the level of individual actions, the complexity of the task becomes an important issue. Gervasio et al [9] found that when trying to predict the actions that a user carries out to create a schedule in a crisis planner, that by reducing the complexity of the task to be predicted - by abstracting classes of actions from the set of available actions - the accuracy of prediction increased. Of course, this increases the workload for the user, as they are required to provide the specific details to the action predicted. This raises the issue of just how effort should be divided between user and computer in such a mixed initiative system.

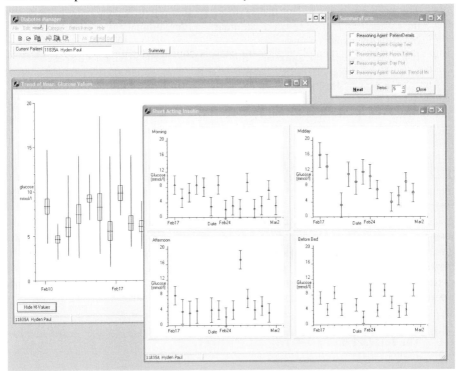

Fig. 1. The Multiagent system in action

The goal in providing adaptivity is to make the user's task easier rather than to actually replace the user. In a mixed initiative system, the user should still maintain control and the system should be simply trying to reduce the complexity of the user's task rather than taking them out of the loop completely. With this in mind, it is perfectly feasible to produce a system that meets the more limited goal of making it easier for the user to obtain the commands they wish to carry out rather than to predict with complete accuracy each command .With this objective, the proposed adaptivity in the system involves a dynamically generated set of options that reflect important aspects in the data available. The system simply provides these options to the user; the user is then free to take or ignore these choices, thus maintaining control. Crucially system generated choices save the user from having to analyze the data to make the choices themselves.

Figure 1 illustrates the interaction from the user's point of view. The interaction follows these stages:

- The user logs in.

- The user selects a patient which causes the patient's dataset ('log-book' record of PDA recorded events) to be loaded, having been either previously or immediately downloaded from the patient's PDA.
- The dataset is analysed (i.e. data agents compute data attributes).
- The user can either select one or more of the system's data visualisations via the system's menu or select a 'summary' – the summary is a prioritised list of the systems visualisations.
- If the user selects the summary, this can be stepped through to display each in turn (the user can select the length of the list from one to the complete list of 16 visualisations).

6.   System Architecture

There are two layers to the architecture produced. The interaction layer contains the agents that interact with the data and the user and brings the results of the interactions together to allow decisions to be made. The control layer contains the agents that manage this process. In addition, a blackboard contains a discourse model to record user actions and a domain model to capture relationships between interface actions and dataset attributes. A blackboard is employed to communicate models because the system is using reactive agents that do not have the facility to store large amounts of data.. Figure 2 shows the system architecture and how the two layers of agents operate within the system.

6.1.   The Interaction Layer

The main part of the functionality of the agent component is found in the interaction layer. The agents here are responsible for interacting with both the user and the data and combining the information from both to make the decisions about the summary that is to be generated. The task to be completed has two distinct parts. As data arrives, it needs to be analysed for patterns and as the system is used, the interface has to monitor the actions of the user, i.e. choices of visualisations. These are very different tasks. Monitoring the data is a discrete process that is carried out whenever a dataset is loaded whereas monitoring the user is a continuous process. It therefore makes sense when employing a community of agents to employ one set to act in a discrete manner and deal with the dataset while another acts in a continuous manner and deal with the actions of the user. While the data and the interface are monitored separately, each needs to feed into the other. Thus an effective way of combining the information from the data and the interface is needed. To allow this, a third set of agents is required that communicates only with other agents. These bring together the information from the data and interface agents in such a way that the patterns in the data can be used both to drive what is important in the summary and to provide a context for the actions that the user is taking.

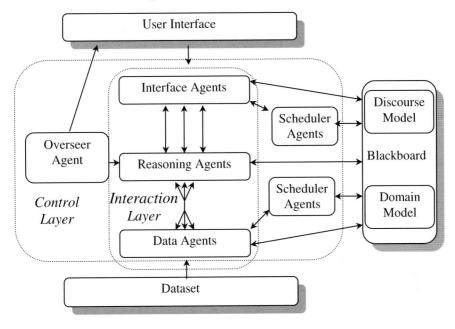

Fig. 2. The Multiagent system architecture

6.1.1. Interface Agents
There is an interface agent associated with each of the relevant interface actions. When the user carries out an action, the relevant interface agent notices this and keeps track of this occurrence. It then looks to see which interface actions preceded it and which follow it. This information is used to update its model about sequential relationships between the action it is associated with and other interface actions. This information can be supplied to the relevant reasoning agent when required. In this way, each interface agent is responsible for building a model of how important its own action is and how it relates to other interface actions.

6.1.2. Data Agents
When a dataset enters the system, some initial calculations are carried out to enable the system to assign attribute values to the dataset. At this time, the data agents will also examine the data. Each data agent is concerned with a particular attribute of the data and looks to see whether the data's value is different from what it normally expects. If the value is beyond a threshold above or below normal, the agent will notify this fact. It will then look to see which other agents have also notified. By taking note of which agents have notified each data agent can build up its own local model of how other data aspects relate to its data attribute. This allows the community of data agents to track correlations and inverse correlations. As with the interface agents, this information can be provided to the reasoning agents when required.

6.1.3.   Reasoning Agents

Reasoning agents do not have any direct contact with the users or the data. Instead they combine the data from interface and data agents. Interface agents can determine patterns of behaviour in the actions of the user and data agents can determine patterns in the data. By combining these, the reasoning agents have a fuller picture of the situation. When the data agents are notifying about changes in behaviour, the reasoning agents take note of this. They also take note of when their associated interface action takes place and look for correlations between the use of their interface action and changes in the data. When a summary is requested, each reasoning agent will attempt to make a case for its interface action. It does this by interrogating its associated interface agent about the associated interface action and by interrogating the data agents to decide whether the current data patterns match with the correlations that it has developed. This information allows the reasoning agent to decide whether its interface action's priority in the 'summary' should be amended (up or down). Once each reasoning agent has made an initial case for its interface action, it can check the strength of belief that other reasoning agents have of their actions and use the information from the interface agent to decide whether to update its belief because of the level of belief in other interface actions to which there appears to be a correlation.

6.2.   Control Level

If one allows a community of agents to alter their behaviour then there is a danger that the system's behaviour will migrate away from what is required. To address this, the control layer has final control over any changes made and so can ensure that the actions of the agents stay within sensible bounds. An overseer agent is responsible for this. In a community of agents there is also the issue of coordinating the communication that takes place. Again the control layer takes responsibility for this by providing scheduler agents to mediate the interaction where required.

6.2.1.   Overseer Agent

The role of the overseer is to keep the system within sensible bounds. This is something that could have been achieved by coding limits into the interaction layer agents themselves or by providing an overall arbiter. It was decided that a central arbiter was a more sensible choice as the control was being applied to the overall decisions being made rather than the individual parts of the process. In a system that utilizes emergence, trying to effectively constrain the system by considering it at an individual agent level would be a difficult task without affecting the ability of the agents to effectively collaborate. Thus providing the control at the community level was implemented as a more transparent way or providing the necessary functionality. The overseer agent responds to the user's request for a 'summary' by interacting with the reasoning agents to compile a prioritised list of visualisations.

6.2.2.   Scheduler Agents

Facilitating the interchange of information in the system are the scheduler agents. While the individual agents can in many cases interact sufficiently without outside interference, it is sometimes the case that an outside entity is required to control part of the data flow. For this reason, scheduler agents are responsible for mediating various parts of the interaction. An example of the use of a scheduler agent is when an interface agent is activated and adds the fact that its action has been chosen into the discourse model. It can then look back over the discourse model to see which actions were carried out previously and use this information to update its model of action sequences. Each agent also needs to know which actions happen after their own action to allow for sequences going forward in time. To provide for this, the interface agents could remain watching the discourse model and take notice of every time a new action was added. This means that a number of agents will be spending time simply accessing the discourse model to see what was happening. However we have seen that it is more efficient to have a single scheduler agent tasked with watching the discourse model and keeping track of which agents' actions have occurred and taking responsibility for sending information to each agent when further actions occur .

7.   Discussion

The system has been informally evaluated in a clinical setting in consultations between health care professionals and diabetic patients.   Three health care professionals used the system and reported that they found the information provided useful. They also reported that they did not find the system intrusive, one clinician reporting that he had viewed the information in one session with a patient but had not found the information useful in this particular instance, importantly he said that had not felt that it had wasted his time asking for the information. All users reported that the system delivered the information in a timely manner and did not detract in any way from their interaction with their patient. In addition, they stated that if the system were made available for their use they would use it in the majority of the sessions they had with patients.

When creating a system such as this, it is very important that the system is able to make accurate judgments as to what the user wants. As discussed, this has been achieved through observing the user choices in response to the data available. In itself, this might seem a logical start but a feedback mechanism is needed to allow it to appraise effectiveness. Using agents to check how the user utilizes the summaries provided achieves this by analysing choices from the summary in the same way that the choices from the main interface are analysed. This allows the system to determine how accurate the summary is. Just as choices made at the interface provide data for adaptation, advice followed, and indeed advice not followed provide the feedback loop to keep the system in check. The control layer agents keep the actions of the agents within sensible bounds but this in itself does not prevent the agents making incorrect choices. Providing an effective feedback mechanism goes towards addressing this problem.

Currently, the feedback mechanism uses whether or not the choices from the proposed summary were selected to provide the information. If the user selects something that is available from the summary directly from the interface, it does not consider the ramifications of this in terms of acceptance of the summary. An analysis of this type involves a much deeper study of the user interface issues surrounding the use of a system of this type. While worthwhile, it is beyond the scope of the current work.

A second issue when considering accuracy of decisions made is the quality of the information upon which the decision was made. Many adaptive systems do not have a strong model of exactly what the user is trying to achieve. A good example of this is the work of Korvemaker & Greiner [10] where they were trying to predict Unix commands. They demonstrated that a system could, in the case of Unix command prediction, attempt to predict the pattern of commands that is to be repeated. However, this does not mean that one can necessarily have any understanding of what the user is trying to achieve. Without this knowledge, the task of prediction is, as shown, very difficult. In the case of web page prediction, the various systems can attempt to match keywords in the available pages to pick their recommendations. This could be seen as starting to move towards trying to understand what the user is trying to achieve and perhaps make it easier to then predict what they require from the system. The agents have some idea about what each page is concerned with and user choices allow them to determine what type of page is of interest. Of course the use of keywords is not perfect. Unfortunately HTML based pages do not allow for much else. With more widespread use of the various XML related technologies [10], we could perhaps be moving towards a situation where much richer knowledge about what the user is attempting to retrieve is available. This could be used to enable agents to produce better-informed choices about what is required.

In our system, a conscious effort is made to try to make the most of the available information from both data streams. The actions of the user are considered alongside patterns in the data. This allows the system to not only observe patterns in what the user does but relate these to the data being considered thus placing these actions within a context.

By using a community of simple agents that communicated with each other, it was possible to consider the actions at the interface and the patterns in the data separately while still having a mechanism in place in the form of the reasoning agents, which allowed these two analyses to be combined to provide the final decisions.

8.   Conclusion

This work demonstrates that the use of emergent behaviour in a community of agents provides a means of driving a self adaptive system. To achieve this using a conventional approach would have required the construction of a far more complex system with the various high level models that such an approach entails. We have shown that a group of agents working at finding patterns can combine together through their interactions to produce a working system. With the relationships between the various patterns in the data and user actions implicitly modelled, one can, at least in some cases, avoid the need for complex high level models.

Hence the agent-based system adapts to the clinician's usage, rather than to his or her implicit directions, in order to provide the clinician with high quality information in a form that is pertinent to their enquiries yet unobtrusive in use.

References

[1] Holman R.R., Smale, A.D., Pemberton, E., Riefflin, A., Nealon J.L. Randomised controlled pilot trail of a hand-held patient-oriented insulin regimen optimizer. In: Journal of Medical Informatics, 21:4, (1996), 317-326

[2] Diabetes Control & Complications Trial Research Group: The Effect of Intensive Treatment of Diabetes on the Development and Progression of Long-Term Complications in Insulin-Dependent Diabetes Mellitus. New England Journal of Medicine, 329(14), (1993)

[3] UK Prospective Diabetes Study (UKPDS) Group. Intensive blood glucose control with sulphonylureas or insulin compared with conventional treatment and risk of complications in patients with type 2 diabetes. Lancet 352, (1998), 837-853

[4] Wooldridge, M. An Introduction to MultiAgent Systems. John Wiley, (2002), 258-259

[5] Muller, J.P. Architectures and applications of intelligent agents: a survey. In: Knowledge Engineering Review, Vol. 13(4) (1998), 353-380

[6] Brooks, R.A. Intelligence without Representation, Art. Intell. 47 (1991), 139-159

[7] Nwana, H., Ndumu, D. A perspective on software agents research. In: Knowledge Engineering Review Vol 14(2), (1989), 125-142

[8] Goecks, J., Shavlik, J. Learning User's interests by Unobtrusively Observing their Normal Behaviour - IUI 2000. In: Proc. Int. Conf. On Intelligent User Interfaces, (2000), 129-133

[9] Gervasio, M.T., Iba, W., Langley, P. Learning to Predict User Operations for Adaptive Scheduling Proc. of the 15th Nat. Conf. on AI (1998), 721-726

[10] Korvemaker, B., Greiner, R. Predicting Unix Command Lines: Adjusting to User Patterns. In: Proc. 17th Nat. Conf on A I (2000), 230-235

[11] Berger, G., Ruddock, N. Is XML the Missing Link in Raising Browsers to a Higher Intelligence, XML99 (1999)

Acknowledgement

The authors wish to acknowledge the collaboration of the Diabetes Research Laboratories and Diabetes Trials Unit of Oxford University.

Sue Greenwood, John Nealon and Peter Marshall, Department of Computing, Oxford Brookes University, Oxford OX33 1HX, UK

E-mail address: {sgreenwood|johnnealon|pmarshall}@brookes.ac.uk

GruSMA1: Experience on the Deployment of Agent-Based Health Care Services

Antonio Moreno, Aïda Valls, David Isern and David Sánchez

Abstract. In this paper we describe an application called *GruSMA1*, which is an agent-based system that provides medical services to its users (the citizens or the visitors of a city). This multi-agent system contains agents that have information about the medical centres, departments and doctors of the city. All these agents coordinate their tasks to provide a set of services to the user of the system, who can search for medical centres satisfying a given set of requirements, as well as access his/her medical record, or make a booking to be visited by a particular kind of doctor. Special care has been paid to the definition of a medical ontology and to the implementation of mechanisms that guarantee the confidentiality in the access and transmission of medical data.

1. Introduction

Imagine that you are attending a scientific congress in a foreign city. It is the first time that you go to that city, so you only know the location of the airport, the hotel and the congress site. After attending a workshop on the morning you don't feel very well, because you have been suffering an increasing pain in your chest for two hours. You have had heart problems in the past, so you are quite worried about this pain. Fortunately, you carry your PDA with you. Your personal assistant (Jimmy) is permanently executing on it. You ask Jimmy about the location of the nearest medical centre in town. In a few seconds, you have in the PDA's screen the details of the closest hospital, along with a map of the neighbourhood and indications about the buses that can be taken to arrive there. Then, you ask Jimmy to find information about the timetables of the doctors of that medical centre that are heart specialists. Your assistant replies with a list of three doctors; one of them performs examinations on the afternoon, and another one on the evening (the third one is on holidays). You request Jimmy to book a visit to one of the two available doctors as soon as possible. Jimmy tries to book a visit to the first doctor by contacting the medical centre's agent, but he is told that the doctor has a full schedule. However, he manages to book a visit to the second doctor at 18:00. Then, you can see in the PDA's screen a confirmation of the booking and the details about how to get to the doctor's office within the hospital. At 18:00 you go to the hospital. After explaining the problem to the doctor, she asks the personal assistant on her desktop computer to retrieve your medical record (which can be accessed with a code and a password that you introduce in the computer's keyboard). In a few seconds she can see your previous heart conditions, the treatments and operations you have had in the past, the medicines to which you are allergic, etc. After a detailed examination, she concludes that the problem is not serious, and that you only need some rest. She also adds the information gathered in this examination to your medical record, so that it can be taken into account in the future.

This scenario is not as far-fetched and futuristic as it may seem at first glance. If agent technology delivers the results it is promising, the facts described in this example could indeed happen in a real setting. The challenges involved are many and come from these main areas:

- Communication between services - e.g. sharing ontologies and semantics, which could be heterogenous even within the health care domain.
- Security/Authorisation - accessing/editing sensitive medical data, such as the medical records of the patients.
- Creating an environment where agents can join/leave the system dynamically, discover one another and access one another's services.
- Communication between users and agents -e.g. graphical user interfaces to communicate with personal assistants, who provide personalised access to information to a user.
- Coordination between distributed services, i.e. making complex distributed decisions (for instance, several units of a hospital might coordinate their activities to schedule different tests to be made on a patient, [1]).
- Deploying personal agents in mobile devices, such as PDAs or mobile phones, so that users may have ubiquitous access to agent-based services.

Our work is a first step towards these future scenarios, with contributions to primarily the first four challenges. In this paper we describe the design and implementation of a *multi-agent system* (MAS, [2, 3]), called *GruSMA1*, that offers some of the services which have been mentioned in the first paragraph. The system contains agents that represent entities such as medical centres, medical departments or doctors. These agents coordinate their activities and knowledge to offer a set of services to the users of the system. The developed system also contains an agent-controlled database in which the medical records of the users are stored. Our main claim in this paper is that, when agent (and telecommunication) technology is a little bit more mature, citizens will be able to access much useful health-related information and facilities all around the world in an easy, dynamic, flexible and cheap way.

The rest of the paper is organised as follows. First of all, we describe the specific objectives of the work and we argue why multi-agent systems offer an appropriate framework for developing health-related applications. After that, a detailed description of the MAS that has been designed and implemented is given. We explain the architecture of the MAS, the ontology used to represent medical information, the security mechanisms that have been put in place to ensure the confidentiality of medical data, and the especific services offered by the different types of agents. The paper finishes with a discussion of the work done and an outline of some potential future lines of research.

2. Background

Agent Cities [4] is an ambitious project whose main aim is the construction of a worldwide, publicly accessible network of agent-based FIPA platforms[1]. In March 2003 there are around 50 active platforms. Each of them supports agents that offer services similar to those that can be found in a real city (facilities, amenities, attractions, information and commercial services). It is expected that, in the near future, it will be possible to implement intelligent complex compound services (e.g. agents that are able to help a user to plan a weekend away, including tasks such as booking air tickets, selecting and booking a room in an appropriate hotel, buying tickets for the theatre and reserving a table in a restaurant that is near the theatre and offers the user's favourite meal).

The main aim of our work was to develop a set of agents that could offer to the citizens and visitors of a city not the usual leisure-oriented services but health-care related services. This interest is related with previous work that our research group had done in the last years in the application of AI techniques (especially agent-based technology) to the medical domain (see e.g. [6]). Therefore, we decided to design and implement a multi-agent system with the following features:

- The user may request information about all the medical centres available in a particular geographical area.
- The structure of medical centres in Catalonia should be maintained (each centre has a set of departments, and each department has a set of doctors).
- It should also be possible to book a visit to be examined by a doctor.
- The user must be given access to his/her medical record. A doctor should also be able to consult and update the medical record of a patient during a visit.
- It must be made sure that nobody can access the private medical information of the users of the system without proper authorisation.

The decision of using a multi-agent system in this medical setting (and not other more tradicional AI techniques such as an expert system or a decision support system) is motivated by the following reasons:

- The information that must be dealt with is geographically distributed, because each hospital or medical centre will keep its own data, each doctor will have his/her personal information (e.g. an up to date daily schedule) in a personal computer, the medical records of the potential users of the system may be located in different databases, etc. Therefore, a distributed AI approach (such as the one offered by multi-agent systems) seems suitable in this case.
- There must be a fluent communication between the user and the medical centres. For instance, the user's personal assistant should be able to ask for a booking with a certain doctor, and be able to react quickly to the fact that the doctor's schedule is full (so another doctor -in the same hospital or in a

---

[1] The *Foundation for Intelligent Physical Agents* (FIPA, [5]) is an non-profit organisation that defines standards for agent interoperation

different one- has to be chosen). Agents are not only *reactive* but also endowed with *social abilities*, so they are able to communicate with other agents in order to negotiate and co-ordinate their activities.

- Existing systems (such as databases containing medical records) may be easily included in a multi-agent system. The standard way of agentifying a database is to put a *wrapper* ([7]) around it. A wrapper is an agent that receives the queries to be made to the database in a standard agent communication language (such as FIPA-ACL [8] or KQML [9]) and is able to translate these requests into queries in SQL to the database. After receiving the reply from the database, the wrapper may translate the answer to the common agent language and send it to the requesting agent.

- Health-oriented agents could perform *proactive* tasks in order to have ready all the information that the user may need at a particular time. For instance, the user's personal assistant may keep, in the user's health profile, the information that he/she has had heart conditions in the past. When the user travels to a foreign city, the personal assistant could immediately (without an explicit demand from the user) search all those medical centres in which there are heart specialists, and have this information ready in case the user needs it. This property has not been implemented in the agents described in this paper, though.

- It is also interesting for the user to be able to access his/her medical record from anywhere. For instance, the user may be on holidays in a rural area, far away from medical centres, and need to be examined by a local doctor. If the user may access his/her medical record from a mobile phone or a personal computer connected to the Internet, the doctor may take it into account in order to make a more precise diagnosis. It must be said that, in the present version of the system, all agents have to be running in standard personal computers.

- Agents are assumed to have an *autonomous* behaviour (i.e. they are supposed to choose their actions on their own, according to their beliefs and the information they receive from the environment, without being externally controlled by a user or by other agents). Therefore, they offer an ideal paradigm when we want to model a domain with different kinds of entities, and each of them wants to keep its independence and follow a particular policy (e.g. each doctor might define a specific way of accepting bookings from patients).

- Finally, perhaps the most important reason for capturing services as agents in this way is to enable the individual medical services to interact with each other at a high enough level to ensure that they can all interoperate. Agent communication languages (such as FIPA-ACL, [8]), content languages (such as FIPA-SL, [10]) and formal ontologies ([11]) are very useful in describing communication between different services at the application level – i.e. in a way which relates to the domain of discourse rather than to any single implementation. Without formal specifications for domain ontologies it would be almost impossible for diverse medical systems to interact with each other correctly.

3. Architecture of the Multi-Agent System

This section describes the multi-agent system *GruSMA1*, which has been designed and implemented by members of the Multi-Agent Systems Group at URV (*GruSMA*, [12]). The primary design objectives of the work were the following:

- To provide a decomposition of the problem that matched agents to entities which could be realistic players in such a domain (e.g. medical centres, personal agents, doctor agents, etc.).
- To provide an ontology for the domain (a detail often ignored in demonstrations, but crucial to provide interoperability between agents).
- To provide security measures that ensure the confidentiality and privacy of medical data.
- To make the developed agent services as reusable as possible by using standard languages - in this case FIPA-ACL for communication and RDF for content and representation of ontologies ([8, 13]) - and providing detailed service models to describe the individual functioning and objective of each agent including descriptions of actions, protocols used and example messages.

These points are particularly important since the aim is to make re-usable service components which could be used in many applications (not all of them necessarily medical).

3.1. Overview of the Multi-Agent System

The basic architecture of the MAS which has been developed in this work is shown in fig. 1 in the next page. This multi-agent system contains six different types of agents:

- The user's *personal agent* (PA), that provides a graphical interface of the MAS with the user. This interface is used to introduce the requirements of a search or to show the results of a query to the user.
- The *personal broker* (PB) is an agent that provides a gateway between personal agents and the rest of the agents in the system. It controls the access of users that are properly authenticated.
- The information of a medical centre is divided in three levels. For each medical centre there is one *medical centre agent* (MCA), several *department agents* (DEPs, one for each department of the centre) and many *doctor agents* (DAs, one for each doctor of each department). The MCA has the general information of the centre (e.g. its address and opening times). Each DEP has the knowledge of a certain department (e.g. all the information of the Ophthalmology department). Each DA maintains the schedule of a given doctor, and is aware of the doctor's visiting times.
- The *database wrapper* (DW) is the agent that controls the access to a database that contains the medical records of the users.

The agents that provide information about the medical services available in a city are internal to an *Agent Cities* platform. Personal agents, that represent the users of the system, are supposed to be running in computers external to the platform.

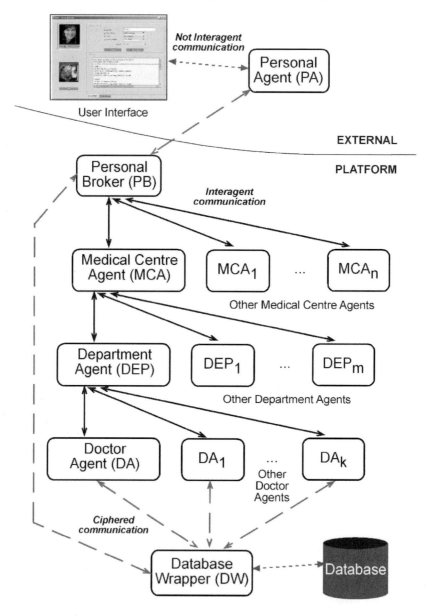

Fig. 1: Architecture of the multi-agent system GruSMA1

4. Definition of a Simple Medical Ontology

There is not a universally accepted medical ontology that may be used in all health care applications. However, there are several standards organizations trying to develop specifications for having uniform ways of storing and managing health care information, such as the *American Society for Testing and Materials* (ASTM, http://www.astm.org, see the XML Healthcare Informatics subcommittee E31), the Technical Committee 251 of the *European Committee for Standardization* (CEN/TC251, http://centc251.org), the Health Informatics Group of the *International Organization for Standardization* (ISO, TC 215, http://www.iso.org) and *Health Level 7* (HL7, http://www.hl7.org). Other interesting approaches in the same field are the following:

- The *Unified Medical Language System* (UMLS, http://www.nlm.nih.gov/research/umls) provides a relational database that connects medical terms from around 60 vocabularies and dictionaries.
- SNOMED (*Systematized Nomenclature of Medical Reference Terminology*, http://www.snomed.org) provides a way of comparing and aggregating medical data, and facilitates the transmission of pacient information through several information channels.
- The GALEN technology has been designed to represent clinical information in a computer readable support. It provides a multi-lingual computerised system for codifying medical terms (see http://www.opengalen.org).

We have found inspiration in these works to define an ontology for the GruSMA1 system which is complex enough to manage the basic information of medical centres, departments, doctors and medical records, but simple enough to be easily implemented.

The HL7 reference information model has been applied to our ontology in order to use a structured way of representing data (including class inheritance). It also offers some examples of the attributes that can be useful to store, for example, the patient record or the result of a visit with a doctor (results, treatment, tests, etc.). The CEN/TC251 standard about electronic health records has been used to specify the structure, classes and attributes about health care providers (organizations, persons, devices, etc.). Moreover, it also provides a model for storing common information about person names, addresses, and telecommunication means. Finally, the UMLS knowledge resource offers a huge vocabulary data base of medical terms, grouped into semantic categories. We have used this information to create some attributes and to define its range of values (ex: medical specialties). In addition, we have also included in the ontology some other frames and slots that allow us to add other functionalities (for example, the working hours for a healthcare party or the department structure within a healthcare organisation). Concerning the patient record, its slots are based on the Catalan medical law about clinical histories [14]. The ontology, a part of which is shown in fig. 2, has been represented using RDF [13].

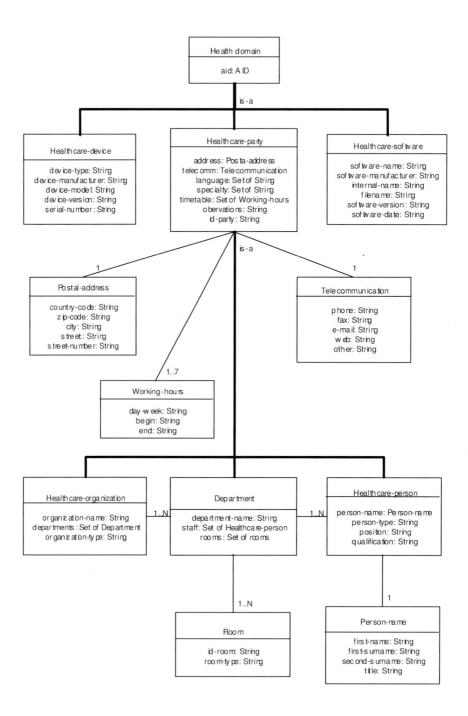

Fig. 2. Part of the Grusma1 medical ontology.

5. Security mechanisms

Dealing with medical records is clearly a very sensitive issue. In 2000 an American law that regulated the treatment of medical data was passed ([15]). This law establishes which rules must be followed by the software business in this field, and the fines that will be applied to those that do not comply with the regulations. This text, however, does not force any specific standard for storing or transmitting data. A Catalan law dealing with the patient's right to access medical information was also recently passed ([4]). Some issues related to secure communication are discussed in [16].

One of the aims of the GruSMA1 system is to guarantee a secure access to medical records, so that only authenticated users, and doctors that examine the users, are allowed to obtain and update this information. To provide this security, a three-level security mechanism was implemented:

- All the messages that are sent between the agents in the system are encoded using SSL (*Secure Socket Layer*) in order to avoid any sniffing attacks on the net. This feature is provided by JADE-S, a plug-in for JADE (*Java Agent Development Framework*, [17], [18]), which is the library of Java classes that we have used to implement our system. This tool eases the process to create a multi-agent system that follows FIPA standards.

- Through JADE-S we can also define different types of users (with login and password), to which we assign various access permissions (like an UNIX based OS). Each agent is owned by one of these users; therefore, the actions that it is allowed to perform are controlled by the list of permissions assigned to this user. For example, the *Personal Agent* (which is an external agent that we don't control directly), only has permission to talk with the *Personal Broker* and with the AMS (*Agent Management System*), but not with the DF (*Directory Facilitator*) or any other agent of the system. This restriction prevents the agent from requesting services such as killing or changing the characteristics of an agent that is advertised in the DF.

- Finally, we have implemented an authentication process based on a public key mechanism on top of JADE-S that allows controlling the identity of the agents that request some critical actions (like asking for medical records or setting up visits with doctors). When an agent (*Personal* or *Doctor*) wants to perform this kind of actions, it has to sign the message sent (to the *Broker* and the *Database Wrapper* respectively) ciphering its content with its Private Key (which is only known by it). On the destination, it is possible to verify its identity by deciphering the message with the agent's Public Key (which can be accessed by everybody) and checking the content. The *Database Wrapper* manages the creation and storage of these keys safely. The specific algorithm used to implement this authentication mechanism is called RSA (Rivest, Shamir, Adlemann, [19]). The code was adapted from a Java library of cryptographic functions [20].

6. Services Provided by the Multi-Agent System

In this section we describe the medical services that the user may access through the personal agent, and we detail the flow of information between the agents shown in fig. 1.

6.1. Searching appropriate medical centres

The *personal agent* offers a graphical interface that allows the user to search for medical centres that satisfy some requirements. This graphical interface is depicted in fig. 3.

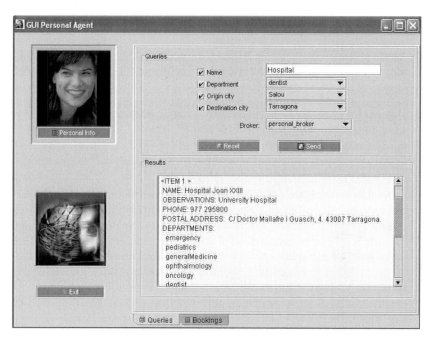

Fig. 3: Graphical interface for searching for medical centres

As shown in the figure, in this kind of request the user has to select the *personal broker* as the recipient of the message. As PB is aware of all medical centres in town, it will find out which of them satisfy the user's constraints. The user may specify (some of) the following four requirements:

- *Name*: the user may provide a string that must appear somewhere in the name of the medical centre (e.g. "Hospital", "central", "memorial", "St.John").
- *Department*: the user may express that he/she is interested in centres having a particular department (e.g. "Cardiology"). The department may be chosen from a predetermined list.

- *Destination city*: the user may be interested only in those centres that are located in a particular town (e.g. "Tarragona").
- User location (*origin city*): in this option the user may tell its actual location to the system (e.g. "Salou"). In this case, the list of all the centres that satisfy the constraints will be ordered according to the distance from the user 's location to the centres. The city of the medical centre and the user's location are also selected from a predefined list, that contains the cities in the area

. This four search criteria may be freely combined. In the most general case, when no constraints are specified, the user is demanding information about all the medical centres known by the broker; in the most specific case, the user may ask for centres containing a given string in the name, that have a certain department and are located near a particular city (e.g. the previous figure shows a search for medical centres having the word "hospital" in their name, that have a "Dentist" department and are located in Tarragona, ordered according to the distance from the medical centre to Salou). The results of the search are shown at the lower area of the window.

The sequence of messages needed to perform the search is shown in fig. 4 (all the messages have a format that follows FIPA specifications). First, the *personal agent* sends a query to the broker, which forwards them to all MCAs (there are five of them in fig. 4). Each MCA checks whether it satisfies the user's constraints. If it does, it returns an *inform* message to the broker; in other case, it returns a *failure* message (in the example shown in fig. 3, two of the medical centres, hospitals one and five, satisfy the user's conditions). The *broker* receives all these messages and sends to the personal agent an *inform* with a list with the positive answers, which is then shown to the user in the graphical interface.

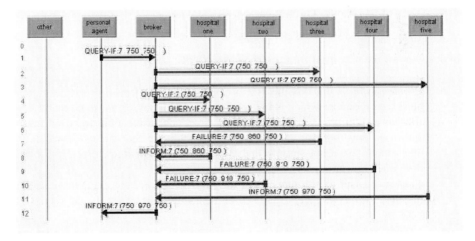

Fig. 4: Search protocol through the broker

6.2. Booking a visit to a doctor

The user may also ask his/her personal agent to make a booking to be visited by a particular kind of doctor. The graphical interface that is shown to the user is the one in fig.5.

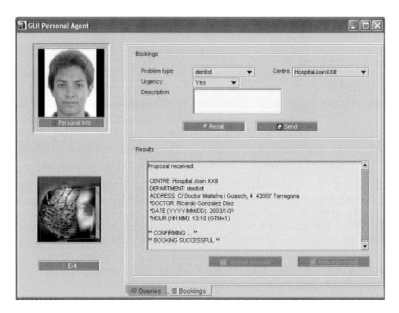

Fig. 5: Booking a visit to a doctor

In this window the user must fill three mandatory slots:

- *Problem type*: in this box the user is offered a list of medical departments, and he/she must choose which is the one in which the booking has to be made (e.g. if it has a sight problem, the "Ophthalmology" department has to be selected). The user may not specify a particular doctor, he/she can only select the department (we are assuming that the user is in an unknown city, so he/she does not know any specific doctor in the city).
- *Centre*: the user must select one of the MCAs registered in the system, shown in a list. This is the agent that will be contacted to try to make the requested booking.
- *Urgency*: the user has to tell the system whether the visit is urgent. If it is, the system tries to make a booking as soon as possible; if it is not, the system tries to make a booking for the following two days.

Finally, the user may optionally give a description of the problem, which can later be included in his/her medical record (when the examination is performed).

The sequence of messages needed to make a booking of a visit is shown in the following figure.

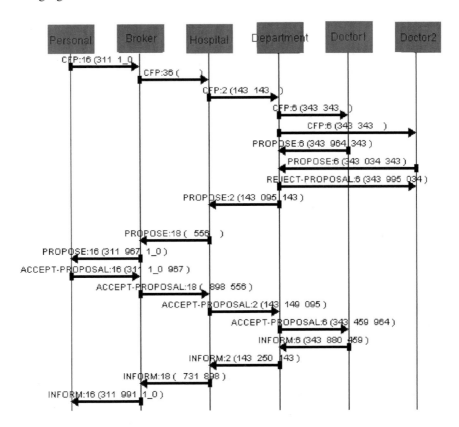

Fig. 6: 4-layer-CFP Protocol for booking a visit

The protocol (called *4-layer-CFP*) involves several types of agents of our achitecture: *personal agent* (PA), *personal broker* (PB), *medical centre agent* (MCA), *department agent* (DA) and some *doctor agents* (DAs). It has the following steps:

- The *personal agent* sends a *call for proposals* (CFP) to the *broker*. The *broker*, after checking the identity of the user, sends a CFP to the chosen MCA. This CFP is forwarded to the department selected by the user.
- DEP sends the CFP to all the doctors of the department. Each DA replies with a proposal, in which it tells when is the earliest time in which the doctor has a free slot for making a visit (or a refusal, if it does not have any available slot).
- DEP rejects all the proposals but the best one (the one in which the visit may be made earlier).

- The chosen proposal is sent by DEP to MCA, which forwards it to the *personal agent* via the broker. PA shows this proposal (doctor, visiting time) to the user, who must confirm his/her interest in being visited by that doctor at that time. If the user accepts, an accept-proposal is sent to MCA by the *broker*, which forwards it to DEP, which in its turn forwards it to the DA of the selected doctor. If the user does not accept the proposal, he/she must try to make another booking with different constraints (in another centre, another department, or with a different degree of urgency).
- Finally, DA confirms that the schedule of the doctor has been updated to add the visit, and this confirmation is sent to the user through DEP, MCA and PB.

6.3. Management of medical records

A medical record contains a sequence of medical visits managed by our system. Each one has a description of the problem and the treatment suggested by the physician. The medical records of the users are stored in a database, the access to which is controlled by DW. There are two services that this agent provides: accessing a medical record and updating it. Imagine that the user has scheduled a visit to Dr. Jones at 11:00. When the booking is made, a low priority Java thread calculates how much time is left until 11:00, and sleeps until that time has elapsed. Then, at the visit's time, this thread awakes and a simulation of the visit is made. The DA associated to Dr. Jones requests the medical record of the user from DW. After that, DA adds to the medical record the (simulated) information gathered in the examination and sends the modified medical record back to DW, so that it can update the database.

The user may also access his/her medical record through the *personal agent*. In the GUI of the *personal agent* (see fig. 3) there is a button named "*personal info*"; if this button is pressed PA requests the user's medical record from DW, via the *broker*, and shows it to the user (see fig. 7).

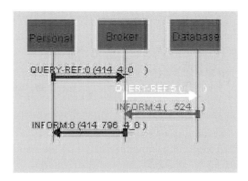

Fig. 7: Access to a medical record

7. Discussion and Future Work

The main aim of the *Agent Cities* initiative ([4]) is to provide agent-based services that improve the quality of life of the citizens and the visitors of a city. The deployed application certainly contributes towards this objective, by giving to the users the possibility of accessing medical data in an easy and efficient way. This system is fully implemented in a prototype version, with all the agents running in standard PCs. The benefits of the system, were it to be implemented in a real setting, would reach two kinds of users:

- Citizens that need medical services, who could access their medical record from anywhere, make appointments with a certain doctor, and obtain any kind of information related to the medical centres, departments and doctors of a given city.
- Health care personnel, who could automatically access and update the patient's medical record during the examination, and would have their workload decreased, due to the fact that citizens could make queries or appointments on their own.

The MAS is accessible live in the *Agent Cities* network of platforms (see access instructions at http://grusma.etse.urv.es/~agentcities/). The ontology that has been designed explicitly for this system is based on the ideas of several proposals for standardising the representation of medical information. It is represented in RDF and is freely available from the same web page.

The agents described in this paper are the first step towards a first generation of intelligent agents providing health-related services. The range of the services that could be given by these agents is as wide as our imagination. For instance, it could be possible to ask for an ambulance from our mobile phone; our personal agent, after consulting a GPS service, would find out which is the closest hospital and would automatically request an ambulance to be sent as soon as possible to our current location.

The MAS described in this paper has been implemented using JADE. The content of all messages is written in RDF ([13]). The medical records database has been implemented using *MySql* ([21]). In the current implementation the user's personal assistant is simulated through a graphical interface, as shown in fig. 3. The examination of a user by a doctor is also simulated by adding the information about the examination in the user's medical record, as described in section 6.3. In this prototype all the agents are running in the same computer.

Some future lines of work are the following:

- It is planned to use the JADE-LEAP framework ([22]) in order to implement personal agents that may be running in mobile devices, such as PDAs or mobile phones with enough computational resources.
- When PB searches the information of the MCAs that satisfy some requirements, it returns a list that is ordered according to the distance of the user with each one

of them. Other preferences could be used to sort this list (e.g. the user may prefer private hospitals to public ones, or it may prefer to go to a primary medical assistance centre rather than to a hospital, if the problem to be treated is not very serious). The personal agent could have some learning procedures to find out automatically which are the user's preferences.

- If PB finds out that none of the local medical centres can solve the user's problem, it could access a regional PB, which should have access to the PBs of the cities in the same zone. In this way, it could find out whether there is a hospital near the current location of the user where he/she can be examined. Following this idea one step ahead, it could be possible to have a whole hierarchy of brokers (city, region, county, province, state, Europe). A search would be sent to the upper level when the medical centres in a certain level do not offer the requested service. In this scenario it would be possible to keep a database of medical records for each area, so that the user may access his/her medical record from anywhere (which is more realistic that the current situation in our prototype, where a single database is assumed to contain all the medical records).

- We plan to add some amount of co-ordination in the medical departments level. For instance, when a patient is being examined, the doctor may decide that a number of medical tests should be made. In this case, the doctor agent could already contact the agents in charge of the involved departments (e.g. Radiology, Blood Tests), and schedule specific times for the patient to undergo the tests. The results of these tests could also be sent automatically to the doctor agent, who would access them directly in the nest visit of the patient.

References

[1] Decker, K., Li, J. Coordinated hospital patient scheduling. Proceedings of the 3rd International Conference on Multi-Agent Systems, ICMAS-98. Paris, France, (1998).

[2] Weiss, G. Multiagent systems: a modern approach to Distributed Artificial Intelligence. MIT Press, (1999).

[3] Wooldridge, M. An introduction to multiagent systems. Wiley Eds, (2002).

[4] *Agent Cities*: http://www.agentcities.org. The set of active *Agent Cities* platforms is available from http://www.agentcities.net.

[5] *FIPA: Foundation for Intelligent Physical Agents*: http://www.fipa.org.

[6] Aldea, A., López, B., Moreno, A., Riaño, D., Valls, A.. A Multi-Agent System for Organ Trasplant Co-ordination. In Artificial Intelligence in Medicine. Eds: S.Quaglini, P.Barahona, S.Andreassen. Lecture Notes in Computer Science 2101, Springer Verlag, (2001), 413-416.

[7] Brenner, W., Zarnekow, R., Wittig, H., Intelligent Software Agents Foundations and Applications. Springer Verlag, (1998).

[8] FIPA Agent Communication Language: FIPA ACL Message Structure Specification. Spec. Number 00061. FIPA, (2000).

[9] Finin, T., Labrou, Y., Mayfield, J.. KQML as an agent communication language. In Jeff Bradshaw (Ed.), Software Agents. MIT Press, Cambridge, (1997).

[10] FIPA Semantic Language: FIPA SL Content Language Specification. Spec. Number 00008. FIPA, 2000.

[11] Fensel, D. Ontologies: a silver bullet for knowledge management and electronic commerce. Heidelberg, Germany, (2001).

[12] GruSMA: Multi-Agent Systems Group - http://www.etse.urv.es/recerca/banzai/toni/MAS.

[13]Alexaki, S., Managing RDF metadata for community webs. Proceedings of the 2nd International Workshop on the WWW and Conceptual Modelling, WCM-2000. Salt Lake City, USA, (2000), 140-151. See also http://www.w3c.org/RDF.

[14] Generalitat de Catalunya. Llei sobre els drets d'informació concernent la salut i l'autonomia del pacient, i la documentació clínica (Law on the information rights concerning tha patient's health and autonomy, and the clinical documentation). Law 21/2000, 29/12/2000, Health and Social Security Department, Generalitat de Catalunya.

[15]US Department of Health and Human Services. Standards for Privacy and Individually Identifiable Health Information. Federal Register, volume 65. December 28, 2000.

[16]Wong, H., Sycara, K.. Adding security and trust to multi-agent systems. Proceedings of Autonomous Agents'99, Workshop on deception, fraud and trust in agent societies. Seattle, Washington, (1999), 149-161.

[17]JADE: *Java Agent Development Environment*: http://sharon.cselt.it/projects/jade.

[18]Bellifemine, F., Poggi, A., Rimassa, G., Developing multi-agent systems with a FIPA compliant framework. Software Practice and Experience 31, pp. 103-128, 2001.

[19]Rivest, L., Shamir, A., Adleman, L. A method for obtaining digital signatures and public-key cryptosystems. Communications of the ACM, 21(2), pp. 120-126, February 1978. See also http://www.rsa.com.

[20]Cryptonite. Package of Java logi.crypto, v. 1.0.7. http://logi.org/logi.crypto.

[21]MySql: http://www.mysql.com.

[22]LEAP: *Lightweight Extensible Agent Platform*. See http://keap.crm-paris.com.

Acknowledgements

The authors would like to acknowledge Steve Willmott for his comments on an earlier version of this paper. This work has been made with the support of the *AgentCities.NET* deployment grant "*Deployment of agent-based health care services*". The authors also acknowledge the support of the Spanish thematic network "*Creación de un entorno innovador para la comunicación de agentes inteligentes*", TIC2001-5108-E, founded by the Spanish Ministry of Science and Technology.

Multi-Agent Systems Group (GruSMA). Computer Science and Mathematics Department. Escola Tècnica Superior d'Enginyeria. Universitat Rovira i Virgili. Avinguda dels Països Catalans, 26. 43007-Tarragona, Spain
E-mail address: {amoreno, avalls, disern}@etse.urv.es

Agent.Hospital – a Framework for Clinical Applications in Agentcities

Stefan Kirn, Christian Heine, Rainer Herrler and Karl-Heinz Krempels

Abstract. Agent.Hospital is an open agent-based (software) framework for distributed applications in the healthcare domain. Previous appropriation of the Agent.Hospital development is the application and examination of agent technology in a realistic business scenarios and the identification of further research needs. This paper introduces the framework developed by the German Priority Research Program 1083. We describe the initial system concept, currently implemented or specified functionalities and the integration of FIPA standardization activities. The example scenario, "clinical trials", illustrates how Agent.Hospital supports distributed clinical processes as well as further research of agent technology.

1.   Motivation and Problem Description

Besides the development of the object-oriented paradigm within software engineering, the area of intelligent software agents was established as a new subdiscipline of artificial intelligence in the late 1970s. In a sense, it can also be understood as an extension of the object-oriented paradigm by introducing "intelligent objects" into this field. Intentional models define agents as software systems which autonomously adjust their behavior in accordance with dynamically changing goals. With this definition, artificial intelligence has taken a step from a technological level to research areas which lie at the heart of economic theories. For example, the concept of limited rationality of software agents on the one hand and the model of the so-called "homo oeconomicus" ground on the same roots, and there are relationships between the manager/contractor model in negotiation- based coordination and the approach of princicpal/agent theory in economics, or between models of cooperation processes in multi- agent systems and transaction-cost theoretic approaches in the New Institution Economics [1]. Different authors report essential improvement of operational flexibility [2], significant reduction of software specific costs [3] or advances by integrating organizations and information technology [4]. But the examination of agent technology so far was restricted to laboratory environments. Valid experiences with the specification and application of large agent based information systems are still missing in the year 2003 [5], [6].

Applications need realistic business scenarios. The healthcare domain with its specific requirements [7] is a predestined world of discourse for building realistic scenarios and the application of multiagent systems. Cost reductions and further quality increase of clinical services have to be adjusted. The demand for economic viability of hospitals requires reengineering of hospital service processes and rethinking of all involved actors [8]. Intra-organizational as well as numerous inter-organizational interfaces to different actors along the "supply chain" (for instance rescue service, general practitioner or specialist, rehabilitation etc.) have to be integrated. Raising importance of information systems is interlinked with specific deviations of the (German) healthcare domain (sectored distribution, decision autonomy of physicians and patients) which blocks top-down-integration of processes and information systems. A successful way of connection could be the definition of public interfaces for local encapsulated systems. It explicitly supports the medical, juridical and economical autonomy of actors. This corresponds to the extremely differentiated healthcare market with nearly exclusive small and medium software houses.

Related questions are examined since 2000 by the German Priority Research Program (SPP 1083). The main goal of SPP 1083 is the examination of agent technologies within large realistic business scenarios and the identification of further research needs. One of the examined domain specific scenarios focuses on the healthcare domain. Basic supposition of the SPP is, that agent-based development and connection of decentralized information systems generates essential benefit by supporting interorganizational business processes and organizational flexibility. Examination of these hypotheses is supported by large agent-based software systems.

This paper introduces essential questions and research approaches addressed by the SPP 1083. By means of the exemplary application framework Agent.Hospital we describe requirements and possible solutions for agent-based development and connection of autonomous multiagent systems. We introduce the research network Agentcities and corresponding FIPA standardization activities. At the end of the paper the example scenario "clinical trials" illustrates how Agent.Hospital supports distributed clinical processes as well as further research of agent technology.

2.   Research Approach: Integrated Application Scenarios and Cooperative System Development

In this context the senate of the DFG (Deutsche Forschungsgesellschaft) decided on the 6th of May 1999 to setup a new priority research program "Intelligente Softwareagenten und betriebswirtschaftliche Anwendungsszenarien" [9]. On this basis researchers from management science, information systems, and computer science are collaborating in order to advance the state of the art in intelligent software agents so that agent technologies for large systems in realistic business application scenarios can be developed and tested. With that one goal is to find and investigate a new approach to the development of application systems and to an improved adaptivity of companies with respect to dynamic market processes. In particular, this approach should more closely meet the requirements of the networking and the dynamics of worldwide distributed business processes than existing proposals.

Concerning the generalization goal of the SPP the manufacturing domain as well as the healthcare domain is analyzed under a logistical perspective. Special area of the healthcare domain is the acute-stationary care. Medical and care processes are especially dependent from the capabilities of the logistic systems (patient logistics, bedside logistics, drug logistics, information logistics etc.) At the same time these processes are extremely interlinked. The competitive use of the external factor patient and limited operational resources like medical or nursing staff, operating rooms or physiotherapeutic is the reason for that. In addition high dynamic of daily events (emergency) influences routine activities [10].

Previous results in modeling, development and application of agent-based information systems are mainly based on laboratory experiences in small and reviewable environments with low dynamics and complexity. These results can thus only be partially transferred to complex operational environments with high dynamics. For instance insufficient research is done about the integration of software agents into legacy systems and their consequences or the scalability of multiagent systems or the prognosis and reliable controlling of the behavior of complex multiagent systems.

One first important task was thus providing realistic business application scenarios and the use for evaluating agent-oriented systems and engineering methods. In result to these attempts numerous project specific, empirical funded and detailed described models of the healthcare domain were developed. By the mean of this every project analyzed agent-oriented modeling methods, model configuration problems etc. on their own. For the examination of general research questions SIG's (Special Interest Groups) were established, for instance for the development of a common hospital ontology – *OntHoS* [11]).

In this context the effort for support and coordination between the project partners raised enormously. To solve this problem the cooperation platform *RealAgentS* [12] was established. To enable SPP-external researcher's access to the results of the priority program *RealagentS* provides a public portal for accessing data and documents [13]. Beyond that *RealAgentS* provides a platform for cooperation with other research groups. Further models and material can be easily included. Research groups like GruSMA1[1] and the CoMAS-project[2] (Control and Management of Agents and their Services) cooperate with the SPP and intend to provide domain specific models from transplantation medicine and patient specific Information Retrieval as well as tools for management of agent-based services.

---

[1] Antonio Moreno, Computer Science and Mathematics Department, University Rovira i Virgili, Spanien - Preisträger der Agentcities Agent Technology Competition 2003
[2] Michael Schroeder, Department of Computing, City University London, Großbritanien

3.   Agent.Hospital

In the context of the working group "hospital logistics" an extensive and empirical funded model called *Agent.Hospital* is being developed. This model is defined as an open Framework with numerous different healthcare actors. *Agent.Hospital* provides empirical funded und detailed described partial models of the healthcare domain. It enables the examination of modeling methods, configuration problems as well as agent-based negotiation strategies and coordination algorithms

The domain specific working group is also responsible for the integration of different partial hospital logistics models created by the participating projects. One important step for the integration was the definition of numerous different gateways between all these models. Beside theses basic process patterns had to be defined (for instance planning and execution of clinical trials with oncological patients). All existing models had to be integrated in a conceptual overall scenario. On the conceptual level *Agent.Hospital* consists of partial models, process patterns and gateway specifications (figure 1). Relevant organizational structures, processes and necessary data models were analyzed, formalized and modeled at several hospitals.

At this point it is important to say, that it was and still is an essential development goal of *Agent.Hospital*, to support an open and extensible agent-infrastructure for the healthcare domain. In the following we present the developed framework and the benefit provided.

3.1.   Framework

If actors under lack of global transparency and control have to interconnect for solving tasks- modular reference models are necessary, which contain a explicit formal representation of the interconnection semantics (interfaces, functionality, meta knowledge)

In *Agent.Hospital* several clinics, departments and wards are defined as service provider and consumer units. Further the offered and requested services are denoted simply as *services*. For a technical interaction between the service providing and consuming units there is a need to use well defined interfaces based on existing agent communication languages, interaction protocols, content languages as well as on common ontologies.

Figure 1 shows the basic structure of the Agent.Hospital framework as well as several selected supply chains. The involved research groups and application parties offer a wide spectrum of relevant clinical processes. Below the integration process of the different systems is described.

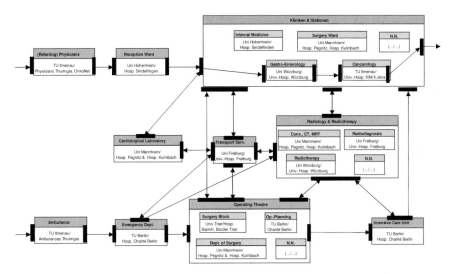

Figure 1. Application diagram of the *Agent.Hospital* framework with several selected supply chains

The figure shows that the *Agent.Hospital* framework covers a broad spectrum of clinical and care processes. At this time the following overall supply chains are implemented: clinical trials (ADAPT), radiotherapeutics (ADAPT), rescue patient (AGIL), lung cancer treatment (ASAinlog), angina pectoris (MedPAge), gallstone therapy, surgery processes (Policy Agents), radiological service processes (EMIKA). More details and references to these projects are provided via the RealAgents interface[3].

3.2. Agent.Hospital Infrastructure Services

The following infrastructure services for the Agent.Hospital framework are planned and partially implemented:

- *Agent.Hospital Directory Facilitator (AHDF[4]):* This is a yellow pages service with extended functions in comparison to AgentCities globaldf. It is used for registration and surveillance of the service agents as well as for visualization of the agents and their services. The main aim of the continuous surveillance is to guarantee availability of the registered agents and to create a robust network. To facilitate network control there is also a web interface of the directory, where all registered agent and their services can bee seen. This service is implemented and deployed.
- *Agent.Hospital EventService (AHES):* an event service that can be used for event based simulation of multi agent systems in the healthcare domain.

---

[3] http://www.realagents.org

[4] http://www-i4.informatik.rwth-aachen.de/agentcities/RWTH_Agentcities_Web_files/hospital.html

Several groups of service agents can register at the event service for generated event streams. The specification of the AHES functionality and a prototype implementation is already completed and now the service has to be
tested in a distributed real-world scenario. This should lead to further refined
specifications and implementation of the service.

– *Agent.Hospital Ontology Repository (AHOR):* a repository providing
healthcare specific task ontologies on demand. The definition of all ontologies should be stored in RDF but a requested ontology can be provided in a
description language specified in the agent's request. The translation of the
ontology definition is going to be made with format adaptors for each specific export format. This approach allows a modular extension and adaptation
to other formats. In addition, the AHOR should provide different versions of
the same ontology in such a way that an agent, who has implemented an
older version of the ontology, can obtain the right one. Therefore, the AHOR
should provide a version control for the stored ontologies. Ontology should
be requested by an agent via a description containing the ontology name, the
ontology version or an informal description. If there is a match for more than
one description of the requested ontology, then the agent should select the
needed ontology from the matching set.

– *Agent.Hospital Knowledge Base (AHKB):* a knowledge base based on the
domain ontology OntHoS. It consists of a T-box and an A-box. The T-box
contains all the concepts and terms of the domain ontology, the structures
defined on them and their semantical definitions. The A-box consists of all
the instances of the used terms and concepts for the description of representative scenarios of the health care domain. On the top of this knowledge base,
different approaches of discerned problems of this domain can be tested and
investigated, and their results can be compared.

– *Agent.Hospital Actor Agent (AHAA):* another common component to all the
involved projects is the actor agent that provides functionality that is often
needed. Instances of the actor agent represent real actors in Agent.Hospital
scenarios. Each actor agent contains the personal data, personal preferences,
and a calendar with the appointments of his principal. The provided Agent
can be specialized or extended for new projects, i.e. by adding a new tab
view containing a project specific user interface and respective agent behaviors.

– *Agent.Hospital CVS (AHCVS):* a repository containing the source files of the
service agents based on the CVS. The repository provides access to its
content via a web interface and command line tools. AHCVS supports code
sharing among the involved developers as well as version management of the
source files. In this way the specified interfaces of all service agents and their
exemplary implementation can be made available at one place.

– *Agent.Hospital Simulation Environment (SeSAm):* The SeSAm-Environment
[14] allows visual modeling of agents and their environment respecting their
properties, abilities and behavior. So it addresses not primarily programmers
but domain experts to create simulation models. There are plugins provided
to support FIPA-compliant communication and to import ontologies modeled

with Protegé. After modeling the agents, simulation situations can be created and can be run from within the environment. Simulation analysis is provided by a flexible component, which allows filtering, processing and generating charts from the simulation data.

In addition to the described services the *Agent.Hospital* infrastructure provides service agents (gateways) for the functionality offered by the agent systems of the different involved projects, i.e. planning, scheduling, coordination, etc. With this approach the heterogeneous field of agents systems was connected based on existing standardized agent communication languages, interaction protocols, and content languages as well as on common ontologies.

The gateway agent's implementation was made with the Java Agent DEvelopment Framework (JADE) [15]. In this way the migration from an existing non-FIPA compliant MAS to a FIPA compliant one was not mandatory. As interaction protocol gateway agents use the FIPA Request Interaction Protocol. That means services of a functional unit can be used sending a simple action request to the unit's gateway agent. A basic requirement for interactions like these is the existence of common task ontologies. All the ontologies used in the Agent.Hospital framework are stored in the Agent.Hospital Ontology Repository.

One of the main components of the Agent.Hospital framework is the Agent.Hospital Directory Facilitator (AHDF). All the service agents are registered at this DF and monitored by him. The functionality offered by the AHDF is described below, i.e. registration, deregistration and monitoring.

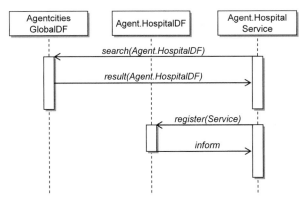

Figure 2. Registration of a Service with Agent.HospitalDF

– *Registration of a service agent with the AHDF:* a service agent registers itself at the AHDF when he is started. Therefore the globaldf (Directory Facilitator from Agentcities) is asked at first for the AHDF agents ID and then the new service agent registers with the AHDF by submitting a description of the offered services and his agent ID.

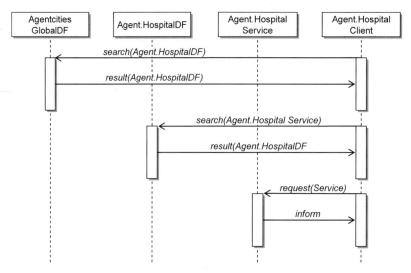

Figure 3. Agents using services of Agent.Hospital

- *Request of a registered service:* an agent looks at first for the AHDF's ID using the globaldf. Then a search query with the description of the service needed is submitted to the AHDF. The AHDF returns the service agents ID and the interested agent can request the service via the FIPA Request Interaction Protocol (Figure 3).
- *Deregistration of a registered service:* in a distributed system like Agent.Hospital we cannot guarantee the availability of a remote hosts, and therefore of services offered by these hosts. We cannot distinguish in a network from the point if view of an agent a split, or a system crash of a host running an agent platform because in both cases the system is not reachable and the offered service not available. In that case the agents can't deregister themselves. Damaged directories can negative affect the remaining agents in the network. Thus we realized an active surveillance of service agents by the AHDF based on periodic control messages. If a service agent doesn't answer to 3 successive control messages the AHDF deregisters the specific service agent (Figure 4). On the other side the service agents expect periodic control messages. If these control messages doesn't reach the agent (for instance the Agent.Hospital platform is temporarily down), it considers being deregistered and tries to reregister through searching for and registering with a new or the same AHDF.

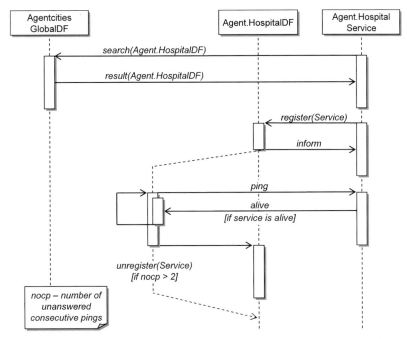

Figure 4. Monitoring of an *Agent.Hospital* Service by the *Agent.HospitalDF*

- *Robustness of AHDF:* The AHDF exports periodical a list of registered service agents. If the primary AHDF crashes another agent platform with a secondary AHDF loads this exported list and continues operating. This mechanism raises the reliability and availability of this service and enlarges it to a High Availability Service (HAS).

Main task of *AHDF* and at the same time delimitation to global DF of the Agentcities-Network is grouping of services with the same context for an application specific service forum. The additional functionality of AHDF became necessary especially through the distribution of service agents on several platforms. The functionality of *AHDF* was domain independent implemented and enabled the utilization also in the manufacturing domain inside the SPP 1083.

Measures of the query response time made on the described Agent.Hospital DF infrastructure are shown in the figures (5 and 6) below. The measures represented in figure 5 are made in the LAN of the University of Aachen and the measures from figure 6 between a host at the University of Aachen and a client at the University of Ilmenau.

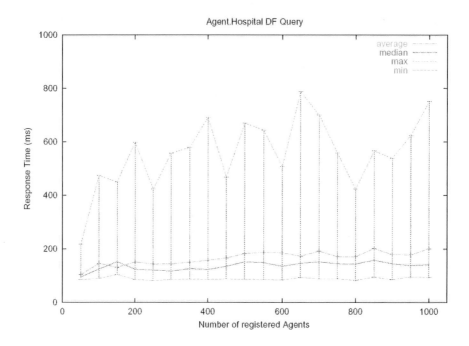

Figure 5. Response Time of the Agent.Hospital DF at the University of Aachen

The query response time was measured 50 times for 20 different configurations, while in each configuration the number of agents was incremented by 50 agents. Interesting parameters of the measures made are maximum, minimum, average and median. Usually the average value can be used as a point of reference of future queries duration but it is often falsified by single very high response time peaks in comparison with the bulk of response times. Therefore the median value was also computed and is shown in both diagrams.

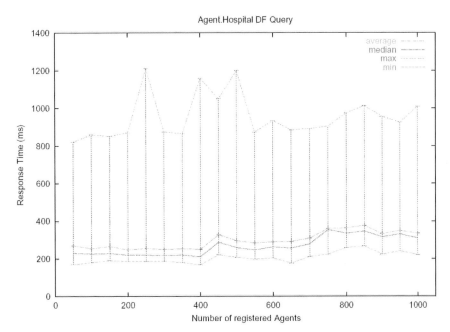

Figure 6. Response Time of the Agent.Hospital DF at the University of Ilmenau

In the local environment (Aachen) the median and the average value of the measured response times are less than 200 ms and in the distributed environment (Ilmenau) less than 400 ms. This values should be considered for query intensive agent applications dealing with time planning, scheduling or resource allocations. Further the maximum values should be considered for real time applications dealing with hard time constraints.

3.3. Agent.Hospital Services

In this section we shortly introduce the focuses of the individual projects and the services realized so far. It is very useful for the tandem projects, to be able to work with the detailed domain models and technical implementations of other projects. So they could avoid making costly empirical investigations for detailed models as well as making big abstractions within the model. The offered services usually are provided by a service agent that represents the interface to the external world and often they are realized internally by a set of cooperationg agents as well. The offered services again can be used in a larger agent network to realize compound services. In the following the focuses and the services realized so far are described.

– *Project EMIKA (University of Freiburg)* The main functionality of the EMIKA-Agents is a message service, that receives messages for actors in hospital scenarios and delivers them via PDA's or mobile phones to the according recipients. One functionality is the wireless localisation/tracking of persons, that can be realized by equiping the actors with RFID-Chips (Radio Frequency Identification). Example implemented service: *NotifyService(Message)*.

– *ASAinlog (Univerity of Potsdam, Univerity of Hohenheim)* Focus of the ASAInlog-Project is the electronical patient record. The record is here seen not as a passive ressource but as an "active document" resp. agent. Services for treatment documentation from admission till dismissal of a patient are provided. Examples for implemented Services are: *AddDocument(Message), ModifyDocument(Message), GetDocument(Message)*.

– *MedPAge (University of Mannheim, University of Hamburg)* Medpage-Agents undertake the task of scheduling of different functional units. Important aspect of the project is coordination between several planners. Different scheduling strategies can be choosen e.g. First-Come-First-Served or the own development MedPaCo. Examples of implemented Services: *AddPatient(Message), GetPatientSchedule(Message)*.

– *Agil² (University of Berlin)* Focus of the domain modells of the project Agil is the emergency room. Central service is the service for the admission of a emergency patient. As gateway to other projects services for the handover of patients to a ward as well as the service for treatment documentation (see ASAInlog) can be accessed.

– *ADAPT (Technical University of Ilmenau/ University of Würzburg)* Focus of the ADAPT-Agents are services for treatment planning and distributed scheduling. They provide decision support in planning and execution of clinical trials as well as services for appointment scheduling for any functional unit. Examples of implemented services are: *RequestStudyPlan(Message), GetStudyPlanEntry(Message)*.

– *Policy-Agents (University of Trier/RWTH Aachen)* The scheduling of operation theatres shall be supported by agents as representatives for the actors in hospitals (personel, patients). This agents act for their principal by contributing specific personal preferences to the planning of the process. The provided services can be used for solving conflicting preferences with negotiations between the agents. Examples of implemented services are: *RequestTask(Message), ConflictSolver(Message)*.

For every implemented service the sourcecode of a service-using agent and the according ontology are publicated in the joint repository. This is necessary for supporting system coupling on all levels, the technical level as well as the content level. Since the already realized services represent just a part of the hospital, we created a executable simulation model with SeSAm, building a szenario that makes use of all the provided services and interconnects the interfaces at that points where the service agents are not able to utilize themselfes mutually at the current stage of development. At some suitable gateways these the serviceagents are already interconnected. Joint goal of the Agent.Hospital group is to extend the szenario by incremental addition of services and the construction of complex and compound services from simple services. This leads to an open and "agent-populated" software framework, in which agentbased prozesses of high complexity and dynamics can be realized and simulated.

3.4.   Agent technology standards, FIPA-cooperation and utilization of the Agentcities infrastructure

An important question for the development of Agent.Hospital is the orientation at currently available standards resp. standards currently in development. The Foundation for Intelligent Physical Agents (FIPA) [16] is responsible for standardizing agent technology. Within the last years this organization has proposed primarily standards for the design of agent platforms as well as standards for communication. Furthermore the FIPA develops application specifications, although there are just a few available. Being a member of FIPA the priority research program (SPP 1083) undertook the task to develop some example application specifications [17] for health care. In parallel the SPP initiated cooperation with the association of information system producers in health care (VHGit), to develop specifications of interfaces between specialized applications (practice systems, patient record, etc.).

Intelligent software agents in application have to be integrated in an existing (often proprietary) information system infrastructure. Broad application of agent technology presumes therefore, to deal with these questions and requirements making efforts of standardization. Therefore the aim of the hospital logistics working group is implementation, evaluation und documentation of agent based health care services, which are supposed to be base of future FIPA-*Application Specifications*. For this reason the SPP 1083 is member of the FIPA and contributes to the development of *Business Application Specifications*.

A further important activity concerns the contribution of the SPP to *Agentcities* [18], an open, worldwide net of FIPA-compliant agent platforms, on which different agent based services - often in the stage of development - are provided. The net currently consists of more than 140 agent platforms with a high concentration in Europe and also several platforms in the USA, Australia and the near east. The application domains of the intended services reach from e-Health to manufacturing control, digital libraries to travel services and many more. Ultimate aim of the initiative is to support the commercial as well as academic efforts for the realization of agent based applications and to make it possible to compose dynamic, intelligent and autonomous agents to complex service agents.

Agent.Hospital is going to be realized as a part of *Agentcities*. Therefore five new *Agentcities* platforms have been set up till now: Aachen, Ilmenau, Würzburg, Freiburg and Hamburg. They are connected by a central directory service (Agent.HospitalDF) in Aachen, that registers all the participating agents (see figure 7).

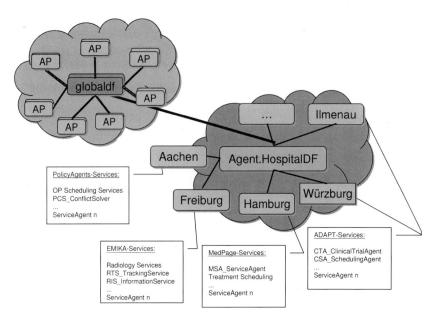

Figure 7. Embedding of Agent.Hospital in the Agentcities.NET infrastructue

4.   Example Scenario "Clinical Trials"

To visualize and test the possibilities for interaction and performance of the multi agent systems integrated in *Agent.Hospital* so far, different use cases have been defined and modeled. Using the example scenario "clinical trials" we want to show in the following, how *Agent.Hospital* is able to support highly distributed clinical processes as well as the ongoing research of agent technology. In execution of clinical studies in real world hospitals interoperation of various clinics, organizational entities and wards is necessary. The coordination of tasks for diagnosis as well as treatment often demands to exceed hospital boundaries for cooperation and is therefore a suitable example scenario for our purposes.

Clinical trials are tests executed with random samples of test persons or patients. Regarding german principals for proper clinical inspection (similar to good clinical practice) we can distinguish between controlled and not comparing trials. In the example scenario "clinical trials" we strictly used controlled trials. Aim of controlled trials is the derivation of general theorems about the benefit-risk ratio of two or more treatments based on a trial result with a given reproducible probability. Regarding the reproducibility of results it is important that the statistically necessary number of cases is determined before the trial is started. Besides medical and statistical requirements for clinical trials in recent times new economical requirements play an important role. These new requirements arise from the economical development in health care in the past years and have to be respected by the management of clinics and hospitals. For instance the participating hospital has to make a prediction for the necessary "patients-good" during the clinical trial (that has to be fit to the criteria defined in the trial protocol) and has to calculate, weather is has sufficient personnel and technical resources to take part in a clinical trial. In some cases it may be necessary to hire a new study nurse or documentalists to prevent resource shortages. Decisions like these are often intentional ad-hoc decisions. International multi-center trials often base on a complex set of rules for restrictions to obey and treatments to execute.

Figure 6 describes an exemplified process part of the integrated scenario "clinical trial". The description of the process is similar to the extended event-driven process chains (eEPC). The strict bipartite change from events and functions is repealed to simplify the description of the processes.

At the beginning of a clinical trial various tasks for diagnosis and treatment have to be coordinated and scheduled resources have to be assigned and if necessary informed (Figure 8 shows an example with CT- (computer tomography) und MRT- (magneto-resonance-tomography) examinations as well as execution of a surgery). In the first step the suitability of the patient for the study is going to be checked. The DAISIY-System (Deliberative Agents for Intelligent Simulation System) appraises the patient data (regarding specific criteria from the clinical study guidelines) coming from a simulation modeled in SeSAm. This appraisal leads to decision weather the patient should take part in the study. The user interface agent of DAISIY presents the patient data and the recommendation to the responsible physician, and asks for the affirmation. If the patient fulfils the preconditions for the study an individual study plan can be created by calling *request(studyplan)*. The concerned documentalists can also integrate own ideas for appointments into the proposed study plan. After planning the medium term study plan (usually four weeks) for the patient and extending the electronically patient data record using the ASAinlog service (*AddNewDocument*) the agent systems of MedPAge and PolicyAgents can start the operative planning and scheduling of the mandatory appointments.

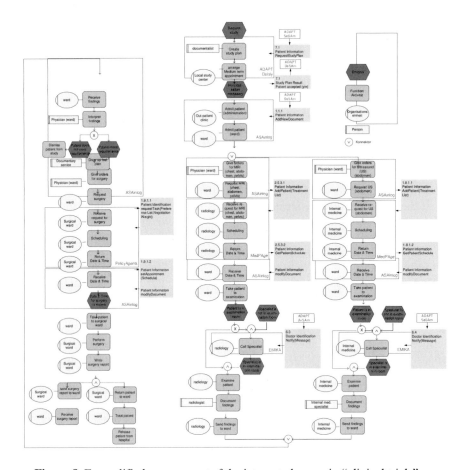

Figure 8. Exemplified process part of the integrated scenario "clinical trials"

When the point of time of a certain examination is reached, the *TrackingServices* of EMIKA are used to find a certain bed or a mobile device or to find the physician and to inform him about the pending appointment. In case of an emergency surgery of a patient it might be necessary that the concerned systems for study management and treatment scheduling change an already planned appointment. The described part of the process ends with the interim dismissal of the patient.

The following interaction diagram (Figure 9) shows a simplified process of the system interactions within Agent.Hospital. Here just the essential steps are depicted and interactions for error handling are not included (e.g. *not-understood, refuse, failure*).

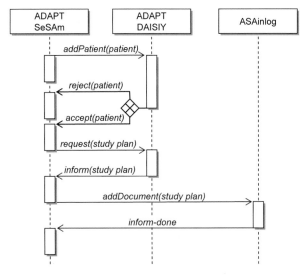

Figure 9. Simplified interaction diagram of the system interactions in the integrated scenario "clinical trials"

In the context of the various imaginable service providers a further research area emerges – benchmarking of agent systems. In general but particularly in Agent.Hospital service providers have to be comparable to competing approaches. The Agent.Hospital framework was introduced to an international community at the Agentcities Information Days 3 in Barcelona (ID3) for the first time and encountered big interest. At the coming annual conference of the german association of computer science (GI) in Frankfurt a simulation scenario using the cooperating multi agent systems of different origin is going to be presented to a broader national public.

5.   Conclusion and Outlook

This paper described the conceptual design and the essential system components of Agent.Hospital, an open agent based (software)framework for highly distributed applications in health care.
Agent.Hospital arose from the projects of the priority research program "Intelligent Agents and economic application scenarios". It serves to test and develop basic concepts and methodology of agent technology. It allows just making tests in laboratory conditions but as well in appropriate big and complex scenarios and under conditions that are close to conditions die of real applications in health care.
The initiated transition from small-scaled agent orient programming to large-scaled agent based development of information systems has far reaching consequences: Information systems science has to develop new theories and

methodologies for the design and use of mostly decentralized aplication systems. Finally computer science has to deal with evaluation of a new software technology with the criterum of economic improvement of business. We have already done the first steps and the gained expiriences are rather encouraging. Some other results contribute to this.

We found international cooperation partners (from Spain and the UK) as a result of the presentation at the Agentcities Information Days in February 2003. There is a close collaboration with the 6th Framework program initiative openNet (Building Next Generation Open Service Environments), that intends to create a worldwide distributed network of big agent based applicatios. Industrial interest for cooperation is shown by the association of IT system developers of in health care (VHitG). Here we have the perspective to use Agent.Hospital as a testbed for a supply chain spanning evaluation of interface specifications of dedicated information systems. In parallel we go about the connection of Agent.Hospital to existing hospital information systems by integrating established standards (e.g. HL7 and DICOM). Furthermore the broad empirical funding (organisation models, data, functions, processes) of the systems contained in Agent.Hospital offers the unprecedented possibility, to gain economic insight to the halth care system.

References

[1] Kirn, St.: Intelligente Softwareagenten und betriebswirtschaftliche Anwendungsszenarien. Vorschlag zur Einrichtung eines DFG-Schwerpunktprogramms, 1999.

[2] Cockburn, D.; Jennings, N.R.: ARCHON: A Distributed Artificial Intelligence System for Industrial Applications. In: O'Hare, G.M.P.; Jennings, N.R. (eds.): Foundations of Distributed Artificial Intelligence. John Wiley, New York et al. 1996, pp. 319-344.

[3] Parunak, V.D.: Applications of Distributed Artificial Intelligence in Industry. In: O'Hare, G.M.P.; Jennings, N.R. (eds.): Foundations of Distributed Artificial Intelligence. John Wiley, Chichester et.al., United Kingdom 1996, pp. 139-164.

[4] Kirn, St.; Gasser, L.: Organizational Approaches to Coordination in Multi-Agent Systems. Themenheft "Intelligente Agenten" der Zeitschrift it + ti. Heft 4, August 1998, pp. 23-29.

[5] Müller, J.P.: Architectures and Applications of Intelligent Agents: A Survey. Knowledge Engineering Review, 1998, Vol. 13, Issue 4, 1998, pp. 1-24.

[6] openNet: "Building Next-Generation Open Service Environments". http://www.agentcities.org/openNet/Documents/opennet_overview_02.02.03.pdf, 2003-03-17.

[7] Winter, A.; Ebert, J.: Referenzmodelle für Krankenhaus-Informationssysteme und deren Anwendung. In: E. Zwierlein: Klinikmanagement: Erfolgsstrategien für die Zukunft, Urban & Schwarzenberg, München 1997, pp. 548-562.

[8] Simoneit, M.: Informationsmanagement in Universitätsklinika : Konzeption und Implementierung eines objektorientierten Referenzmodells. Dt. Univ.-Verl. Wiesbaden 1998.

[9] SPP 1083 "Intelligente Softwareagenten und betriebliche Anwendungsszenarien",
     http://scott.wirtschaft.tu-ilmenau.de:8080/htdocs_wi2/schwerpunkte.xml, 2003-03-17.

[10] Eichhorn, S.: Integratives Qualitätsmanagement im Krankenhaus: Konzeption und
     Methoden eines qualitäts- und kostenintegrierten Krankenhaus-Managements.
     Kohlhammer, Stuttgart et al. 1997.

[11] Becker, M.; Heine, C.; Herrler, R.; Krempels, K.H.: OntHoS – An Ontology for
     Hospital Scenarios. Technical Report No. 300, Julius-Maximilians-Universität Würz-
     burg, Institut für Informatik, September 2002.

[12] Anhalt, C.; Kirn, St.: RealAgentS - Realistic Agent Application Scenarios.
     http://141.24.72.19/realagents/geturl.php?ID=120, 2003-03-17.

[13] RealAgentS-Plattform. http://www.realagents.org, 2003-03-17.

[14] SeSAm - Shell for Simulated Agent Systems - Multi-Agent Simulation Environment.
     http://ki.informatik.uni-wuerzburg.de/sesam/, 2003-03-17.

[15] JADE – Java Agent DEvelopment Framework. http://sharon.cselt.it/projects/jade/,
     2003-03-17.

[16] FIPA ACL Message Structure Specification. http://www.fipa.org/specs/fipa00061/,
     2003-03-17.

[17] FIPA Application specifications.
     http://www.fipa.org/repository/applicationspecs.php3, 2003-03-17.

[18] Willmott, S.; Constantinescu, I.; Dale, J.; Somacher, M.; Marinheiro, R.; Mota, L.;
     Bothelo, L.; Bonnefoy, D.; Picault, J.; Poslad, S. ; Tan, J.; Bothelo, L.: Agentcities
     Network Architecture Recommendation. http://www.agentcities.org/rec/00001/actf-
     rec-00001a.pdf, 2003-03-17.

Stefan Kirn and Christian Heine, Technische Universität Ilmenau, Department of
Economics and Business Administration, PoBox 100 565, D-98684 Ilmenau,
Germany
E-mail address: {stefan.kirn|christian.heine}@tu-ilmenau.de

Rainer Herrler, Universität Würzburg, Chair of Information Systems, Am
Hubland, D-97074 Würzburg, Germany
E-mail address: herrler@informatik.uni-wuerzburg.de

Karl-Heinz Krempels, RWTH Aachen, Chair of Computer Science, Ahornstraße
55, D-52074 Aachen, Germany
E-mail address: krempels@i4.informatik.rwth-aachen.de

OntHoS – an Ontology for Hospital Scenarios

Marc Becker, Christian Heine, Rainer Herrler, and Karl-Heinz Krempels

Abstract. The goal of this paper is to present an ontology for hospital scenarios (called OntHoS). It was developed by a couple of research projects dealing with the application of agent systems in hospital scenarios. The aim of OntHoS is to establish a basis for a description of these scenarios and to facilitate their inter-operability. Therefore, we classify types of ontologies and approaches to ontology design, we focus on constructing a domain ontology and discuss the proceeding as well as the encountered problems. Finally, an overview about the future work is given, focussing especially on opening the scope to task ontologies for special project-specific purposes.

1. Introduction

The goal of the research project "Intelligent Software Agents in Economical Applications" is the improvement of applications through the deployment of agent systems. The project incorporates several specialized subprojects with different goals that focus on logistic systems in either the medical or the manufacturing domain. The main prob-lems identified are the incompatibility between the individual agent systems and the different interpretation of terms in the domains of economics and computer science. In computer science and especially in distributed artificial intelligence and knowledge management ontologies have been studied in various contexts. Recent work in Distributed Artificial Intelligence is exploring the use of formal ontologies as a way of specifying content-specific agreements for the sharing and reuse of knowledge among software entities. There is a great variety of definitions for the term ontology [13, 14, 15, 16, 17]. In order to communicate about (a part of) a hospital's real world, the knowledge about this part has to be represented by some kind of model on which all participating agents agree. The main purpose of these models is to find an effective communication between various agents by providing a method for a concise and un-ambiguous representation of the domain knowledge to be transferred. Thus, the agents are able to communicate and possibly argue about the part of the world described by the model. The chosen solution is to deploy FIPA-compliant agent systems and the development of common ontologies for the investigated domains and tasks. The de-veloped ontology was already successfully used to create an integrated scenario called "Agent.Hospital" and to link services of the projects together. In the first part of this paper we present the idea and motivation of *Agent.Hospital*. Then we take a closer look at the concept of an "ontology" including

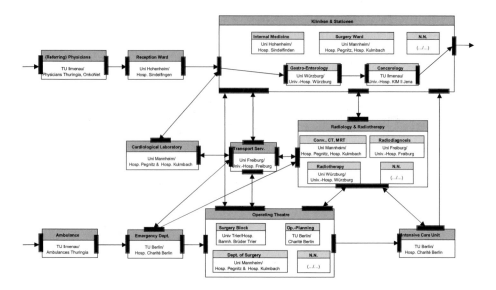

FIGURE 1. Application diagram of the Agent.Hospital framework with several selected supply chains

the definition, existing types of ontologies, and approaches and tools for ontological design. The subsequent part addresses the development of the ontology "OntHoS" used for knowledge acquisition in the hospital domain and for the modeling of two application scenarios, "Policy-Agents" and "ADAPT". In the final part we describe the future work with respect to ontology development for different tasks in the project and we outline the behavior of agents with different kind of goals.

2. Integrated Scenario Agent.Hospital

In the work of the participants of the SPP 1082 numerous partial models of the health care domain have been developed. Relevant organizational structures, processes and necessary data models were analyzed, formalized and modeled at several hospitals. On the other hand agent based systems and services have been developed to solve problems of the domain. Now the aim was to link the systems as well as the partial models together and to create a complex integrated model. So the idea of "Agent.Hospital" was born. *Agent.Hospital* is intended to provide empirical funded und detailed described models of the healthcare domain and open and extensible agent-infrastructure to integrate new health care services. It enables the examination of modeling methods, configuration problems as well as the evaluation of agent-based negotiation strategies and coordination algorithms. First steps for the integration was the definition of a common ontology. Secondly numerous different gateways between all these models have been identified (see figure 2). Beside these gateways basic process patterns had to be defined (for instance planning and

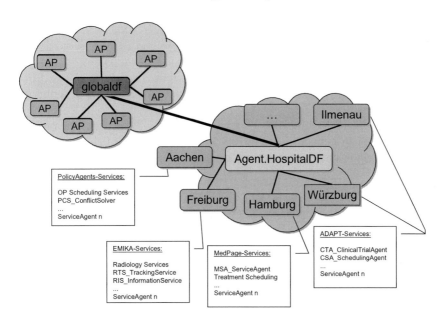

FIGURE 2. Embedding of Agent.Hospital in the Agentcities.NET infrastructue

execution of clinical trials with oncological patients). All existing models had to be integrated in a conceptual overall scenario. On the conceptual level *Agent.Hospital* consists of a joint ontology (OntHoS), partial models, process patterns and gateway specifications.

In *Agent.Hospital* several clinics, departments and wards are defined as service provider and consumer units. For a technical interaction between the service providing and consuming units there is a need to use well defined interfaces based on existing agent communication languages, interaction protocols, content languages as well as on common ontologies. Figure 1 shows the basic structure of the *Agent.Hospital* framework as well as several selected supply chains. The involved research groups and application parties offer a wide spectrum of relevant clinical processes. Below the integration process of the different systems is described.

The figure shows that the *Agent.Hospital* frameworks actually covers a broad spectrum of clinical and care processes. At this time the following overall supply chains are implemented: clinical trials (ADAPT), radiotherapeutics (ADAPT), rescue patient (AGIL), lung cancer treatment (ASAinlog), angina pectoris (MedPAge), gallstone therapy, surgery processes (Policy Agents), radiological service processes (EMIKA). More details and references to these projects are provided via the RealAgents interface[1].

Technically *Agent.Hospital* is realized as a part of Agentcities. Therefore five new Agentcities platforms until now have been set up: Aachen, Ilmenau, Würzburg, Freiburg and Hamburg. They are connected by a central directory service (Agent.HospitalDF) in Aachen, that registers all the participating agents (see figure 2). Several infrastructural

---

[1] http://www.realagents.org

services have been set up to support the technical integration of the systems like for example a central Directory Facilitator, with extra functionality and a service dedicated to event based simulation. The example scenario was modeled in SeSAm, a powerful environment for visual agent modeling and simulation. Agent services provided in *Agent.Hospital* were utilized from the simulation communicating via FIPA ACL using the terms defined in the common ontology.

Obviously the task of integrating agent systems prerequisites to agree on an ontology. This and the current lack of alternatives regarding ontologies in health care were the main motivations for developing OntHoS.

3. Ontologies

The term "Ontology" seems to generate considerable controversy in discussions about Artificial Intelligence. "Ontology" is used in different research areas with different meanings. It was first used, and has a long history, in philosophy, in the context of aspect of being and individuality. It is also often confused with epistemology, which is about knowledge and knowing. In artificial intelligence the term ontology is used for a formal, explicit specification of a conceptualization [1]. This interpretation is used in the technical areas, e.g. agent technology.

3.1. What is an ontology

An ontology is a set of primitive concepts that we can use for representing a whole domain (or part of it) for which the ontology was designed, while a concept is a world-view that defines a set of objects, relations between and subsets of those in the respective domain. An ontology is also a man-made framework that supports the modeling process of a domain in such a way a collection of terms and their semantic interpretation is provided.

We define ontology as a conceptualization with regard to a domain [11], where every ontology defines:
- a vocabulary - the set of terms used for modeling,
- a structure of the statements in the model, and
- the semantic interpretation of these terms.

The main benefit of ontology usage is that software systems can share the ontology of a domain, so that they yield the same world-view and the ability to share their knowledge about the given domain.

3.2. Types of Ontologies

Ontologies can be made for various spheres of validity. Although the purpose is always to define terms and their semantics, they differ in scope. The following classification can be made:
- *General ontologies* - are definitions of general concepts that have a wide scope and are applicable for several domains. Examples of general ontologies are ontologies for general theoretical concepts like automata, time, data structures (list heap, queue, stack), school grades, geometric representation, states etc. General ontologies can

be prerequisite of the more specific domain and task ontologies described below and referenced by them.

- *Domain ontologies* - are knowledge domains for a specific area (ship design, airplane design, electrical connectivity, etc.). A domain ontology is useful for the modeling process of several representative scenarios and for information acquisition in the domain. A domain ontology provides the vocabulary and the concepts that have to be used in the modeling process of real scenarios of the given domain and which are described with instances of the provided terms. The use of common domain ontologies facilitates interoperability between applications. An example will be shown in Chapter 4, where we describe the modeling process and the usage of the domain ontology OntHoS.

- *Task ontologies* - are the most specific type of ontology. They describe terms and concepts of individual problem-solving methods. Examples include negotiations with preferences or assignments from customers to suppliers. Mutual understanding at the level of task ontologies allows a very high grade of interoperability but is also very hard to achieve, because it restricts application to special problem solving methods. Task ontologies can also be domain independent (negotiation with preferences/constraints between agents) and be valid in several domains (negotiation of appointments for examinations).

Some other classifications of ontologies are possible, for instance based on their structure or design. This paper discusses the efforts to construct a common domain ontology for hospitals and outlines a proper distinction from the individual project-dependent task ontologies. As far as possible it was tried to reuse and extend existing general ontologies (for example, for the time concept) that were already established in other domains.

3.3. Approaches to Ontology Design

An ontology design-process consists of several phases [9], [10], [11], [15]:

- *Decision of ontology's purpose* - in this phase the deployment area and the purpose of the planned ontology should be specified. Both should influence the ontology's level of formality and the decision which design-tool should be used. The more an ontology has to support automated tasks, the more formal it will be.

- *Ontology modeling* - this phase deals with the most difficult part of the ontology design process - the modeling part. Modeling a task, a process or a concept is difficult because the resulting model should represent and contain only those attributes of the modeled entity that are necessary for the emulation or description of its characteristical properties. Ontology modeling starts with the analysis of specific scenarios of a domain or a task, and the identification of terms and concepts used. Analysis and abstraction can be done in the same way as in object oriented programming, so that existing approaches can be used like cookbooks. For the identified terms we have to specify their semantical definition, and for the identified concepts we have to build models. The modeling task cannot be handled in the same way as analysis and abstraction because at this point we need experience in building models. We know that things can be modeled more or less elegantly and that there is no "correct" way of how we have to design models. A convenient definition of the term "modeling" can be found in [12], where "modeling" is defined as "the art of building models". The art of modeling is enhanced by the modeler's ability to abstract the essential features and characteristics of a concept. A modeling task should begin with a small model that should be enhanced recursively until a one-to-one mapping between the modeled concept and the real concept is possible.

- *Ontology evaluation* - in this phase the new ontology should be tested with a sample or representative scenario of the given domain. If the scenario can be modeled without problems, the ontology design process is completed. Otherwise the ontology should be re-designed in such a way, that the sample scenario can be modeled.

There are several approaches for ontology design depending on the size of the development team and the starting point of the design process. Each approach [2] or a combination of them can be used as a guideline in the ontology design process:

- *Inspirational approach* - starts from the purpose of the ontology and is developed by a single person. The resulting ontology reflects an individual viewpoint of the given domain.
- *Inductive approach* - starts with the analysis of a case in a given domain. The resulting ontological characterization of the case is then applied to other cases of the same domain.
- *Deductive approach* - starts with adopting some general principles and adaptively applies them to construct an ontology applicable for a specific case.
- *Synthetic approach* - starts with a base set of "small" ontologies. An ontology can cover parts of others, but none should be a real subset of another one. The concepts are synthesized from the existing "small" ontologies and are then included in a new "big" ontology. The resulting ontology reflects a common viewpoint of the users of the initially used "small" ontologies.
- *Collaborative approach* - is useful for the development of big ontologies. The development process can be performed either stepwise through parallel contributions followed by a commitment step or through leader rotation in a way that guides the development by different developer, each of whom is specialized in a specific part of the investigated domain. The resulting ontology is widely accepted if the involved developers are from different research areas, because this implicitly supports a committed viewpoint from the represented areas.

3.4. Tools for ontology design

Several tools support ontology design, each of them with its own pros and cons. The deployment area of the new ontology (agent systems, semantic web services, knowledge bases), its estimated size and complexity, and the level of formality should influence the decision-making. The following tools are the most popular in this area:

- *Ontolingua* - was developed at Stanford University [20]. The Ontolingua ontology development environment provides a suite of ontology authoring tools and a library of modular, reusable ontologies. The tools in Ontolingua are oriented towards the authoring of ontologies by assembling and extending ontologies obtained from the library.

- *Chimaera* - was also developed at Stanford University [18] on top of Ontolingua. The software system supports users in creating and maintaining distributed ontologies on the web, and in tasks such as loading knowledge bases in different formats, reorganizing taxonomies, resolving name conflicts, editing terms, etc.
- *OILEd* - was developed at the University of Manchester [19] and is a simple ontology editor that allows the user to build ontologies using OIL. The development of large-scale ontologies is not actively supported. This means that ontology migration and integration, versioning and argumentation are not supported. The OILEd tool should be a "NotePad" for ontology editors, offering just enough functionality for building ontologies and to check their consistency.
- *Protégé 2000* - was developed at Stanford University [21] and is a tool for ontology construction, customization of knowledge-acquisition forms, and domain knowledge acquisition. The functionality of Protégé is continuously improved through the offered API. Several plugins are available, e.g., for merging ontologies, database import and export, XML export, graphical visualization of ontology trees, interaction with Jess (Java Expert System Shell), addition of several first order logic languages etc. When Protégé is deployed in the development process of ontolgies for FIPA (Foundation for Intelligent Physical Agents) compliant agent systems, the BeanGenerator plugin will speed up this process because of its export function of an ontology as Java class files.

4. OntHoS - a domain ontology for hospital scenarios

The OntHoS-ontology is a collection of terms and definitions relevant for modeling scenarios of hospital logistics. This kind of modeling is - more or less explicitly - necessary for the development of clinical information-systems or hospital simulation models. Programmers engaged in such tasks often directly derive a program's class-structure from mental abstraction of the real world problem. However, it is useful to make some effort and develop, and commit to, a common ontology, as this makes comparing results and integrating systems more feasible. The ontology has been developed by several academic organizations that work together in the project "Intelligent Software Agents in Economical Applications" of the German Research Foundation DFG. Researchers from six subprojects (ASAinlog, PaGS, Policy-Agents, Med-Page, ReStLA, Aurecon) develop agent systems for different scenarios in the hospital environment. Many aspects from document management to scheduling are covered in the selected scenarios. Some of them are similar enough to benefit from interoperability of the systems or use approaches that are interesting to be compared. This requires on the one hand technical interfaces, for example the use of standardized agent platforms, but also a common ontology. Therefore, OntHoS was developed in several workshops, intended to take into account as far as possible the requirements of every individual subproject. In the following sections the OntHoS-Ontology is presented, and the proceeding as well as the encountered problems are described. Finally, two example scenarios illustrate the use of the ontology in different projects.

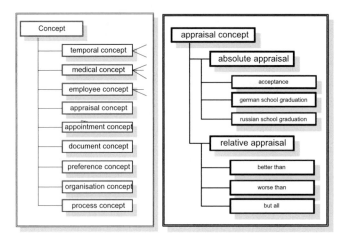

FIGURE 3. Left: Main hierarchy of concepts Right: Concept hierarchy of appraisals

4.1. Proceeding and Description

The Ontology is modeled with Protégé [18]. It was chosen because of its ability to process and convert the results (OntoViz, XML), and because of the availability of an interface to FIPA-compliant agent systems. Protégé supports graphical ontology design and modification (see Section 3.4). The process of design and construction was mainly collaborative (see Section 3.3), but also inspirative. The domain was decomposed in several concept categories, and an agreement on the basic hierarchy was found. The top level of this hierarchy is shown in Figure 1. At these first two hierarchy-levels the mechanism of sub-classing is used, not for inheritance but for classification and structuring.

In some parts we tried to adopt already existing ontologies or parts thereof, for example regarding the temporal concept that is mainly influenced by the Dharma Guideline Model [23]. Currently, some parts are still rather immature, for example the document concept - OntHoS is still work in progress. Other parts, primarily including those concerning scheduling, are developed very precisely. In the following a short introduction to the various concepts is given:

- *Temporal concept* - The terms defined here are domain-independent definitions of temporal concepts, like dates, fixed and relative time points, time intervals or durations. Also abstract terms like "today" or "now", without any given reference-point, are described including their semantic meaning. The definitions of this concept are needed and referenced in many of the other concepts.
- *Medical concept* - Here, terms for describing medical knowledge are defined. This reaches from a model to describe clinical guidelines to a meta-object-model for the definition of symptoms, diagnosis and therapies. By creating instances of the defined classes one can develop a knowledge base that he needs for his particular scenario
- *Employee concept* - Here, some terms for abstract concepts for the description of hospital staff are defined, like, e.g., qualifications, and roles.

- *Appraisal concept* - For scheduling and planning in hospitals, or more generally for all decision purposes, we need some terms that specify how someone appraises a certain alternative. To be most flexible we distinguish between absolute and relative appraisals. An absolute appraisal might be expressed through grades, whereas "better than" represents a relative appraisal that needs a reference. Absolute appraisal can implicitly assign a full order to things, although this is often not intended. This means that a bijective mapping to the order of the same things in the real world is not possible, and that absolute appraisals can be considered as a restriction in modeling, e.g. for modeling things in a semi-ordered way.
- *Appointment concept* - For scheduling of treatment and examination tasks some further terms are needed. They describe what is necessary for an appointment, tasks, times, present persons and necessary resources. With respect to appointments it must also be distinguished between already agreed appointments and proposals that might be appraised.
- *Document concept* - The form and content of various typical types of clinical documents, like diagnostic findings or patient data, is described here. Standards for clinical information systems (HL7) should be considered here.
- *Organization concept* - To describe an hospital scenario it is essential to include the underlying organization and its entities. Usually we find functional units that provide services for examination and treatment, wards, administration, and special entities like, for example, a pharmacy or an orthopedic service. Functional units have resources and provide several types of actions (see Process concept below).
- *Process concept* - Terms that describe processes composed from atomic actions, sequences and alternatives are described here. Since it is intended to support domain modelers with different ways of process modeling, the process concept provides a meta model with adaptations to specific modeling languages, e.g. a EPK-like or a petrinet-like description. Atomic actions of these processes might be medical and logistic actions. Medical actions are further classified as examinations, treatments, or actions regarding care. Many actions need to be processed by functional units, others require special resources or persons to be present (see Object concept below).
- *Object concept* - In contrast to the terms described above that describe abstract, non-existing objects, this defines terms for real objects or persons. Real objects include, for example, rooms, medical and general devices, supplies, and chattels. Objects can be necessary resources for actions, or they can be subject to appraisals. There are many interdependencies between the various parts of the ontology. Persons like patients and hospital staff are also subjects of this category, as they exist as touchable "objects" as well.

For more details the OntHoS-Ontology can be downloaded from its home page [22]. The next section describes the experiences that were made during the development of the ontology.

4.2. Experiences with ontology design

As already mentioned the collaborative approach was used in designing the hospital ontology. This works well as long as the developers' interests are in different parts of the ontology, according to their respective project. Yet, there were technical barriers to be overcome. For instance, it is very difficult to integrate different versions of an ontology with Protégé. There can be name-collisions when importing a second ontology, and references between the packages have to be updated manually. Often it is easier to migrate the modified parts manually or to serialize the development process (although this takes more time).

Another question often discussed during development was in which cases "terms" - should be represented by classes in an ontology, and in which cases by instances. Sometimes both are possible, but have different consequences on how to model the scenario. For example, the term "functional unit" and the representing ontology class are defined by offering some services and by owning several resources, and - of course - a name. When defining a "radiology unit" we have to decide if it should be an instance or a subclass of a functional unit. Both approaches have advantages. If we let these particular functional units be instances, and therefore part of the scenario, we sustain a self-contained ontology. Whatever kind of functional units we may find in a hospital, they can be modeled, and mutual understanding by different system is assured. If we let certain functional units be subclasses, and therefore part of the ontology, we might have to extend the ontology whenever we want to model new scenarios. However, the advantage is that common functional units of the hospital domain are represented in the ontology, and that additional properties can be respected. Similar decisions have to be made when defining medical actions and their semantics.

In consequence, some further confusion can emerge from the different approaches. In some cases a term describes a class, in others an instance. For examples, if we talk about diagnostic actions it makes a difference if we talk about defining "x-raying", a generic action or "x-raying a particular patient at a particular time", a very concrete action. This also has to be taken into account especially in the collaborative design because the practice shows that ontology-developers often mean different things when discussing "terms".

The question "sub-classing or instantiation" is also related to the question of abstraction level. There is an incredible amount of domain-specific terms in the hospital domain. The important question is which of these are relevant to be understood by information systems, and to be represented in the modeled scenarios. For example, we need to know some constraints about tasks (or actions) for scheduling purposes, but we usually do not need to know the real difference between a surgery to fix the achilles tendon or a surgery to the cruciate ligament. Hierarchical modeling of the ontology with the option to improve and to add details can be a convenient way to meet the demands of different scenarios. Right now we have a very simple way to describe clinical documents, since there was no participant in the developer group who was concerned with such documents in his scenarios. Thus, there is still work to do and only evaluation and application of the ontology in many scenarios can show how good the current approach is.

4.3. Tools for Ontology support in MAS

Besides the pure ontology development there are also other activities regarding ontology support in multi agent systems. To meet the new requirements of *Agent.Hospital* ontology support was integrated in SeSAm [28] and extensions for FIPA-compliancy have been made. SeSAm enables rapid development of multi agent models on base of existing ontologies. Ontologies created with Protegé [21] can be imported and accessed within the environment. Agents classes can be automatically created from ontology concpts. The SeSAm-Environment then allows visual modeling of agents and their environment respecting their properties, abilities and behavior. The visual programming abilities do not primarily addresses programmers but domain experts to create simulation models. Basic representation of the agents behavior are UML-activity diagrams (see figure 1). They are easy understandable and a common and well known notation. Activity diagrams consist of activities and transition rules. Activities can be seen as states containing a series of actions, that are executed until an exit rule activates the next activity. An agents behaviour might be described by one or more activity diagramms that are executed in paralell. Several features to handle complex models like healthcare scenarios are integrated in the environment. So among various other features it provides a mechanism to compose simple activities to compound activities as well as to compose primitives for sensing, effecting and computing to compound user primitives. Another important feature in connection with ontologies is the support of FIPA compliant communication. Messages can be send to and received from external systems. This makes the creation of testbed-scenarios for external agent applications possible [29]. After modeling the agents, simulation situations can be created on a two dimensional map. For simulation of a scenario this model representation is compiled and can be run from within the environment. Simulation analysis is provided by a flexible component, which allows filtering, processing and generating charts from the simulation data. To get reliable evaluations often a lot of experiments are needed. Therefore SeSAm allows the distribution of multiple simulation runs on different computers within the local network. So the available computing power can be accessed easily.

Another development regarding ontology support shall be presented here. The *Agent.Hospital* Ontology Repository is going to be a repository providing healthcare specific task ontologies on request. The definition of al lontologies should be stored in RDF but a requested ontology should be provided in the description language specified in the agent's request. The translation of the ontology definition should be made with a format adaptor for each export format. This approach allows a modular extension and adaptation to other formats. In addition, the AHOR should provide different versions of the same ontology in such a way that an agent, which has implemented an older version of the ontology, can obtain the right one. Therefore, the AHOR should provide a version control for the stored ontologies. An ontology should be requested by an agent via a description containing the ontology name, the ontology version or an informal description. If there is a match for more than one description of the requested ontology, then the agent should select the needed ontology from the matching set.

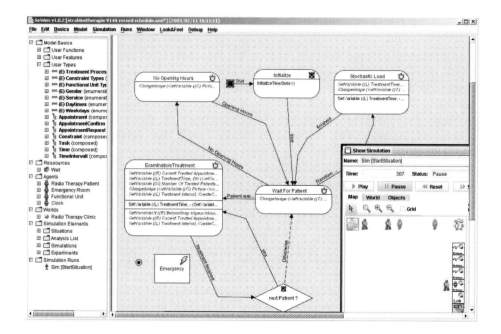

FIGURE 4. Model of a radiation therapy unit

4.4. Modeled scenarios

In the following a short description of the goals and the underlying scenarios is given. To show the connection to the hospital ontology referenced terms are written in italic letters.

4.4.1. THE ADAPT SCENARIO   Regarding health care scenarios a main focus of the ADAPT-project lies on coordination of *appointments* for treatment and examination *actions* in hospitals. The goal is to develop and provide flexible and adaptable coordination strategies that can be applied in real world hospitals and informations used in this environment. Different strategies and their consequences are evaluated within computer-based simulation models (that are as well part of the *Agent.Hospital*-Scenario) and can have influence on future development efficient agent applications for hospitals.

The treatment of hospital *patients* requires complex coordination of many autonomous *organizational entities*. Special requirements to coordination emerge at the intersection between *wards* that have to organize patients' appointments, and *functional units* that provide medical services for treatment and examination. The capacities of these functional units are limited by their resources (*medical devices, personnel, rooms*). Coordination strategies can vary from simple queues to a precise anticipatory scheduling that also considers shifting of *appointments*. In particular, we want to evaluate the benefit of complex distributed coordination strategies using negotiation to meet all the actors' interests and goals. These interests may conflict, and can be formally expressed by *appraisals* for appointments and local *restrictions* that are valid for a certain entity. For example, a high load might be desirable by a functional unit, whereas patients prefer short waiting periods. To evaluate the effects of different strategies we focus on patient *processes* of selected standardized medical guidelines. These are used to create realistic demands in the scenario. In addition to these standardized *guidelines* and general medical knowledge there are parts of the scenario which are highly individual and typical for the specific considered hospital. This includes the structure of the organization and the preferences and restrictions of the different actors.

All this was taken into account in the development of the ontology. Thus, various scenarios regarding scheduling of treatments and examinations can be described and we achieve a high grade of flexibility without having to change the ontology.

4.4.2. THE POLICY-AGENTS SCENARIO   The primary goal of the policy agent project is to develop a scheduling system for centralized operating theaters based on "intelligent" software agents. In comparison to decentralized operating rooms, which are directly related to their medical *departments*, a centralized operating theater forms an organizationally independent complex of *operating rooms* that are used by the different *medical departments* of the hospital. This should result in a better utilization of *rooms*, *devices* and *personnel*, as well as to higher flexibility of planning in case of emergencies. In contrast to these benefits, the transaction costs for manual planning strongly increase as conflicts about the use of resources and operating room staff arise, which have to be solved through various negotiation processes between the different medical departments [26].

The investigated system is based on negotiating software agents which intend to remove the conflicts of the scheduling-process with minimal human interaction, while taking care of the individual interests of all participants. Therefore, every human actor is represented by his own software agent which negotiates autonomously in the interest of his human principal. As the involved medical departments and their individual actors show a high degree of autonomy and have differing goals and intentions, a great variety of conflict-situations can arise, which can not be handled by simple reactive or goal-based agents [27]. Instead, this leads to the necessity of using utility-based agents which contain a representation of the relevant part of their principals utility function [25].

To derive a valid utility function different *preference-* and *appraisal-concepts* were integrated into the ontology, which allow the modeling of the users preferences. In the current ontology-design relative and absolute preference statements are implemented. This allows a great flexibility for deriving preference or utility profiles. An absolute preference statement, i.e. a cardinal statement of partial-utility for every decision relevant "economic good", can be easily transferred into an agent utility function but lacks some sense of reality. Relative preference statements resemble human decision making much better than cardinal designs, but are more difficult to derive and aggregate into a useful utility-function [24].

5. Future Work

The work presented here is still work in progress. There are open tasks in ontology- refinement, building knowledge bases and extending the integrated scenario to receive a complex and reliable reference scenario close to reality. The first step is the incremental construction of a broad knowledge base. This includes defining typical medical actions and restrictions, the modeling of medical guidelines, and defining types of medical devices to achieve a useful library for constructing hospital scenarios. The next step will be the construction of an exemplary realistic hospital scenario that will be useful for benchmarking information systems in the hospital environment. This might indeed be a difficult task, since the requirements and prerequisites of the different systems (or projects) are very diverse. This leads us to the next problem, the separation between individual task ontologies and more general domain ontologies. It is often unclear where to define certain concepts.

5.1. Task ontologies

As mentioned before (see Section 3.2), only the problem-solving knowledge should be contained in a task ontology. This knowledge is specific for the tasks of each project, but there is one common part because of the common domain ontology and the common goal to deploy FIPA-compliant agents systems. The knowledge base built on the top of the OntHoS ontology should provide all information of the modeled scenarios and the specialized agents should use it with the help of their specific task ontologies.

5.2. Ability-dependent agent behaviors

An agent should represent the interests of his principal in different situations, like negotiation, consummation, travelling, etc. For each situation type a task ontology is needed. It should give an agent the ability to make the same decisions and to have the same behavior as his principal, and to request the required information from the available knowledge base. Therefore, the terms used for the interaction between agents and the knowledge base must be specified in the task ontology, as well as the problem solving method for the given task. The next question is now, in which way the behavior of a real existent principal can be specified in a knowledge base and be reproduced by the agent. There are several existing approaches, like statistical analysis and the usage of probabilistic functions, learning systems based on long training periods, and preference/constraint based systems. A combination of these is possible as well.

Depending on the investigated task the must promising approach should be used. In the Policy-Agents project the preference/constraints based approach is used. This decision was made because there is insufficient time for training and analysis of the agents principals behaviors, because they are patients and medical personal and aren't available long time for such tasks. The design process of the task ontology for a negotiation behavior is in the evaluation phase. A redesign of this ontology is planned because there are many possible interactions with task ontologies from other projects, discovered during and after the first design phase. After work completion a more comprehensive description will be created.

5.3. Utility function

The main problem is that the agent needs a "feeling" for the appropriateness of a decision that should be made. For this reason utility functions are used. They should help the agents' behavior to fulfill the paretocriteria. This means that the value of the utility function f at time t should be greater or equal to its value at the time $t+1 : f_t(x_1, \ldots, x_n) >= f_t+1(x_1, \ldots, x_n)$, where $x_1, \ldots, x_n$ are measures for the importance of a specified preference. An other problem is the consideration of a decision made by one behavior in the other behaviors of the same agent.

6. Outline & Conclusion

In constructing OntHoS it was possible to integrate the aspects and domain description of several independent projects. They are all developing applications in the hospital domain, and the hope is to obtain comparability and interoperability between the developed systems.The development of OntHoS was the first step towards the integrated scenario *Agent.Hospital*, including several projects in one simulation.

Further general questions in the ontology design and possible elegant solutions were shown. The ontology is modeled in Protégé, a tool widely used for ontology modeling, results can directly imported into the simulation environment. Besides this it provides a couple of additional advantages: a variety of plug-ins enables graphical visualization, export to XML, and even generating Java-code, that can easily be integrated in software basing on the JADE agent platform.

Therefore, the implementation of agent based information systems in the hospital domain is facilitated, especially in the early development phases. Similarly to design tools for UML, it is more difficult to maintain changes in the later phases of system development. Thus, ontologies can also be seen as a further tool for software engineering.

Moreover, we can benefit from constructing ontologies, because concepts are presented, compared and discussed from researches with different ideas. An ontology supports the communication between the researchers of different expertise. In our case it mediates between medical, economic, and computer scientists. It mediates between a formal, computer-understandable world and the informal world of mental concepts and natural language.

The most important thing regarding ontologies is that we have the chance to build interoperable and comparable systems. Especially in hospitals efficient interoperation is hampered by isolated computer systems that are quite common in the current situation. We hope to make a small contribution to make information systems in hospitals be more accepted and efficient in the future.

References

[1] Gruninger, M.; Lee, J.: Ontology - Applications and Design. Communications of the ACM, Vol. 45, No. 2, February 2002.

[2] Holsapple, C. W.; Joshi, K. D.: A Collaborative Approach to Ontology Design. Communications of the ACM, Vol. 45, No. 2, February 2002.

[3] Kim, H., W.; Lammers, D.; Lippe, W.: Predicting how Ontologies for the Seman-tic Web evolve. Communications of the ACM, Vol. 45, No. 2, February 2002.

[4] Everett, J- O.; Bobrow, D. G.; Stolle, R.; Crouch, R.; de Paiva, V.; Condoravdi, C.; van den Berg, M.; Polanyi, L.: Making Ontologies work for resolving Redun-dancies across Documents. Communications of the ACM, Vol. 45, No. 2, Febru-ary 2002.

[5] Guarino, N.; Welty, C.: Evaluating Ontological Deciscions with Ontoclean. Communications of the ACM, Vol. 45, No. 2, February 2002.

[6] Noy, N. F.; Fergerson, R. W.; Musen M. A.: The knowledge model of Protégé-2000: combin-ing interoperability and flexibility. 2th International Conference on Knowledge Engineering and Knowledge Management (EKAW'2000), Juan-les-Pins, France, 2000.

[7] Noy, N. F.; Sintek, M.; Decker, S.; Crubezy, M.; Fergerson, R. W.; Musen. M. A.: Creating Semantic Web Contents with Protégé-2000. IEEE Intelligent Sys-tems 16(2) : 60-71, 2001.

[8] Musen, M. A.; Fergerson, R. W.; Grosso, W. E.; Noy, N. F.; Crubezy, M.; Gen-nari, J. H.: Component-Based Support for Building Knowledge-Acquisition Sys-tems. Conference on Intelligent Information Processing (IIP 2000) of the Interna-tional Federation for Information Processing World Computer Congress (WCC 2000), Beijing, 2000.

[9] Grosso, W. E.; Eriksson, H.; Fergerson, R. W.; Gennari, J. H.; Tu, S. W.; Musen, M. A.: Knowledge Modeling at the Millennium (The Design and Evolution of Protégé-2000). 1999.

[10] Devedzic, V: Ontologies: Borrowing from Software Patterns. Communications of the ACM, 1999.

[11] AI Watch - The Newsletter of Artificial Intelligence. Vol. 4-6. AI Intelligence, Oxford, UK.

[12] Knuth, D. E.: The Art of Computer Programming; Volume 2: Semi numerical Algorithms. Addison Wesley, 1981.

[13] Guarino, N.; Giaretta, P.: Ontologies and Knowledge Bases - Towards a Termi-nological Clarification. In: Mars, N.J.I. (ed.): Towards Very Large Knowledge Bases: Knowledge Building and Knowledge Sharing. Amsterdam 1995, 25-32.

[14] Guarino, N.: The Ontological Level. In: Casati, R.; Smith, B.; White, G. (eds.): Philosophy and the Cognitive Sciences. Wien, 1994 (revised version 1995).

[15] Guarino, N.: Understanding, Building, And Using Ontologies. International Jour-nal of Human-Computer Studies 46 (1997), 293-310.

[16] Studer, R.; Fensel, D.; Decker, S.; Benjamins, V.R.: Knowledge Engineering: Survey and Future Directions. In: Puppe, F. (ed.): XPS-99: Knowledge-Based Systems - Survey and Future Directions. 5th Biannual German Conference on Knowl-edge-Based Systems, 03.-05.09.1999 in Würzburg, Proceedings. Berlin et al. 1999, 1-23.

[17] Gruber, T.R.: A Translation Approach to Portable Ontology Specifications. Knowledge Ac-quisition 5 (1993) 2, 199-220. See also: Gruber, T.R.: A Translation Approach to Portable Ontology Specifications. Knowledge Systems Laboratory Technical Report KSL 92-71, Computer Science Department, Stanford University. Stanford 1993 (revised version).

[18] Chimæra Home Page: http://www.ksl.stanford.edu/software/chimaera/

[19] OILEd Home Page: http://oiled.man.ac.uk/

[20] Fikes, R.; Farquhar, A.; Rice, J.:. Tools for Assembling Modular Ontologies in Ontolingua. Knowledge Systems Laboratory, April, 1997.

[21] Protégé Home Page: http://protégé.stanford.edu/

[22] OntHoS Home Page: http://l6-spike-dos.informatik.uni-wuerzburg.de/Ontologie/

[23] Dharma Guideline Model: http://smi-web.stanford.edu/projects/eon/DharmaUserGuide/

[24] Samuelson, P. A.; Nordhaus, W. D.: Economics, Boston et al. 1998, 80-101.

[25] Russel, S. J.; Norvig, P.: Artificial Intelligence - A Modern Approach, London et al. 1995, 31-50.

[26] Seidensticker, A.: Organisation des Operationsbereiches im Krankenhaus - Eine empirisch-explorative Studie zur Beurteilung zentralisierter versus dezentrali-sierter Operationsbere-iche, Frankfurt a.M. et al 1984.

[27] Czap, H.: Policy-Agents as Personal Assistants: The Case of Hospital Schedul-ing. D-CSCW 2000 Deutsche Computer Supported Cooperative Work Fachtagung - Verteiltes Arbeiten - Arbeit der Zukunft, Workshop-Proceedings: Agents and CSCW: A Fruitful Marriage? , München 2000.

[28] SeSAm Home Page: http://www.simsesam.de/

[29] Klügl, F.; Herrler, R.; Oechslein, C.: From Simulated to Real Environments: How to use SeSAm for software development accepted at: First German Conference on Multiagent System Technologies (MATES03), Erfurt, 2003

Marc Becker, University of Trier, Department of Business Information Systems,, Universitätsring 15, D-54286 Trier, Germany
E-mail address: mb@wiinfo.uni-trier.de

Christian Heine, Technical University of Ilmenau, Department of Business and Administration,, PoBox 100 565, D-98684 Ilmenau, Germany
E-mail address: christian.heine@tu-ilmenau.de

Rainer Herrler, University of Würzburg, Department of Computer Science, Informatik VI, Am Hubland, D-97074 Würzburg, Germany
E-mail address: herrler@informatik.uni-wuerzburg.de

Karl-Heinz Krempels, Aachen University of Technology, Department of Computer Science,, Informatik IV Ahornstr. 55, D-52074 Aachen, Germany
E-mail address: krempels@i4.informatik.rwth-aachen.de

Agent-Based Up-to-date Data Management in National electronic Library for Communicable Disease

Patty Kostkova, Jane Mani-Saada, Gemma Madle, and Julius Weinberg

Abstract. Modern healthcare specialists are overwhelmed with medical information available on the Internet. However, it is difficult to find a particular piece of information when and where they actually need it. The National electronic Library for Health (NeLH) is addressing this issue by providing a single-entry portal to evidence-based medical information on the Internet enhanced with a quality tag assigned by professional experts in the field. In order to fully utilize the potential of an Internet-based library, the NeLH is distributed and consists of a number of Virtual Branch Libraries (VBLs), each dedicated to a particular disease or a medical area. Our team is responsible for the development of the communicable disease branch of the NeLH, calledNeLCD (National electronic Library for Communicable Disease). VBLs are dynamically updated and their design reflects the needs of each particular user base. However, users accessing a single VBL may want to search the entire NeLH or should have the option of being able to search the entire NeLH. Therefore, support for a distributed search according to an adopted topology ofVBL servers is essential. Intelligent interface agents are essential for the development and runtime of the library as they perform autonomously a number of tasks related to the search, assist humans in information publishing, the document review process and data exchange and retrieval. In this paper, we present an agent-based solution to assist in distributed search across the NeLH, and customization and personalization in the NeLCD.

1. Introduction

Modern healthcare specialists as well as general public are overwhelmed with medical information available on the Internet. However, they cannot find a piece of information when and where they need it [1]. Therefore, Department of Health (DoH) UK proposed a development of a National electronic Library for Health (NeLH) [1], a gateway to the evidence-based medical knowledge on the Internet. This paper focuses on agent-based development of the National electronic Library for Communicable Disease (NeLCD) [2], one of the virtual branch libraries (VBLs) forming the NeLH and the issues of distribution in the NeLH.

One of the crucial requirements of the NeLH is providing the *best available evidence* and *quality-tagging* the medical information for all user groups. By the term "quality" we mean information giving the level of evidence, the source of the evidence, consistency, completeness, reliability and "up-to-date-ness". This will distinguish the NeLH from many other existing medical sites (such as Medline [3]) which typically offer comprehensive search for documents available on the Internet without giving the user an insight into the level of evidence and quality of the presented information [4].

One of the key applications of Intelligent Agents, a fast-growing area in software technology, is information retrieval and assistance in searching information in the Internet [5]. In addition, agents autonomous behaviour enables them to assist in various search-related processes on the users behalf, however, without human intervention. These features make them particularly exciting for health care applications and in various health-related fields in general. However, there is no common agreement on ontology, nor agreed standards in health care (coding standards, data representation standards and common legal and ethical recommendations). For example, there is no common internationally accepted clinical coding scheme - currently, several coding systems are being used by different organizations: MESH, CTLV3/SNOMED and ICD10. This is not only a UK but an international issue.

The NeLCD, communicable disease branch library, investigates the application of intelligent agents in information retrieval, user customization and other aspect of the NeLH library, as being implemented in the UK.

This paper focuses on technical aspects of the distribution of the library into the Virtual Branch Libraries (VBLs), each dedicated to a specific area or a disease. There could conceivably be areas of overlap for example between the VBL for communicable disease and the VBLs for public health or primary care. The need for distributed search across the NeLH is essential in order to allow users to fully utilize the Internet-based resource. However, there is a trade off between flexibility and implementation simplicity.

This paper starts by giving a brief overview of the NeLH project (section 2), and then focuses on various aspects of the NeLH (section 3). Autonomous Intelligent Agents – supporting intelligent searching, enabling user profiling and managing the document review process, as being implemented in the NeLCD, are discussed in greater detail in section 4. Further, in section 5, our current work in progress is introduced demonstrating the usage of multi-agent systems (MAS) in information exchange within the scope of the entire NeLH project. Then, a discussion of various aspects is presented in section 6. Finally, in section 7 we discuss the project status, in section 8 the related work, and in section 9 we conclude.

2.   The NeLH Background

The three major goals of the NeLH are [6]:
- To provide health care professionals and the public with knowledge and know-how to support health care related decisions.
- To provide easy access to best current knowledge and know-how on the Internet.
- To improve health and health care, clinical practice and patient choice.

The focus on clearly defined quality by stating a level of evidence will distinguish NeLH from other medical portals (Medline, PubMed, etc). In addition, the goal of NeLH is to provide the best available evidence, unlike many high-quality medical initiatives, such as Cochrane library, that provide the golden standard but omit many issues where the evidence is insufficient.

The main source of medical evidence are books, journals, and Internet-based sources. These include: Public Health Laboratory Service [7], Cochrane database [8], NHS Centre for Reviews and Dissemination, Effective Health Care Bulletins, British National Formulary, Centres for Disease Control, British Medical Journal, and others. However, the quality, reliability and "non-biasness" of provided information significantly vary. For example, studies of Mulrow [9], Oxman and Guyatt [10] have revealed how unreliable some editorials and review articles can be if they are not prepared systematically. In particular, although readers rely on journal review articles and editorials, the scientific evidence of these is inherently unreliable and biased towards a positive and optimistic view of the effectiveness of intervention [11].

The key approach supported by the NeLH framework is evidence-based healthcare that aims to clearly identify the level of evidence of a study or recommendation. As defined in [12]: *"evidence comes from a range of activities such as randomized controlled trials (RCTs), consensus statements, observation studies and surveys of patient views. Meta-analyses and large sample RCTs are considered to provide the highest quality evidence, with expert opinion and clinical experience at the lower end of the evidence hierarchy."*

Therefore, in order to overcome the problem of bias and unreliable medical evidence, and to ensure that the best current knowledge is delivered, NeLH aims to fully support evidence-based healthcare [13]. However, in order to achieve this goal autonomous agents need to be implemented to ensure that the available information is up-to-date, to manage and automate the documents review process and to respond to users' specific needs.

The NeLH consists of virtual branch libraries (VBLs), each dedicated to a particular disease or a group of diseases. As has been said above, we are responsible for development of the NeLCD, the Communicable Disease branch of the NeLH, addressing issues of prevention, investigation and treatment of communicable disease.

3.   Structure of the NeLH

NeLH is a single information gateway, a portal, to evidence-based information related to communicable disease with respect to all user groups – clinicians, GPs, public health professionals, environmental health officers, infectious control nurses, general public and others. In this section, we will look at the general issues of the NeLH digital library and discuss internal data representation in the NeLCD.

3.1. Overview of the Library

The NeLH Knowledge Base is now a dominant commodity and knowledge distribution is so vital that the contribution made by computing, telecommunications and the World Wide Web are obviously of increasing importance. The development of knowledge management within healthcare is both necessary and possible [14]. It is based on existing medical evidence-based sites, PubMed, Cochrane Library database, etc.

The core content of the NeLH can be likened to a central reference library and Virtual Branch Libraries to local branches, which serve the needs of the communities in which they based. So far, a number of prototype VBLs are being developed, such as Cancer, Child Health, Communicable Diseases, Diabetes, Diagnosis, Emergency Care, Health Informatics, Heart Disease, and others.

Our team is responsible for development of the NeLCD [35], the Communicable Disease branch of the NeLH, which addresses issues in prevention, investigation treatment and control of communicable disease. This is a single information gateway, a portal, to evidence-based information related to communicable disease with respect to all user groups – clinicians, GPs, public health professionals, environmental health officers, infectious control nurses, general public and others.

Figure 1 illustrates the NeLH framework. NeLCD stands for the National electronic Library for Communicable Disease, NeLC is the National electronic Library for Cancers, and the NeLPC is the National electronic Library for Primary Care.

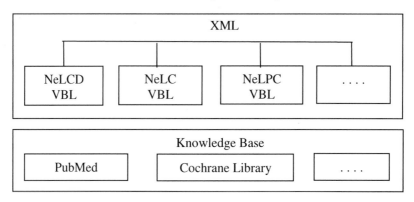

Fig. 1. The NeLH Structure

3.2. Knowledge Sources

The evidence available from NeLCD is obtained from high quality evidence-based directories, journals, and other databases. These include: PHLS [15], Cochrane database [16], NHS Centre for Reviews and Dissemination, Effective Health Care Bulletins, British National Formulary, Centres for Disease Control, BMJ, and others.

3.3. Data Representation

In order to support a user-customizable search, documents in the library need to be precisely described. The Dublin Core Metadata initiative (http://www.purl.org/DC) defines a list of fields characterizing an electronic document for cataloguing and search purposes. The NeLH adopted and extended this framework to better meet the requirements of quality and "up-to-date-ness". Issues related to metadata are covered in greater detail in the paper by Kamel Boulos describing a preparatory study of metadata, RDF and problem-knowledge coupling for the NeLH [17]. MESH medical ontology is used for indexing all documents in NeLH that is expressed in the field "Subject" of the Dublin Code metadata definition. Every document in NeLH will be described by the following fields - called "electronic catalogue card".

Table 1. Electronic catalogue card

Dublin Core Field	Description
Title	Title of the document
Creator	Author(s) of the document
Subject	Keywords for indexing
Publisher	The publishing organization or the Internet site

Date   - publishing
                    - posting
                    - expiry
	Date of publication
	Date of NeLCD posting
	Date for review

Type	Publication type
Format	Software format
Identifier	Identifier (ISBN, URL)
Source	Document Bibliography
Language	Document Language
Relation	Reference to related documents
Coverage	Medical "category"
Quality Tag	Level of evidence
Check List	Answers to Check List Questions
Description	"Reviewers Assessment" summarizing the document
ID	Unique identifier

3.4.   The Appraisal Process

As each VBL serves specific group of healthcare professionals with particular information needs , there is a need for variations in the document appraisal process to meet the specific needs of each VBL's user base.

In this section, we will describe the appraisal process as it is set up within the NeLCD. The model of collaboration with professionals involved in the appraisal process may vary among VBLs, however, the key issues regarding the support for evidence and quality-tagging are agreed by all VBL teams.

As only pre-processing and quality-tagging of available information before incorporating it into NeLCD could ensure the required quality of the site, the core of NeLCD will consist only of appraised documents which have passed the NeLCD editorial procedure. This does not restrict the physical location of the actual documents – they could be local or accessed at their original source. Nor does it restrict the type of document available – the NeLCD attempts to present the "best available evidence", this could be a meta-analysis, or where there is little literature, a case report (but this is clearly indicated by the Level of Evidence, that is the Quality tag in the Dublin Core definition). The Timestamp attached to every document in NeLCD will consist of three data items:

- Publication date (date of the document publication or "Access date" where no publication date is available),
- Posting date (date when document is added to the NeLCD database), and
- Expiry date (date when document is reviewed by the NeLCD team, usually 1 year after posting and annually there after).

As all information posted to NeLCD must be kept up-to-date, it is essential to review the core material regularly, even when no contradicting evidence has been found. For this reason every document has to go through a review process when its "Expiry date" (Table 1) has passed which is performed by the Expiry Agents. This is usually one year from the date of posting and then annually thereafter. Each document considered the best available evidence on a particular subject is assigned a *quality tag,* by a member of a professional society or expert group. The quality tag consists of:

- Level of Evidence (meta-analysis, Randomized Control Trial, Clinical Trial, Cohort Study, Case Control Study, Peer Leader Opinion, Personal Experience or Unspecified),
- Reviewers Assessment critically summarizing the paper, and
- Checklist, which answers brief questions about the methodological issues, level of evidence, potential biases and applicability of the results [18].

The resultant quality tag and a signature of the particular society are attached to the document and made available through the NeLCD.

4.   Agents in the NeLCD

Agent architecture is described at two sections of this paper: firstly, agents supporting the information management within the NeLCD, and secondly, a set of agents responsible for distribution is discussed in the next section.

There are currently four basic agent concepts in the NeLCD. First two, Intelligent Search Agents and Pro-active Alert Agents, are involved in the search process and user profiling and customization. The later, Reactive Review Agents and Reactive Expiry Agents, are in change of various aspects of the library review process. The NeLCD is illustrated in Figure 2.

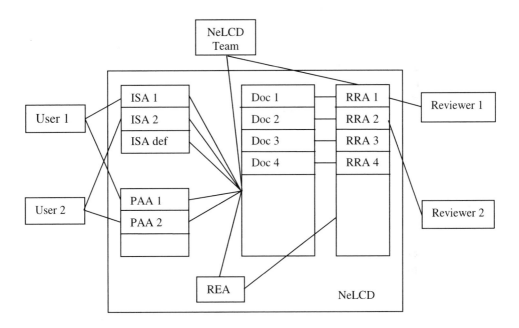

Fig. 2. Agents in NeLCD

4.1.   Intelligent Search Agents

The primary goal of the library to provide a single portal for searching for an up-to-date medical information. Special types of Intelligent User Interface (IUI) agents [19] and Intelligent Search Agents (ISA) are used to provide the search-related functionality.

Tasks

- Presenting users with a user-friendly adaptive interface to define his or her query for searching medical information in the library.
- The ISAs perform the searching functionality according to the given criteria.
- In addition to defining keywords for a query and their combination by logical operators, users can customize the search by restricting the resultant set to certain criteria, as indicated by the Dublin Core fields. For example, the agent can search for all documents regarding meningitis and children and display only Randomised Control Trials, or Case Studies.
- In addition, we are currently investigating a framework for adaptive ISA agents learning user profile - special interests, and preferences - to customize the interface and search capabilities to better meet user needs.

Number

There is an ISA for each registered user to allow the customization of the interface and the search,. In addition, as registration is not compulsory, there is a default ISA providing standard search and presenting default interface to non-registered users.

Interaction and Coordination

Each ISA interacts with one user - that is, a customized ISA dedicated to a particular user provides the customized functionality, and a number of default ISAs serve non-registered users.

In addition, they also communicate with the Knowledge Sources to perform the search and return the results back to the user.

When a user logs in the site the dedicated ISA is activated and the user interface and search is customized accordingly. A new default ISA is created when a new user logs in.

4.2.   Pro-active Alert Agents

Pro-active Alert agents (PAA) are performing tasks on users-behalf.

Tasks

- Users can instruct PAAs, to perform given tasks on their behalf autonomously or alert them accordingly. For example, the PAA is monitoring the library and informing users about new postings or comments related to specific issues.

Number

There is a PAA for each registered user to perform the alert functionality. Non-registered users have no PAA agents.

Interaction and Coordination

PAAs interact with users - one PAA per registered user. In addition, they communicate with the Knowledge Sources to check changes in the database interested to each particular user.

PAA act autonomously with a frequency given by the particular user – e.g., every day, once a week, etc. Users can set the PAA to alert about several issues, each with different frequency. PAA is in control of its activation according to the settings.

4.3. Reactive Review Agents

As a part of the appraisal process, experts from professional societies review each document by assigning it the quality tag. This process is managed by Reactive Review Agents (RRA).

Tasks

- RRAs are responsible for ensuring that each document is assigned a reviewer when its DC information is entered, and posting it to the library as soon as the review is delivered.
- In addition, the Review Agents remind the reviewers and the NeLCD team when the quality tag is not obtained within a given deadline.

Number

There is one RRA for each document in the database.

Interaction and Coordination

RRAs interact with reviewers and the NeLCD team (a special type of user) – a RRA sends off a request for a review to dedicated reviewer and wait for the reply. They send out another request and a notification to the NeLCD team if the review is no received within the given deadline. In addition, they interact with Reactive Expiry Agents (REA) which will be discussed below. RRA have three states:

- "deactivated" (when the document is reviewed), is activated by entering a new document by the NeLCD team or by the REA
- "waiting - first request " (waiting for review when the first request has been sent out),
- "waiting - second request" (waiting for review when a second request and the information to the NeLCD team has been sent out). If the review is still not received, the NeLCD team needs to interfere to sort it out by choosing a different reviewer or finding an alternative solution.

4.4. Reactive Expiry Agents

Each document posted on the library is assigned an "expiry date" to ensure that all information is always up-to-date. This is the responsibility of the Reactive Expiry Agent (REA).

Tasks
- checking all documents for their expiry date
- the particular Reactive Review Agent is activated to inform the reviewer that the document needs to be reconsidered. It will take on the task and will remind the reviewer when the reply is not obtained within the given deadline, as is the case with new documents.

Number
The is only one REA in the database.

Interaction and Coordination
The REA collaborates with the Knowledge Sources to check expiry dates for all documents. In addition, it interacts with RRAs by activating them to take on the document review process. The REA runs autonomously once a week.

4.5. Example

There are some typical examples of the functionality of these agents as for the user perspective and document workflow perspective.

User perspective
Users typically set up their PAA by indicating the keywords defining their professional interests (based on MESH ontology), for example, meningitis in children & investigation, TB & treatment, Hepatitis A, etc. The PAA then searches the Knowledge Source for new entries related to these topics and sends an email to the user if a new document of his interest has been inserted. In addition, users have their ISAs set up to search for information in the library. For example, the ISA is looking for documents on "journal papers" dealing with "prevention" of "HIV" as this is the user specialty. Obviously, the user setting could be overridden for any new search request. Then the ISA searches the Knowledge Source and presents the user the relevant documents. More advanced personalization, allowing users to customize the MESH-based keyword tree, is being investigated.

Document Perspective
Documents described by DC have phases they have to go through in the NeLCD that define the document workflow. Firstly, if a published document is considered the key

evidence, it is included in the NeLCD and a new RRA is created. It sends an email to the appropriate professional society for request for the appraisal (the Reviewers Assessment). It is in the state "waiting - first request" until the Reviewers Assessment is submitted (by an online questionnaire) and then the agent go to the state "deactivated". Alternatively, it can request the RA once more if it was not received within a month – goes to the state "waiting - second request" which can lead into "deactivation" of the agent if the RA is received, Alternatively, an email to the NeLCD team is sent informing that the review is still pending, if there is no response from the processionals within another month. Another core functionality performed by the REA, running once a week, is to ensure that all documents are reviewed again according to their "expiry date". The expired document's RRA is activated to submit the document for a review which follows the same process as in the case of a new document.

5. Distributed Search across the NeLH

The previous sections of this paper have focused on interface and reactive agents related to medical information retrieval from the NeLCD. However, the NeLH contains a number of dedicated libraries (VBLs), as discussed at the beginning of this paper. The need for common ontology and data exchange specification as well as a framework for technical collaboration among the libraries is obvious.

The above section discussed technical aspects of the search for medical information within the NeLCD. Each VBL team is responsible for implementing the search facility within their virtual branch library, while accomplishing the requirements on data representation using the agreed Dublin Core-based electronic catalogue card. These are exchanged in XML format.

Medical ontology of data exchange and technical aspects of the interoperability among VBLs and the actual topology of VBLs are investigated in this section.

5.1. NeLH Topology

The NeLH architecture is being designed not as a simple client-server, but a set of VBL servers communicating with users who wants to search all available information within the NeLH. Therefore, the first technical issue to enable a distributed search is the topology of the digital library.

We are investigating a *star topology*, that is, a VBL processing a search will contact the NeLH server, which acts as a mediator, to obtain search results from all other VBLs. Another solution would be to implement a *Peer-to-Peer* communication where each VBL would separately contact every other VBL to receive all potential results.

We opted for the star solution for its implementation simplicity and easier consistency maintenance. The star topology of the NeLH is illustrated in Figure 3.

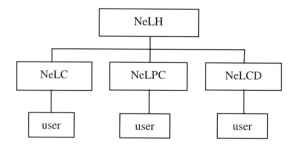

Fig. 3. NeLH Star Topology

5.2.   Cross-search

As for the technical issues, NeLCD team is currently investigating the application of Distributed Cooperative Multi-Agent System (CMAS) [20, 21] to the NeLH using a star topology. At each VBL, in addition to the Intelligent Agents discussed above, there are also Intelligent Search Agents for Distribution (ISA-D). In addition, there is the Central Intelligence Search Agent (ISA-C) at the top NeLH site [22]. These agents provide the additional functionality essential for the cross-search across the entire NeLH and are not needed within the NeLCD branch library - therefore, for reasons of clarity, ISA-C and ISA-D are introduced here and were not discussed in the previous section dealing only with a single VBL.

Intelligent Search Agents for Distribution (ISA-D)
ISA-Ds are present at each VBL and are responsible for ensuring the distributed search.
- They communicate with the particular user ISA to search the local VBL and, secondly, request results form remote VBLs via ISA Central (ISA-C) present in NeLH (discussed below).
- When the results are returned from the ISA-C, the ISA-D is also responsible for combining all results together (local and remote) and presenting them to the user.
- It is activated by a user request to receive all available documents in the NeLH, as the default is to search only the local VBL.

The Central Intelligent Search Agent (ISA-C)
The central NeLH site contains a ISA-C agent responsible for the following tasks:
- Keeps up-to-date information of the location and availability of all VBLs (and references to the default ISAs),
- is responsible for combining the results coming from the VBLs ISA agents,

- is responsible for filtering out duplications in search results before these are sent back to the user, and
- sending the results back the end user, via his VBL ISA-D.
- They could be activated by any ISA-D in VBLs or directly by a user accessing the search facility at the top NeLH site.
- It also communicates with the Negotiation Agent present in NeLH, discussed in the next section.

The architecture is illustrated in Figure 4. Other agents are omitted for reasons of simplicity. The numbers next to communication lines illustrate steps in which the communication takes place.

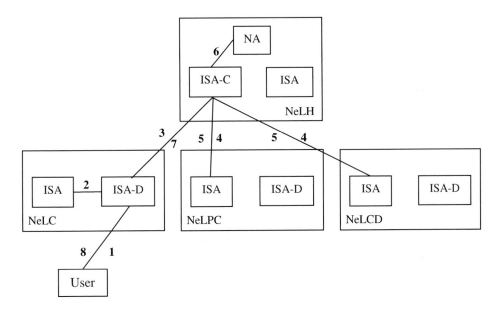

Fig. 4. Agents Performing a Distributed Search

Technically, an agent-based query producing an XML output is a robust and flexible solution for all technical platforms used by VBLs. The XML, defined by DTD/schemes based on the discussed DC, Table 1, could be rendered by the receiving VBL to meet the particular VBL requirements on look and feel, thought customisable ISAs, as discussed in [35]. In addition, server-side scripting should be adopted where possible to avoid browser-related problems. Therefore, the output XML sent to the receiving VBL for rendering is transformed into the resulting HTML which is then sent to the client.

5.3.   Conflict-resolution

However, a single paper or medical document could come up in several VBLs and could be assigned different a quality tag in each VBL, as their appraisal procedure may vary.

There are two solutions to this problem. Firstly, there is a Negotiating Agent (NA), provided by the NeLH, which will autonomously step in and negotiate a common level of evidence. If agreement cannot be achieved without human intervention, the Negotiation Agent could request the check lists and an additional information from the VBLs involved in order to help the end user to make the final decision on validity of the evidence.

The second approach would be always presenting the user all search results, including those of contradicting quality in order to allow the professional to make the final decision. For these cases, providing the check list (which defines the criteria on which a certain level of evidence was assigned), is essential.

In addition, we are investigating the option of enabling users to customise their search so as they can define whether to authorize the NeLH to perform the negotiation, or whether they prefer to receive all contradicting results and decide themselves.

5.4.   Example

For example, a user of the NeLCD is searching for "investigation documents on small pox of "Randomized Control Trial" level of evidence, however, is interested in evidence available in the entire NeLH, not just the NeLCD branch (where this would be performed by the ISA agent, as discussed above). In this case, the ISA-D is activated and calls the ISA to retrieve the relevant local documents. Then, it calls the ISA-C at the main NeLH server with the same request and waits for the result. In parallel, ISA-C, having the knowledge of the location and availability of all VBLs, sends a search requests to all ISAs in VBLs and waits for all responses. As for the ISAs in other VBLs, the search is performed in the same manner as if it was initiated locally. The results are sent back to the central ISA-C which can contact the Negotiation Agent to deal with possible inconsistencies in the review of the same document; however, the specification of this agent is currently being investigated. Then, all results are returned to the originating ISA-C that is responsible for combining the results and presenting them to the user. The numbers at the Figure 5 represent the order of these operations.

6.   Discussion

The distributed star topology solution was investigated by the NeLCD team. Here we discuss other possible approaches to the library design.

6.1.   A Centralized Library

A centralized library would be the best value for money. However, the users vary widely across the libraries (VBLs), and the libraries vary widely in scope and types of content – it is important to maintain the ability of each VBL to respond to the strategic needs of their user base. Therefore, an independence of VBLs in terms of implementing their database structure and search engine, as well as defining the look and feel of the VBL, the user interface and navigation strategy are essential. Also, having a direct control we have more flexibility to adapt and respond to our user base.

6.2.   A Peer-to-Peer Topology

As has been discussed above, an alternative solution to the adopted star topology would be a Peer-to-Peer communication. The simplicity of maintaining consistency by the central NeLH server is the main reason for our approach. Therefore, there is just single point of information on VBL location, access, current availability, etc. Also, all VBLs have to be contacted each time a cross-search is performed to receive all results. As the data are being frequently updated, it cannot be known in advance whether a certain VBL can provide information on a particular subject. On the other hand, the drawback of this approach is that the NeLH server being as a single point of information is also a single point of failure. Therefore, in case of the NeLH server being unavailable, the cross-search, as discussed above, would not work.

6.3.   Search Definitions

We believe that all user queries could be expressed as combinations of logical operators on columns (or full-text search), and therefore, the ODBS type of solutions are not needed. In addition, a number of the libraries have adopted the Lotus Domino database as their implementation platform, therefore, there is no need to provide cross-SQL queries as Lotus database is not relational.

6.4.   Sharing User Profiles

Also, user profile could be exchanged among the VBLs to ensure the same functionality regardless of the actual VBL a particular user has logged in. The user could define his preferences regarding resolving conflicts, as discussed above, as well as user interface preferences. This area is also currently being investigated.

7.   Project Status

Currently, we have finished our prototype phase and are developing the core library. The distributed search has been investigated by a number of VBL teams and currently we are in the process of finding a mutually convenient technical solution which will be implemented. As for the cross-search, currently, many VBLs are providing only a search of their local database, some support an explicit call to a server script to perform search in a particular remote VBL, such as VBLs which adopted standardized technical solution called the NeLH Toolkit [23]. However, a coordinated cross-search across all VBLs is still in the design and development phase.

7.1.   Collaboration with Professional Societies

The major professional societies involved in the practice of communicable disease have indicated their support to the project and an initial model of collaboration have been set up. It is chaired by the Federation of Infection Societies, and secretarial support is provided by the Public Health Laboratory Service. The technical research and development of the project is provided by The City University [24].

7.2.   Ethical Issues

Ethical aspects of any Internet-based healthcare project need to be addressed. In the case of NeLCD, no private patient data are gathered or processed. User profiles collected by Information Agents are kept and used with the owner consent. Personal data, such as names and e-mail numbers are kept by agents on local servers and not shared with agents in other VBLs. In addition, copyright aspects are not an issue either as the library provides links to documents which are already in the public domain [25].

7.3.   Implementation Issues

The prototype of the NeLCD library (http://www.nelcd.co.uk) has been built using CGI scripts to implement the basic agent functionality. Also, many other VBLs have adopted proprietary solutions. The top NeLH site could be found at http://www.nelh.nhs.uk.

Currently we are porting the system to Lotus Domino R5 platform, which was chosen as the common environment for all VBLs in the NeLH. Lotus Domino built-in agents support is used for implementing the agent functionality discussed in this paper. The Lotus Domino agents provide the reactive and proactive functionality and are a substantial part of the development environment. Technically, agents are being written in Java Script and act as state machines being triggered by an event (user input – ISA) or a time definition (document expired - REA).

The prototype of the NeLCD library was built around the 10 high-priority areas, identified in a national prioritization exercise [26], and later populated with core evidence-based documents with relevance to the infections diseases, syndromes and presentations. Documents in NeLCD are represented in XML (relevant DTD is defined for validation purposes). Common DTD across NeLH will allow extensive document exchange and cross-VBL search performed by Information Agents. The separation of the content from style allows flexible manipulation with data, easy modifications of the display format, as well as object-based data representation suitable for data search and document exchange. The documents available at the prototype site are in the editorial process now and the first Reviewers Assessments have been received.

Also, as some VBL teams are not fortunate in having technical expertise available, a toolkit platform has been developed [27]. This resource is essential for some teams, however, as has been said above, as a great number of libraries adopted a proprietary solution. Therefore, the interoperability issue is crucial to ensure data exchange and distributed search among all VBLs.

As has been said above, the physical distribution of VBLs and full control over technical development of each library is important to ensure flexibility and to respond to specific needs of each VBL users. However, in addition to a communication overhead, there are indications that this solution is not long-term viable for funding reasons. Therefore, it is a matter of discussion whether this project will realize the investigated distributed approach or whether less flexible solution would be the case.

7.4.   Future Work

Currently, we are finishing of the MAS architecture described in this paper. In our future research, we will investigate the negotiation agents in greater detail, look at user profiling and more complex customization of ISAs and PAAs. Also, we will be looking at the personalization of the MESH-based ontology through ISA profiling allowing users to select keywords according to their specialty by pruning the MESH tree. Finally, we will investigate automatic download of new documents from PubMed based on data mining Intelligent Agents regularly reviewing new entries at PubMed.

8.   Related Work

Autonomous gents providing various functionality in health care applications have been an interesting area of research in recent years in academia and industry. For example, agent project by Honeywell is investigating applications of autonomous agents in elderly patients nursing [28], agentcities-funded (www.agentcities.net) healthcare project is looking at implementing MAS for negotiating patients visits to specialists according to his or her condition and physical location [29]. Agents-assisted recommendation for screening of cancer patients and other projects were investigated by Cancer Research Fund, UK [30]. However, the NeLCD seems to be the only project using agent technology in medical digital library.

As for the distributed communicate aspect of the library, there are a number related digital libraries providing a collection of cross-searchable documents in the Internet. The Z39.50 [31] standard specifies an abstract information system with a rich set of facilities for searching, retrieving records, browsing term lists, etc. At the server side, this abstract system is mapped onto the interface of whatever specific database management system is being used. The client application is unaware of the implementation details of the software hiding behind the network interface, and it can access any type of database through the same, well-defined network protocol. On the client side, the abstract information system is mapped back onto an interface which can be tailored to the unique requirements of each user. This provides a well founded universal solution, conceptually similar to the one in NeLH, however, the NeLH is a proprietary database which does not aim to provide universality. The same is the case for the general SDLIP communication protocol [32].

A similar approach, looking at a tree hierarchical topology for communicating agents was investigated by Kostkova as the MAGNET Architecture [33].

Also, commercial Web publishing products, such as developed by Interwoven [34], do not provide the additional autonomous functionality required by the NeLH document quality review and appraisal process, as discussed in [35].

Finally, a related non-agent knowledge representation project from NLM: the Unified Medical Language System (UMLS) develops and distributes multi-purpose, electronic "Knowledge Sources" and associated lexical programs to enhance systems focused on patient data, digital libraries, Web and bibliographic retrieval, natural language processing, and decision support. UMLS [36] includes a list of vocabularies in the UMLS Metathesaurus.

9.   Conclusion

NeLCD, a virtual branch library of the NeLH, is developing an information gateway, a digital library, providing the best available evidence-based knowledge, enhanced with medical quality tags, to a wide spectrum of users: clinical experts, public health, general practitioners and general public. In this paper we have introduced this project and discussed the application of Intelligent Agents in information retrieval, user profiling, and the assistance in the documents review process in the NeLCD virtual branch library. In addition, we have introduced and discussed the star topology for NeLH enabling a distributed search across all libraries in the NeLH, based on MAS.

References

[1] Gray, J.A.M., S de Lusignan. *National electronic Library for Health (NeLH)*. BMJ, **319** , 1476-1479, (1999).

[2] P. Kostkova, J. Mani-Saada, J. R. Weinberg. *.Do you read the literature properly, and if you do how can others benefit from it?..* PHLS Annual Scientific Conference 2002, Warwick, UK, (2002).

[3] Medline. http://www.medline.com

[4] M.N. Kamel Boulos., A.V. Roudsari,, C. Gordon, J.A.M. Gray. *The Use of Quality Benchmarking in Assessing Web Resources for the Dermatology VBL of the NeLH,* Journal of Medical Internet Research 2001; 3(1): e5, (2000).

[5] N. J. Davies, R. Weeks and M. C. Revett. *Information Agents for the World Wide Web*. BT Technical Journal, **14: 4**, (1996).

[6] J.R. Weinberg, J. Mani-Saada, K. Smith. *The National electronic Library for Communicable Disease (NeLCD)*. Poster. FIS Conference, UK, (2000).

[7] Public Health Laboratory Service. http://www.phls.co.uk

[8] Cochrane Database. http:// www.cochrane.co.uk

[9] C.W. Mulrow. *The medical review article: state of the science*. Ann. Intern. Med., **106**, pp 485-8, (1987).

[10] A.D. Oxman, G. H. Guyatt. *Guidelines for reading literature reviews*. Can. Med. Assoc. Journal, **138**, pp 697-703.

[11] NeLH Team. *The Knowledge and Know-how Platform*. Internal document (1999).

[12] Health Technology Board for Scotland. *Guidance for manufacturers on submission of evidence to Health Technology Assessments,* http://www.htbs.co.uk/docs/pdf/Consultation%20draft.pdf, (2002)

[13] Health Technology Board for Scotland. *Guidance for manufacturers on submission of evidence to Health Technology Assessments,* http://www.htbs.co.uk/docs/pdf/Consultation%20draft.pdf, (2002)

[14] The NeLH Architecture Paper. http://www.nhsia.nhs.uk/nelh/background/arch_index.asp

[15] Public Health Laboratory Service. http://www.phls.co.uk

[16] Cochrane Database. http:// www.cochrane.co.uk

[17] M.N. Kamel Boulos. *A Preparatory Study on the Dermatology Virtual Branch Library of the NeLH* (MSc Thesis in Medical Informatics), GKT School of Medicine, KCL, University of London, UK, (2000)

[18] http://www.staff.city.ac.uk/~jane/check.doc

[19] S. Green and F. Somers. *Software agents: a Review*. Intelligent Agents Group, Computer Science Department, Trinity College Dublin and Broadcom Eireann Research Ltd., http://www.cs.tcl.ie/research_groups/aig/iag/iag.html

[20] K. Sycara. *Multi-agent Infrastructure, Agent Discovery, Middle Agents for Web Services and Interoperation*. M. Luck et. Al. (Eds.): ACAI 2001, LNAI 2086, 17-49, Springer-Verlag Berlin Heidelberg (2001).

[21] M. Genesereth and S. Ketchpel: *Software Agents*, Communications of the ACM, **37**, No 7, pp. 48-53, (1994)

[22] P. Kostkova, J. Mani-Saada, J.R. Weinberg. *Distributed Search in National electronic Library for Health*. In the Proceedings of the IEEE DCADL, ICPP 2002, Vancouver, Canada, August 2002. 122 Patty Kostkova, Jane Mani-Saada, Gemma Madle, Julius Weinberg

[23] http://www.nelh.shef.ac.uk/nelh/front.nsf/LL?openform

[24] R. Weinberg, J. Mani-Saada, P. Kostkova. *Development of a National electronic Library for Communicable Disease*. IDSA Conference, Chicago, USA, October 2002

[25] P. Kostkova, J. Mani-Saada, J.R. Weinberg. Ethical Issues in Health Care on the Internet: .Much ado about nothing?., In the Proceedings of the Nordic interdisciplinary conference and workshop at NTNU .Making Common Ground: Methodological and Ethical issues in doing Internet research., Trondheim, Norway, June 2002.

[26] P. Horby, A. Rushdy, C. Graham, M. O.Mahony, et al. *PLHS Overview of Communicable Diseases 1999*. http://www.staff.city.ac.uk/~jane/ovcd.pdf

[27] http://www.nelh.shef.ac.uk/nelh/front.nsf/LL?openform

[28] K.Z. Haigh, J. Phelps, C.W. Geib *An Open Agent Architecture for Assisting Elder Independence*. In the Proceedings of the AAMAS 2002, Bologna, Italy, July 2002.

[29] Antonio Moreno, David Isern. *A first step towards providing health-care agent-based services to mobile users*. In the Poster session of AAMAS 2002, Bologna, Italy, July 2002.

[30] J. Fox. Understanding intelligent agents: analysis and synthesis In the Proceedings of Agents applied in Health Care, 15th European Conference on Artificial Intelligence, ECAI-2002, Lyon, France, July 2002.

[31] http://www.biblio-tech.com/html/z39_50.html

[32] http://www-diglib.stanford.edu/~testbed/doc2/SDLIP/

[33] P. Kostkova, J. A. McCann. *Inter-federation Communication in the MAGNET Architecture*. In the Proceedings of the Grace Hopper Celebration of Women in Computing Conference 2000, Cape Cod, Massachusetts, USA, (2000).

[34] http://www.interwoven.com/products/content_management/key.html

[35] P. Kostkova, J. Mani-Saada, J. Weinberg. *Agent-based Up-to-date Data Management in National electronic Library for Communicable Disease*. In the Proceedings of Agents applied in Health Care, 15th European Conference on Artificial Intelligence, ECAI-2002, Lyon, France, July 2002.

[36] http://www.nlm.nih.gov/research/umls/umlsmain.html

Patty Kostkova1, Jane Mani-Saada, Gemma Madle, Julius Weinberg
Institute of Health Sciences, The City University, Northampton Square, London, EC1V 0HB, UK
E-mail address:
{patty|J.Mani-Saada|G.C.Madle|J.R.Weinberg}@soi.city.ac.uk

Wound Care Documentation in Municipal Elderly Care

Hans Kyhlbäck and Hannes Persson

Abstract. This ongoing R&D project is about design of a peer-to-peer groupware aimed to support wound care documentation. Nurses decentralized control is recognized as a crucial factor for transition from a single paper print form to a distributed electronic case book. The use of digital photographs has been introduced revealing a developmental potential in this Swedish municipal elder care. In an evolutionary design approach the project is trying to accomplish a mapping between the work activity and the core features of the software system. An *authorization layered model* and *peer membership rules* are suggested and elaborated in the design work as key elements in a developed peer-to-peer network architecture. The article reports on utilizing ethnographic field studies and nurses participatory design work as contributions to the software development. The opportunity of improving work and learning by means of the peer-to-peer environment is discussed as additional aspects of software development work.

1. Introduction

The aim of the project is to map decentralized network solution to a decentralized wound care work practice. It will be argued that central in the work practice is the issue of the nurses' control of their work activity, and therefore the core issue of the design challenge is to map this control aspect. Focusing on the control aspect, our approach is, first, to find out which aspects of control are central according to information captured by ethnography and participatory design methods. Second, we attempt to "build in" the same "control aspects" into the technology, fully aware of the fact that when we introduce a new powerful technology new circumstances emerge and, consequently, a new work practice will occur.

1.1. Sharing and Remembering Wound Care Information

The Wound Care Documentation project is an ongoing project established since one and a half year in the actual work practice of nurses in a Swedish municipal elder care. So far the use of a digital camera and the task of taking digital photos of wounds have been introduced and accommodated to the nurses' documentation work. In conjunction with initial field studies, a stand-alone software, called "Hedvig", was designed and tested at location as a prototype for a future digital wound document-ation system [1]. Currently users and developers cooperatively construct a decentralized network solution to a decentralized wound care work practice. The special features of digital images are perceived as a promising technique that will be integrated in a new way of sharing and remembering information related to wound care treatment.

The design approach of this project is not to invent a large size and self sufficient system intended to compensate human work. On the contrary, it sets off small and simple to find a way of supporting intelligent human work. The aim of the intended software is not to automate human actions as a kind of an agent system but provide a technological space that facilitates wound care measures and the organizational memory of provided treatment.

1.2.   The Challenge of Introducing a Network Solution

Thus, the Wound Documentation Project is facing a challenge of introduction a distributed network solution in a health care work practice. The introduction of network technology may result in distrust, non-acceptance and frustrating experiences for the health care personnel. What seems to be an important reason to failures of deployment is the human's lack of control of the new technology. In their book *Information ecologies* [2] Nardi and O'Day describes how the activity in an operation room at a hospital was affected by the introduction of a central monitoring system where the neurophysiologist could monitor several operations at once from his office. The introduced system fed all the data of interest to neurophysiologist outside the operating room, including operation room audio and video, in addition to the instrument data. As they write "It was an invasion of privacy. It threatened the sanctity and balance of the social practices that made the difficult work of neurosurgery possible" [2, p. 178]. The authors claim that the "remote broadcast changed the nature of communication inside the operating room in significant ways" [2, p. 179]. They no longer made jokes or talked about their weekend plans. This maybe seems harmful but as the authors states "the banter and fun in the operating room provided social cohesion in a stressful situation that required meticulous teamwork" (ibid.). The personnel who were monitored had no control over who had the access to watch the records of them. It was even so that anyone who got access to the computer network was able to see the broadcast from the operating room. This feeling of being out of control can demolish most introduced systems. As Nardi and O'Day point out, the introduction of a new artifact inevitable will lead to changes in the current work practice, and in some cases it leads to the emergence of a whole new practice. The new technology makes things possible that were not possible before and therefore affect the activity in the work setting where the artifact was introduced. By the deployment of such a central artifact as our designed peer-to-peer groupware system, the daily activity in the elder care is likely to be affected.

1.3.   The Mission and Suggested Concepts

The mission of our R&D project is to support, and avoid making things worse in the elder care. We hope that our contribution will help to make the work activity more sound and flourishing at the same time as we understand that our peer-to-peer system is not the one and only solution to problems of well-being for the care recipients and the health care staff. We have identified a set of goals for what to accomplish in making real our over-all mission for the R&D project. In the developmental work we consequently have created or selected a number of measures for realizing how to accomplish the implementation and deployment of our: decentralized network solution to a decentralized wound care work practice. Our design work focus on a transition of a paper print case book to make a distributed electronic version. The ubiquitous Internet is a technological grounding on which we build an implementation of our designed peer-to-peer groupware. Findings from ethnography on how the local team work is organized, we try to map by means of our suggested concepts for this peer-to-peer groupware. The *authorization layered model* realizes our understanding of core characteristics of wound treatment documentation. Some parts of the information are not needed for assessment and analysis of a particular wound healing process. Leaving personal data out will make it possible to share anonymous information with personnel in the periphery of the work practice. In making a distinction between different information content, we find a way to distribute information and in effect the system might promote learning on a distance to the actual work practice. The authorization model is followed up by the *peer membership rules* and found as a sufficient match to actual division of labor in the health care practice. Those concepts are key elements in our peer-to-peer network architecture which is currently developed further in our R&D project. In developing an *ontology* [3] we might find an artifact that facilitates communication among nurses and software designers, as well as product to be utilized in our design.

1.4. Allowing the Nurses to Maintain Control of Wound Care Information

However, for now this article reports on an on-going project where the peer-to-peer groupware is planned to be deployed allowing the nurses to maintain control of wound care information content in a digital environment. The software under development will allow for the nurses to first invite themselves as members of a specific network community, or more precisely, to a peer group as described in following paragraphs. The nurses and other personnel provide wound care tasks as motivated by the individual care recipient's need to get her or his wound healed. For those mostly elderly people in the municipal special accommodation, it is painful and takes a lot of patience and time to successfully treat wounds. In this writing we refer to wounds in general but adhere to descriptions like: "chronic wounds such as pressure, diabetic and venous ulcers" or "non-healing" alternatively "hard to heal" leg, foot and pressure wounds that need recurring treatment. The municipal wound care work is characterized by skilful assessment and giving 'hands on' measures at the care recipient's home.

1. 5. Integrated and Unified Case Book

A supposition of the R&D project is that the nurses will learn and feel familiar with the peer group software and further get confident about adding more people to either be full members of the group or only as restricted "to just look" at some specific parts of the information. The idea of the extension of the documentation artifact is to let people look and learn and this is found to be a secondary motive for the Wound Care Documentation project. In supporting documentation work an integrated and unified case book is asked for as the central artifact. A nurse in the municipal elder care and member of the Special County Wound Treatment Group pointed out: "There is a need of a unified documentation. Today we have a number of home-made case books" (interview May 2002). Additionally, the General Practitioner Ruth F. Öien that has developed a work practice on pinch grafting at a primary care centre in a neighboring municipality, highlights the importance of improved education in a recent doctoral thesis: "Monitoring standards for assessment of ulcer aetiology through repeated questionnaires and educating medical staff seemed to assure more accurate diagnoses, a prerequisite for effective leg ulcer treatment"[4, abstract].

1.6. Evolutionary Design Approach

The methodological approach of this project is to develop the system in an evolutionary way as inspired in the Scandinavian tradition of participatory design work. The idea is to integrate feedback from the field continuously into the design process. Nurses and software designers and engineers currently interact to get work practice experiences and the design made more specific and fine tuned. The technique of using mock-up's, that is low fidelity prototypes of user interfaces, is a way of facilitating communication between end users and designers. This approach of our R&D efforts seems well suited to applying new technology to an established human work practice. According to Tom Gilb the evolutionary process "… is particularly suited to complex technology, fast-moving environments, large scale projects" [5], this approach seems to make sense also in our project. Analysis and design is in a way adapted to the articulated needs as picked up by ethnographic studies and joint design sessions. Further on, delivered software will be tested and evaluated in the real work setting of the end users.

2. Wound Care in a Swedish Municipal Health Care

In municipal elder care within special accommodations, people live and receive bodily care and help with ordinary things to do in a home, and in some cases they are given medical care treatment. In the Municipality of Ronneby about 500 individuals live at eleven special accommodation units. A total of twenty-three nurses provide medical care treatment. They work as generalist with many different tasks to carry out. A particular task is to provide wound care treatment.

The use of computers is not prominent in this work-at-home-setting while this municipal elder care requires a lot of "human touch" and sensitive attention to the elderly in need of help and proper treatment. Bandaging and dressing of a wound is a routine task that involves assessment, decisions and co-operation between all involved people. The task is far from trivial but a time consuming work concerning life of a human being and the particularities of a specific wound.

2.1.   Nurses on the Move with the Bag on Wheels

Quality of treatment is dependent of mutual understanding which is built when nurses, doctors and other personnel cooperate. Learning about the individual care recipient in general and about a specific wound is an every day issue of wound treatment. Embedded in the infrastructure of the work practice are artifacts as the case book. In the today paper version it contains heterogeneous information about the individual's personal data, status of health, diagnosis and instructions of the specific wound treatment and also written notes on periodically taken measures. The personnel learn about the development of individuals and of the healing process as close and intimate aspects of life as such. New practices, new medicals and specific wound treatment tools and materials emerge, and consequently, the work has a potential to make treatment to be beneficial for the care recipients.

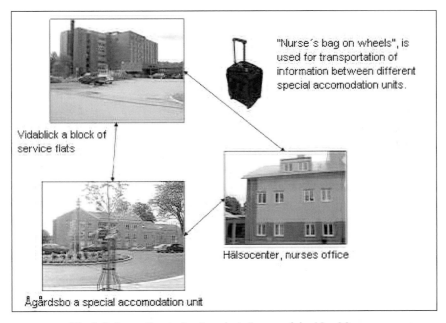

Vidablick a block of service flats

"Nurse´s bag on wheels", is used for transportation of information between different special accomodation units.

Hälsocenter, nurses office

Ågårdsbo a special accomodation unit

Fig. 1. Information technology in today municipal health care.

At the special accommodation the care personnel are integrated nearly as family members. Social relations develop in the intimate interactions between the care recipient and, in the first place, the nurses and the assistant nurses. Vocabularies develop to facilitate hands-on actions and communication. The casebook mediates some aspects of this culture. The case book serves the interest to maintain remembering and assessment of wound healing among those that directly take part in the treatment activity. Apparently the actual paper casebook supports the interest of the closest work team. It can then be seen as an important component in the over-all infrastructure of the municipal work practice. As the health care work is regulated according to national legislation, it is argued to extend the local infrastructure and connect it to adjacent health care institutions and to governmental bodies in the administrative and political system. In trying to realize such extension there is however a lot of baggage to deal with. Information is often thought of to be made available in other locations than where it is created. We believe that it is first necessary to consider the information and communication technology in the primary location. In Figure 1 is indicated the nurses work as on the move and making visits to several homes of elder people on an ordinary day. Each nurse have a "bag on wheels" in which is found four to five ordinary loose leaf binders containing paper prints of information, a diary and some medical equipment. The actual content of the bag is about planned care service to provide fore elderly people as the nurse pay a visit to. Information about wound treatment is only a part of all this paper work. Deploying wound documentation software will not in it self replace the use of a bag on wheels.

This wound care work we believe might be supported by an enhanced and computerized Wound Treatment Documentation System. The use of a digital camera and digital photographs as a part of the documentation work is introduced among the nurses since about one and a half year ago. Fully aware of the risk of reducing freedom of the course of actions of the health care workers while they are dealing with a very rich and diverse reality of elderly care, we try to make a computer support system successful by a sufficient match between the construction of a computer peer-to-peer system and the world as perceived by the end users.

3.   Design of Network Architecture

When we designed key elements of the system architecture we adopted three levels of authority, *apprentice* [6], *credential member* [7]) and *group manager.* We deliberately deviate from the conventional term user and from now on suggest the terms above. These terms would be in better accordance with the common vocabulary in the context of the actual work practice. We use the term peer as a generic term when we don't want to distinguish their level of authority. Those levels, or identified sorts of health care personnel, make up our peer membership rules.

3.1.   Distinction between Different Levels of Authority

This distinction between the different levels of authority is a direct mapping of the relationships in the work context. In the local work setting a nurse is a member of a health care team. In the application the team is mapped into a peer group and the nurses in the team are mapped into credential members. The nurse that is the responsible nurse for a specific care recipient ("PAS" is the Swedish acronym) is flagged as group manager and has the power to let other persons join the group (i.e. become credential members). To make sure that the peers in the system receive the same privileges as in their local work setting we introduced the model of authorization layers [1] (also see Figure 2). This model determines which person is authorized to see (and modify) information about a specific care recipient.

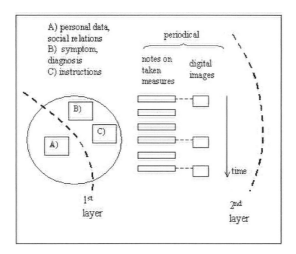

Fig. 2. Model of case book authorization layers

The 1st layer is the protected information that only the credential members have access to. The information in the 2nd layer is for both credential members and apprentices. However, the PAS might prevent the apprentice's access to the 2nd layer information due to the individual care recipient's wish.

It is the PAS that determines which peer is a credential member or which peer is an apprentice (today all peers in the system are apprentices until a PAS let them into their group). As can be seen in Figure 3, a peer can be both a credential member and an apprentice, although not within the same peer group.

At the first degree of extension peer 3 is an apprentice concerning care recipient A ("cr A" in the figure), but a credential member concerning care recipient B. At the second degree peer 2 is a credential member in the peer groups for both care recipient A and B. Peer 4 and 5 is apprentices in the first extension but in the second peer 4 has become a credential member in the peer group for care recipient A while peer 5 still is an apprentice concerning both care recipients. As mentioned earlier peers within the system who are not credential members for a specific care recipient peer group are treated by the system as apprentices.

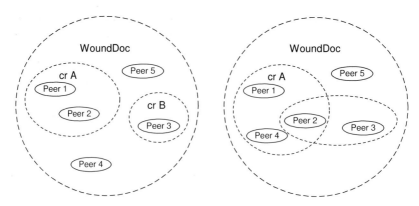

**Fig. 3. The WoundDoc system at two different degree of extension
reflecting the dynamic character of peer membership rules**

As can be seen in the Figure 3, *WoundDoc* is the group that contains all sub peer groups building up the system. Each peer group within the main group WoundDoc corresponds to the concept of a virtual private network (VPN) [7, 8]. The WoundDoc group is a part of the default World peer group [7]. By the nature of the information handled by the system all network traffic and data are encrypted. Encryption together with the introduced authority model helps maintaining the status as a secure VPN.

3.2.   Distribution of the Administration Task

This system model sketched above distributes the administration tasks to each PAS. The system therefore becomes less dependent on central administration authority. The role of the latter will be restricted only to assign a PAS to each care recipient and reassign a PAS to a care recipient when necessary, making sure that each care recipient has a PAS all the time. The municipal nurse unit manager (MnUm) has the responsibility for this task today in their local work setting, and therefore we have introduced another level of authority in our system: the MnUm. The tasks and the role of this peer are derivable from the local work setting and mapped into the system. The MnUm is actually passing over the control of the system to all peers flagged as PAS. Consequently it is the PAS who got the distributed (decentralized) control over the system.

3.3.   The Information Owners Control

The PAS get control over which peers are credential members or which are apprentices in this specific peer group. The benefit of this solution is that it is the information owners (PAS) her/himself that get the control over who is authorized to access the information. An exception thou is the information in the 2nd layer that even the apprentices get access to. This information is totally de-personified and could make no harm, except you have access to the 1st layer information containing personal particulars. The purpose with letting this 2nd layer information free is to support the learning process within the organization: other nurses can read care treatment instructions and see images of critical wounds and learn by other nurse's experience. That's also why we decided to name this level of authority *apprentice*.

Since the PAS now get the control over the specific peer group it is up to her when letting other peers into her peer group. It is expected that the peer groups gradually will expand over time. What's important is that the control of this expansion is distributed to each PAS and not to some central administration authority.

4. Design Considerations Facing Work Practices

A problem of today practice with use of a single paper case book is that it is casually not accessible when it is asked for. This is due to the contradictory character of the information about sensitive and taboo issues. Wounds are not something the care recipients are likely to talk about with somebody else and even less something to show and make visible. It is essential to respect privacy and follow legislation about secrecy. That is why the paper case book is only made available for authorized care personnel. Partly because the municipal nurses are on the move and pay visits to several individuals in different special accommodations on every day, the paper case book might not always be available. The sensitive information content is secrete and because of that less available. As a work-around, the nurses, therefore frequently write notes on "post-it" pieces of paper and for a while put them in their pocket. Later on when there is some space in time, the nurses update the paper case book by with help of those "post-it" notes. To remember is that on an ordinary working day, the nurses plan a number of visits to provide several kinds of treatments, of which wound treatment is only one of them. Typically the nurses try to keep up with the plan but are now and then interrupted by events that "pop up". The nurses are most of the time on foot making rapid shifts of focus and instant switches between different services. In respect of wound treatment, things might be significantly changed if a high level of privacy is maintained and access to a reliable information system is improved by means of a peer-to-peer computer network.

4.1. Crucial to Provide for Nurses Decentralized Control

The crucial design task for our peer-to-peer groupware is then to provide for decentralized control. A paper case book is stored in an ordinary loose-leaf binder of A4-size. It is an artifact with physical properties that is for long accepted as secure in the municipal health care. We expect that if the software fulfills functional requirements for smooth and stable performance and a decentralized control, then the computer artifact also can be regarded as safe and reliable. All of this can not be foreseen in advance but might be created, provided the nurses in the first place are able to experience that they are at least in the same control of the digital case book as with the today's paper version. If they have control of who will access what, it will be possible to create and share information on the computer network. The nurses, in particular the PAS, create documentation to support their own day-to-day actions but as the information owners they fulfill an agency in the interest of the individual care recipient. The relationship between a recipient and a provider is socially constructed and if the health care matters are carried to an extreme, the recipient is in his or her full right to refuse care treatment. In the same manner, the individual might refuse documentation about her or his wound to be made available for others than a select few. This is also supported by Swedish legislation that explicitly states that information across health care institutional boarders have to be carefully approved. The individual care recipient has to actively confirm approval as a condition for distribution to adjacent hospital care system or any other health care authority.

4.2.   Other People might be Members and Peers

The municipal nurse carries a key role in maintaining an intimate and trustful relation as a first hand partner in providing hands-on treatment, as well as a mediator to other potential care providers. If the responsible nurse is able to instruct on proper treatment, assistant nurses and relatives might be involved in the actual wound care treatment. The wound care case book might also be subject to such a cultural constructed health care practice and other people than nurses might have a legitimate interest to become members and peers in appropriate peer groups. Obviously, doctors in the primary care system currently have interest in both the care treatment and in the case book. In the municipality in question, there is an agreement to divide nurse's responsibility on the municipal organization and doctors tasks of mainly making diagnosis and prescriptions on the primary care organization. The doctors come at planned visits to the special accommodations and fulfill a role as a "patient responsible doctor" ("PAL" is the Swedish acronym). Following the rules, there are one PAS and one PAL on each care recipient. The today's paper case book is then available for the adherent PAL at a visit but it is not available at the primary care location, which is the "home" of the doctor's ordinary working time. With our network solution and the individual's approval, the digital case book might be accessible for the PAL at the primary care locations as well. The nurse (as a PAS), given the control of the peer group, might then experience that the relationship with the care recipient is not violated even if the case book is made available in other locations. This possible extension to the primary care has to be carefully considered in deployment of the software.

If the peer-to-peer system will meet an initial acceptance by the nurses, and in compliance with their agency also by the care recipients, several peer groups will be dynamically constructed. On the designed condition the PAS invites and adds her nurse colleagues who replace her at time when she is not on duty. Such flexibility to form peer groups match the current working teams that provide wound treatment for an individual at the special accommodations. The added members of a peer group are those that have the day-to-day primary responsibility for provision of care. They will have full access to the case book which is needed to follow rules of making notes on periodically taken measures of wound treatment. Those notes make up a history of the healing process that also might be further enhanced by digital photos integrated into the electronic case book. Taking pictures with a digital camera is already experienced as a promising technique to enhance wound documentation and is already part of the work practice.

4.3. One Peer Group on Each Individual Suffering of a Wound

In deployment of the peer-to-peer system, a peer group will be created for each individual suffering of a wound, and consequently, the number and size of the peer groups will reflect the practice of those that are close to the individual care recipient. The nurses are as employees obligated to follow the conduct of a hierarchical line organization but there is usually no practical or legal reason to share treatment information with e.g. any superior manager. The provided health care work is inherently decentralized in respect to its location to peoples home and how it is culturally developed and motivated by the needs of the individual care recipient [9]. As our ethnographic studies reveal, the municipal personnel are employed by a large organization comprising one principal authority, however, in respect to most work practice tasks, they are members of several culturally developed *activity systems* [10]. A municipal nurse might be a designated "patient responsible nurse" (PAS) and as such carry a key role. Around the individual are other people involved in providing care treatment. Rules and artifacts are to be followed or utilized – all referring to the care recipient as the central and communal object of an activity system. For short, the municipal elder care as an official line organization is *one* large system, but seen as activity systems, there are *many* decentralized working teams defined by each individual care recipient. Provided that the peer-to-peer system will be accepted and the PAS will be given the decentralized control of the software, we expect that the added peers to each peer group will match the actual members of each activity system. A successful deployment will in a first phase be constructed by the nurses and matching each care recipient as the object of each decentralized working team. In a second phase, also the adherent doctor as a PAL will be added to the appropriate peer group, provided that legally difficulties in crossing institutional boarders are overcome.

4.4. Design Principles for the Graphical User Interface

In our project we emphasize the visualization aspect of the electronic case book. The diversity of information types range from check boxes to free text descriptions including digital images of the wound in question. The graphical user interface is being made to follow design patterns that clearly divide one coherent concern on one distinct display. As the interface is visualized in full authorization mode on a standard desktop screen, it shall also be clear that the information is about only one specific care recipient. Name and other information that reveal the identity is therefore not necessary to blow up for everyone to catch at a glance. On the other hand it is stated as a requirement that a significant part of the interface shall display names and some representative object for each credential member in the actual peer group. It is expected that visualization of all authorized peers support a user experience of the interface that confirm which particular wound and care recipient that is the common object of the group. Additionally, there will also be indicated which one of the peers that is the PAS with power to manage membership in the group. These design principles for the user interface is set up to promote a functional requirement to display only one case book for one care recipient at a time and in effect also support a user experience of a decentralized control of the peer-to-peer system. This design make justice to object oriented software concepts that we believe will serve the purpose of integrating the user interface and the software system into the mature social activity systems.

4.5.   The Scale of the System

Following a guiding-star of humans conduct over an advanced technology, our project utilizes the Internet infrastructure and provides it as a support system to be controlled by the members of a purposeful human work practice. Peoples decentralized distribution of power to accept membership, refuse or restrict access to resources is not a task to automate. Given the foundational principle to support and not reduce peoples conscious work we believe a successful approach allow the end users to learn and get familiar with the new system. If the members of the municipal elder care control what, when and who to be integrated and made connected to the potential of a large technology system, the scale of it will be balanced to the needs and perspective found in the local circumstances of a decentralized work.

Starting in very small scale we expect each peer group of credential members to grow to a size that match the culturally matured activity systems. It might take some time to get to a balanced situation. It will involve breaking principal organizational barriers between the municipal care, primary care and specialist hospital care. By the time when members learn and accept the peer-to-peer groupware they might be encouraged to let size grow in terms of making anonymous information available for apprentice peers. The very existence of the software within the frame of the municipal elder care will make people in adjacent care systems interested, and probably some will insist to share text and images about the wounds. Provided that the care recipient allows his or her information to be shared, it can be made available for the apprentice peers in the system. It is then possibly for apprentice members to "just look" at those parts of the information as we define belonging to only the 2nd layer of information in the electronic case book (see Figure 2). Probably a doctor only needs this anonymous part of the information to be able to make advice from a distance. Students of health care are another group that might have a legitimate interest to look at a series of digital images that reflect the healing process of a wound. We believe the peer-to-peer groupware have the potential as a wound care documentation support system and possibly it also open up for new and improved ways of learning and performing work.

5.   Holding it All Together

Internet infrastructure provides a horizontal zone of expansion beyond the organizations local intranet. Already today the underlying network platform makes it possible to connect to the system from anywhere in the world, as long as the computer has an Internet-connection. We use the worldwide Internet to connect our peers. The built-in mechanisms in the system together with the JXTA-platform[1] enable us to shape a virtual network of geographically distributed clients. The figure below is a general model of how geographically distributed computers and networks establish a virtual network.

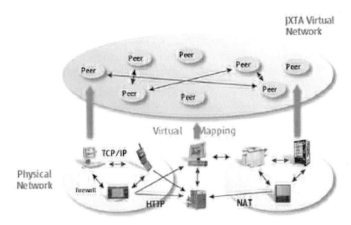

Fig. 4. General model of mapping between physical and virtual networks (JXTA press kit[2])

In our model the WoundDoc main peer group containing all the dynamically created care recipient groups represents the JXTA Virtual Network layer in the picture above. It is this boundary (group) that delimits the peers from the rest of the peers in the default world peer group. The municipal fiber network connecting all the special accommodations in Ronneby represents the physical network in the figure. The fiber ring obtains connection to the global Internet for the public authority buildings within the municipal. As mentioned the access to the WoundDoc system is via Internet, the fiber ring is only used to provide the computers with Internet access. This enables other networks to connect to our virtual network such as the county computer network in Ronneby primary care or at the hospital in Karlskrona or even a dial-up modem connection from the home of a relative as long as the computers got an Internet connection.

JXTA is a set of open-source protocols for building peer-to-peer applications. The following description of JXTA is from the introduction of the JXTA protocol specification:

> The JXTA protocols are a set of six protocols that have been specifically designed for ad hoc, pervasive, and multi-hop peer-to-peer (P2P) network computing. Using the JXTA protocols, peers can cooperate to form self-organized and self-configured peer groups independently of their positions in the network (edges, firewalls), and without the need of a centralized management infrastructure. [11]

---

[1] www.jxta.org
[2] http://www.sun.com/aboutsun/media/presskits/jxta/

In this particular project we use the Java implementation of this API. JXTA gives a potential of unlimited numbers of peers but the decentralized control delimits the actual number of members in our WoundDoc application. With a match to a relevant activity system a particular peer group in our system will be self-organized and consequently it will find its proper size. Nurses and doctors belonging to different principal institutions do have the individual care recipient as their common object and therefore they will become members of the same peer group. Barriers between institutions might be overcome with thanks to the JXTA technology and a match motivated by the common object will balance the size and extent of the peer groups. This dynamic relationship between the humans and the technology seems likely to holding it all together.

5.1. Design of a Digital Case Book

In the course of our evolutionary design the scope and content of the current documentation work is questioned by the nurses as a result of our interest in the paper case book. It is now regarded as a "home-made" variant of a case book adopted five years ago in the municipality. The case book now in use has an origin in another municipality's elder care and it has been disseminated in various forms to several municipalities. Still, it is a point of departure for our design of the digital version, but as a result of our presence in the field, another paper case book was brought up by the nurses: a one-page form, originated from primary care wound treatment work at nearby primary care [4] At location in Ronneby elder care, the nurses made editing work with handwritten markings and notes on both paper case books with the intent to feed information into or wound documentation project. The expected outcome is that the planned software will realize a more uniform and integrated documentation form. Interpretations and compilations of this empirical material are considered as valuable for the developed design.

To be noted is a potential conflict between concepts developed in two different work cultures, that of municipal care on the one hand and primary care on the other hand. A direct translation of the Swedish word "journal" (a word found in both title names of the paper case books) associates to the legally and legislation ruled understanding of a *medical record*. This is not perfectly valid in our case when the wound care documentation shall not be regarded as a medical record in such a strict legally sense. Instead it is a systematically used tool for documentation of municipal wound care treatment and intended to mediate necessary information among those who provide wound treatment.

Our developmental design work is prepared for and allow for new material to be adopted as we now try to merge the most appropriate parts out of two different paper case books. The nurses in the municipal elder care have an active participating design role together with our team of software developers. However, a possible and typical risk of introducing computer artifacts in a work practice is to standardize too much and in effect restrict the existing work culture of providing health care. At the special accommodation, social relations develop in the intimate interactions between the care recipient and the nurses. Vocabularies develop to facilitate "hands-on" actions and communication. The case book serves the interest to maintain remembering and assessment of wound healing among those that directly take part in the treatment activity. To find a balanced way of making a unified case book but not reduce too much of established work culture is an issue of great importance for the health care work.

5.2. Ontology Design supporting a Balanced Standardization Work

We believe that the development of an ontology might work as a bridging process of shared conceptualizations between members of the health care and the developers in order to understand the task at hand. Our approach to ontology design might be different to much other work in the health care domain. We are not satisfied with a simple reuse of a possible available ontology. To avoid a drawing board product we find it essential to make an ontology grounded in a real work setting. In our case we have access to experiences of health care personnel with specific knowledge in wound documentation. An ontology seems as a potential rich artifact that might be developed in joint sessions with both nurses and developers taking part in cooperative work. We expect that ethnography and participatory design to develop an ontology, will effectively help in mapping between the real world practice and a formalized representation. To anchor ontology design in the real work setting seems beneficial even if there is a ready made version produced somewhere else to use as a point of reference. For sure, our project requires learning to successfully integrate the peer-to-peer system in the municipal elder care. To meet the request of enhanced learning of wound treatment, ontology design might mirror the work practice in making explicit the concepts of wound care documentation. Through interaction between developers and members of the health care, a balanced standardization in work can be agreed upon. The nurse's participation in merging the actual paper case book together with the one brought up from the nearby primary care is the primary point of departure for the development of our ontology. In parallel, this ontology will feed structure and concepts into the ongoing design of the electronic case book.

6. Discussion

In the continuation of the Wound Care Documentation Project there is planned a trial period with testing and evaluation of the peer-to-peer system in the real health care work setting. A lot will be in a research interest to observe, and more empirical data have to be analyzed for next phases of R&D work to do. At the moment, we are able to summarize the R&D challenge of designing a decentralized information system solution to a decentralized documentation work. As also can be seen in Table 1 we summarize our mission to accomplish a contribution to support a desired development of municipal health care work. In this article we have suggested and discussed some key design issues that might explain how to realize our mission, of which the most important computer science issues are also depicted in Table 1.

Table 1. Mapping a decentralized solution to a decentralized care documentation work

What to accomplish:	Wound Care Documentation	*How to accomplish:*
Supporting sound and flourishing elder care activity systems	Mapping of technological solutions to health care work practices: ethnography, participatory design and evolutionary software development	Peer-to-peer grouping in a self-organized way implying decentralized software control
A recognized decentralized work practice		
Nurses in control of wound documentation work		Peer membership rules for credential, apprentice and group manager members
Privacy for the care recipients		Separation or loose coupling between personal data and specific wound treatment information
Learning in wound care		Authorization layers
Crossing institutional barriers		Ontology design
		Use of ubiquitous Internet infrastructure

In a number of small activity systems, nurses decentralized control of wound care work is depicted in the first three cells of first column in Table 1. We consider privacy of the care recipients as a fundamental concern to respect in any distribution of the information. Sharing an electronic case book is then possible and improved learning might be supported in wound assessment and care treatment. Privacy is also required for any attempt in making information accessible across institutional barriers. In the rightmost column of the table we indicate peer-to-peer grouping in a self-organized way as an over-all sufficient solution. Web technology and use of the ubiquitous Internet infrastructure we believe opens up for novel designs. The project's implementation of the software is built on a combination of general available technologies and our particular concepts of authorization layers; peer membership rules for credential, apprentice and group manager members and the separation or loose coupling between personal data and specific wound treatment information. Ontology design we expect as a supportive method to facilitate our central task to map a technological solutions to a health care work practice. Future work will reveal the fulfillment of the projects expectations on the design and deployment of a peer-to-peer groupware in a wound care documentation work.

References

[1]   Kyhlbäck, Hans (2002) Utilizing a Peer-to-peer methodology in municipal health care work - a design challenge. Accepted for proceedings of ISCRAT 5th Congress / Amsterdam / 2002

[2]   Nardi, Bonnie A. and O'Day, Vicki L. (1999) Information ecologies: using technology with heart, MIT Press, Cambridge, Mass.

[3]   Fensel, Dieter (2001) Ontologies: A Silver Bullet for Knowledge Management and Electronic Commerce Springer-Verlag, Berlin Heidelberg, Germany

[4]   Öien, Ruth F. (2002) Leg ulcer management in primary care with special reference to pinch grafting, Department of Community Medicine, Malmö University Hospital Lund University, Malmö 2002. Thesis, Sweden.

[5]   Gilb, Tom (1997) Evo: The Evolutionary Project Managers Handbook, unpublished manuscript, publicly available at http://www.result-planning.com/

[6]   Lave, Jean and Wenger, Etienne (1991) Situated learning: legitimate peripheral participation, Cambridge Univ. Press, Cambridge.

[7]   Brookshier, Daniel (2002) JXTA : Java P2P programming, Sams, Indianapolis, Ind.

[8]   Stallings, William (2000) Local and metropolitan area networks, Prentice Hall, Upper Saddle River, N.J.

[9]   Westerberg, Kristina (2000) The important Activity - work, tools and tensions of municipal middle managers in elder care. Department of Applied Psychology, Umeå Universitet, Umeå 2000. Thesis, Sweden.

[10]   Engeström, Yrjö (1987) Learning by expanding: An Activity-Theoretical approach to Developmental Research, Orienta-Konsultit, Helsinki, Finland.

[11]   Project JXTA (2003) JXTA v2.0 Protocols Specification, publicly available at http://spec.jxta.org/v1.0/docbook/JXTAProtocols.html

Hans Kyhlbäck and Hannes Persson, Dept. of Software Engineering and Computer Science, Blekinge Institute of Technology, Box 520, SE-37225 Ronneby, SWEDEN

E-mail address: {Hans.Kyhlback|Hannes.Persson}@bth.se

An Agent-Based Intelligent Tutoring System for Nurse Education

Marjan Hospers, Erna Kroezen, Anton Nijholt, Rieks op den Akker,
Dirk Heylen

Abstract. This paper describes the development of a teaching environment that uses agents to support learning. An Intelligent Tutoring System will be described, that guides students during learning. This system is meant for nurse education in the first place, but it is generic in the sense that the core is separated from the exercise modules and user interfaces. This means that the system can also be used for other (non-nursing) exercises. Exercises can be provided to the system in the form of XML data-files. A user interface can be text-based or 2D, but it can also be a 3D virtual reality environment. An application of the teaching environment for nurse training is described.

1. Introduction

This paper describes the development of a teaching environment that uses agents to support learning. A software system called Ines will be described, that guides students during learning. This means that students can use the system to train certain tasks. Before the Ines project started, the idea was to make an Intelligent Tutoring System for nursing students. The reason was the lack of time, material and room at nursing schools. Because of these lacks, nursing students have too little possibilities to do practical exercises during their study, and they still have to learn a lot when they start working in a hospital. The intention of this project is to improve this situation. Hence the name: Intelligent Nursing Education Software.

The main goal of the Ines project is to provide an effective teaching environment. For an environment to be effective as a teaching environment, it has to fulfill two conditions. The first condition that has to be satisfied is that the teaching environment provides a correct and logical guidance system for the student. This means that a teaching system must be able to provide sensible feedback, demonstrations and/or explanations. The second condition is that the user interface of the system is as optimal and accessible as possible. For this purpose, one could for example use a simple 2D graphical interface, but the interface could also consist of a highly accurate 3D virtual environment.

Until now, the Ines project has mainly concentrated on the first condition. Independent of the task trained, the system is capable of providing feedback, explanations and demonstrations. For this purpose, a number of agents, which together form the main part of Ines, are implemented. The agents observe the students actions and check whether they are performed correctly and in a correct order. In the future, the intention is to concentrate more on the second condition.

Ines is a generic teaching system in the sense that the core is separated from the exercise modules and user interfaces. The exercises can be provided to Ines in the form of data-files. The information from these files is used to check if the actions from students are right, and to provide explanations and demonstrations if necessary. An exercise will typically consist of subtasks with some partial ordering defined for them. The tags in the data-files are general, and can be filled in for repairing a punctured tyre as easy as for a nursing task, for instance.

Adding a new teaching task to Ines also means adding a new interface. A new interface may be text-based or 2D, but it can also be a 3D virtual reality environment. Even haptic feedback devices and a head-mounted device can be used, without making changes to the Ines system itself.

The implemented system is applied to a nurse training task. To demonstrate how the system works, an exercise-file and an interface were made for the subcutaneous injection.

The organization of this paper is as follows. First, in section 2 some Intelligent Tutoring Systems that gave the inspiration for the design of Ines are described. Section 3 contains a description of the architecture of Ines. Then, the most important part of the system, the cognition, is described extensively in section 4. A description of the implemented exercise, the subcutaneous injection, is given in section 5. Section 6 handles about the methods that are used by Ines for planning the order of the subtasks. The paper concludes with a section about testing and evaluation of the system and a section about future work.

2. Existing ITS's

There are a lot of programs that already teach certain tasks to users. The most important systems that gave the inspiration for the design of Ines will be mentioned in this section.

The Parlevink group, researching language, knowledge and interaction at the University of Twente, combines research on human-computer interaction, dialog systems, autonomous agents and virtual worlds. The group has built the VMC (Virtual Music Centre), which is a replica of an existing music centre and serves as an environment to experiment with multi-modal interaction with agents or other visitors to this virtual world [5]. In this context, Jacob was built, an instruction agent that helps users to solve a mathematical puzzle in virtual reality [2].

Based on the experience with Jacob, the idea arose for creating ADRI (Artificial Didactic Recital Instructor), a system intended to aid people learning to play the piano [1]. A 3D-world with a virtual piano and visualization of notes is connected with a real synthesizer using Midi to interact with the user. Also a multi-agent platform is used within the system. Each agent has a special expertise and knowledge domain and can give information or act when it decides that it is appropriate.

Other instruction agents that inspired the design of Ines are Steve [3], [7], [8] and Adele [3], [10]. Steve is an animated pedagogical agent. It gives instruction in procedural tasks in an immersive virtual environment. To allow Steve to operate in a variety of domains, its architecture has a clear separation between domain-independent capabilities and domain-specific knowledge. Adele (Agent for Distance Learning Environments) is developed by the USC/Information Sciences Institute's Center for Advanced Research in Technology for Education (CARTE). Adele runs in a student's web browser, and is designed to be integrated into web-based electronic learning materials. Adele-based courses are currently being developed for continuing medical education in family medicine and graduate level geriatric dentistry.

Another important system that inspired the design of Ines is LAHYSTOTRAIN [4]. This is a training system for two types of minimally invasive surgery techniques. It combines a Virtual Reality Simulator, a Basic Training System that provides web based theoretical training, and an agent-based tutoring system, the Advanced Training System, oriented to supervise the execution of practical exercises. Training in LAHYSTOTRAIN is carried out in two temporal consecutive phases: acquisition of theoretical knowledge with the Basic Training System, and acquisition of practical skills with the Advanced Training System.

3. System Architecture

For Ines, an architecture is proposed that is based on two architectural styles [11]. The first architectural style that is embedded into Ines is the 'data abstraction and object-oriented organization'. This means that single components within the Ines system will be represented by objects that have their own attributes and methods. These objects will be implemented by using several classes within the Java programming language. Objects that can be identified within Ines are, for example, all physical objects in the teaching environment (needles, swaps, and so on), but also the agents that are used are represented by objects.

The other architectural style that is used is the 'event based, implicit invocation' architecture. This architecture is mainly used to implement the agents in the Ines system. Each agent is capable of transmitting messages to other agents on a one-to-one level or a broadcast level. In addition, each agent is capable of receiving messages by observing all messages that are sent to that agent or that are broadcasted to all agents. The agent can then decide what to do for each type of incoming message.

Figure 1 shows the main parts of the Ines system. The patient model and the items in the abstract user interface are specially for nursing exercises. For other exercises, another model and other items can be used. As can be seen from the figure, the architecture of Ines consists of four main parts: input from devices, a concrete user interface, an abstract user interface and the cognition of Ines. The Ines Interaction API[1] is used for the communication between the concrete user interface and the abstract user interface.

---

[1] Application Programming Interface. The programmer of the user interface should only use methods from the API to provide knowledge to Ines.

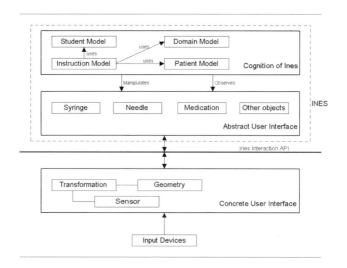

FIGURE 1. The system architecture of Ines.

3.1. Input from Devices

The first main part is formed by the input from the real world. This can be any input from any device, such as input from datagloves, mouse/keyboard, or haptic devices. The input is used to perform actions in the concrete user interface. For example, moving around in a virtual 3D user interface by means of a dataglove will change the viewpoints of the user interface. In this way, the concrete user interface can be manipulated by the user.

Since Ines is completely separated from the concrete user interface, Ines does not care which kind of input device is used, but only expects to receive the necessary data from the concrete user interface, such as the position of objects like syringes and needles within that concrete user interface. The choice of input devices is thus dependent on the concrete user interface that is used, and not of Ines itself. Currently, Ines can display a user interface that is controlled by keyboard and mouse.

3.2. Concrete user interface

The concrete user interface takes care of the visualization of the exercise. This is a very broad definition, which allows a great freedom for the system implementer to alter or create a user interface for an exercise. Any user interface can be implemented, from a simple dialog interface or a 2D graphical interface, to a highly accurate 3D virtual environment. To this point, Ines contains a user interface that mainly uses text and buttons to communicate with the user. In figure 2, the user interface that was implemented for the nursing application can be found. The left side of the figure contains data from a patient, the right side contains descriptions of all subtasks. The middle part displays the subtask that is currently executed by the student. In this case, the student has to give the angle in which the syringe has to be injected. This angle should be between 30 and 45 degrees. The bottom part contains buttons that can be used to ask for explanations.

The architecture of Ines allows to have several different user interfaces for the same exercise. This comes in handy when a different user interface is required for the same task at beginner or advanced level. Therefore, the contents of the concrete user interface as shown in figure 1 is merely the contents of an example user interface (in this case a virtual 3D environment).

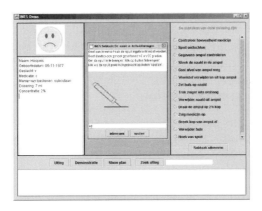

FIGURE 2. User interface of the nurse training application.

All user interfaces that are to be used by Ines should be able to communicate important information to Ines. Without this information, it is impossible for Ines to perform her task. For example, Ines needs to know when the student has picked up an object before it can decide whether that is a correct action or not. To establish this communication from the concrete user interface towards Ines, the programmer of the user interface has the Ines Interaction API especially designed for this purpose at his/her disposal. This API is further explained in section 3.3.

3.3. Abstract user interface

The abstract user interface is a high level model of the concrete user interface. The abstract user interface is, contrary to the concrete user interface, a part of Ines herself. This means that the communication between the two interfaces in fact constitutes the communication between the concrete user interface and Ines. Important changes in the concrete user interface are reported to the abstract user interface and vice versa.

The concrete user interface directly communicates with the abstract user interface, with help of the methods from the Ines Interaction API. This API contains a number of methods that have to be called by a concrete user interface, because otherwise Ines will not be able to perform her teaching task. Every time the student takes an action, one of the methods is called. Example actions of the students are start and stop subtasks, or make an object sterile or not sterile. In this way, the system gets information about the actions from the student, and the agents in the instruction model use this information to decide what actions they should take.

By separating the concrete user interface from the abstract user interface, Ines does not have to contain the exact representation of each user interface, but only the general aspects that are applicable to all user interfaces, for example the position of important objects. Ines should know if a needle is on a syringe or not, but it is not important for Ines how the syringe and the needle look.

The fourth part in the Ines architecture is, from a teaching perspective, the most interesting part. This part represents the knowledge and skills of Ines and is therefore the core of the Intelligent Tutoring System. Section 4 will deal with this cognition of Ines.

4. The core of Ines: the cognition

The cognition of Ines consists of four models as can be seen in figure 1: the domain model, the student model, the instruction model and the patient model. This last model was added to Ines for the purpose of exercises for nursing students. The patient model is an agent that at the moment only describes all knowledge that is known about a patient, like age, sex, religion and so on. In the future, this agent can be extended so that the patient can react to actions from the students, for example pull back his or her arm in anxiety when a virtual reality representation is used. When exercises for non-nursing tasks are added to the system, the patient model can be ignored or replaced by a similar or other model. This is also the reason why the patient model is not a part of the domain model.

4.1. Domain Model

The domain model in Ines encapsulates knowledge about the exercises that should be practiced. Because Ines must be capable of training several different tasks, and because it is unknown which tasks Ines should train in future, it would be very awkward to program all data about all exercises in the system itself. This would lead to such a large amount of data within Ines, that it would become impossible to handle the data in a structured manner. The solution developed for this problem is to only define the elements of the domain model. These elements do not contain any exercise data yet. The real data can be read from an external information source: an XML-file. Thus, instead of programming each exercise into the system itself, a general domain model is used that is filled in by data presented to Ines.

The XML-file contains all the information that Ines needs to know about subtasks, their order, their constraints and explanations and demonstrations. All subtasks have preconditions and postconditions, and these conditions are used by an algorithm to check the order of the subtasks and also to check if errors are made within the subtask. The preconditions describe the conditions that have to be present before the subtask is eligible for execution, and the postconditions describe the condition changes that should have happened after the subtask has been completed.

Explanations associated with conditions will usually mention why a certain condition has to be met before the subtask can be performed. Explanations associated with a subtask itself will describe the necessity of the subtask within the exercise, but can also explain what the student has to do during the subtask. The XML-file also contains references to files that can be used to demonstrate how a subtask has to be performed, and references to the necessary user interface. It is possible to have several different user interfaces for the same exercise, for example for beginners, medium and advanced level students. These references are preventing Ines from containing all user interfaces and demonstrations herself.

When adding a new exercise to the system, the data should be added to an XML-file with exercise data. This can be done by hand, but since an average exercise consists of a lot of data, this task can be very error prone. To prevent mistakes from being made, an editing program has been created that can be used to alter or to create an exercise file.

The "Ines Exercise Editor" provides an environment in which the user can create and alter exercise files in an obvious manner. For this, the INES Exercise Editor presents the user with a user interface in which the user can create the alterations in a graphical environment. Within this graphical environment, an exercise is represented by a tree, where each node represents a subtask and each arrow represents a relation between two nodes. An arrow from subtask 1 to subtask 2, for example, represents a relation between the two subtasks in which subtask 1 provides a postcondition that is a precondition of subtask 2. Thus, subtask 1 has to be executed before subtask 2.

The domain model used by Ines will only collect the information that is needed by the model to carry out its function from the XML-file. After reading the necessary data, Ines is able to perform her teaching task. The contents of the domain model are used to observe the abstract user interface. All actions within the interface are interpreted by Ines, and Ines will respond to certain events. This conduct of Ines is determined by the instruction model.

4.2. Student Model

The student model is a model of the user's characteristics and performance. This model contains data about all students that work with the program: all the information that is needed in order to identify the students and to interpret the results of the students.

For the same reason as with the domain model, the student model is also defined in terms of elements that can be filled with data from an XML-file. Examples of data are student numbers, grades, and which exercises have been performed by the student. The results of the student are used by Ines to determine how often Ines has to provide feedback or explanations.

A list of exercises is kept for each student. This list contains all the exercises that the student has done in the past, and the results that are achieved for these exercises: the number of times that the student has tried the exercise and, when the exercise is finished successfully, the grade that the student received for the latest attempt. This grade is calculated by one of the agents in the instruction model (the Examination Agent) and then stored in the student XML-file. Also for each subtask, the number of tries is kept, and for each try if the student has passed the subtask successfully.

4.3. Instruction Model

The instruction model observes the world, the task and the user's actions. It can manipulate the world and the user through utterances and actions. These actions include giving a demonstration of the next step of the task, telling what the next step is, or explaining a certain step.

Ines is intended to be used to train nursing exercises. This type of exercise usually consists of several subtasks that have a predefined order amongst them. Ines should teach such an exercise, in that the student learns to perform the subtasks in the correct order and in the correct way. The teaching strategy that is used is the practice and drill teaching method [6]. With this practice and drill method, the student has to perform the exercise over and over again, until (s)he masters the task.

Although not implemented in the Ines prototype, one could propose to add the problem solving teaching strategy to Ines, in that the student will be presented with a problem during the nursing task. An example of such a problem could be a non-cooperating patient or an unsuitable environment to administer the injection. By using problem solving in the learning process, the student will obtain better learning results, because the student has to think of a solution himself. Adding problems to the exercise should be fairly simple, since the system is already equipped with an additional agent that represents the patient.

In addition of adding problem solving, one could also add questioning to the Ines system. In this case, Ines could present the student with a number of questions during the execution of the exercise. One could think of questions like: "How many ml of fluid do you have to inject into the patient?", "How can you observe that the injection site has been well chosen?", or "What is the correct order in the following subtasks?". Adding these kinds of questions to the Ines system poses a problem, however. Since Ines is a very general teaching system, she has no idea herself of the answers to these questions. It is thus necessary to add the questions to the exercise data. This can be done by specifying some questions with each subtask. Ines could then read the questions and the answers into her domain model and can subsequently use them to ask to the student.

Ines is an Intelligent Tutoring System based on agent technology. This means that agents are used in the instruction model to provide the instruction to the student.

One could also use simple method calls, implemented within normal Java classes, to provide this instruction. In that case, however, Ines can only be run on single machines. Since Ines is an ITS and will therefore be used by a lot of students on several different machines, one can imagine that it would be very convenient to have the Ines software distributed over several different computers. In case of distributing Ines over several machines, Ines must work with agent technology in order to provide instruction.

In addition, agents can be easily turned off or on by Ines whenever necessary. In future, for example, Ines could consist of several groups of agents, where each group provides instruction for a certain subject matter. One group of agents could be specifically for nursing tasks, whereas another group of agents could be for carpentry tasks. When a certain group of tasks has to be trained, Ines can turn on the agents concerning that group and turn off all other agents.

All agents within Ines are divided into two groups: sensor agents and processing agents. For the implementation of the agents, the agent platform developed by the Parlevink group is used. In this platform, there are two kinds of agents: proactive agents and reactive agents. Reactive agents only take actions if they receive messages from other agents, while proactive agents take actions once in a particular amount of time, for example per second. The sensor agents in Ines are proactive agents, the processing agents are reactive agents.

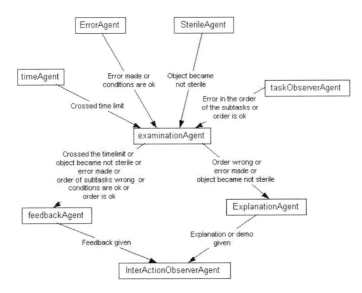

FIGURE 3. The agents. An arrow between two agents means that the first agent sends messages to the second agent.

Each proactive agent observes the user interface with respect to one single aspect. When such an agent has made an observation, it will send it to a reactive agent. Reactive agents receive the observations and respond to it. In figure 3 can be found which agents send messages to which other agents.

Proactive agents

Distinction is made between four different proactive agents: the Time Agent, the Error Agent, the Task Observer Agent and the Sterile Agent.

The Time Agent keeps an eye on the elapsed time during a subtask. To do this, the Time Agent uses information from a time logger. This logger will log the time every time a subtask is started or finished. In addition, the subtasknumber is logged. All log-information is time-dependent, that is, if subtasknumber two is logged after subtasknumber one, then the latter subtask has been started/finished before subtasknumber two. The Time Agent will look for subsequent subtasknumbers. If a pair has been found, then a subtask has been completed (due to the time-dependency of the log-information) and the agent will call for the time values of those subtasknumbers. The time values are then used to compute the time-difference and thus the time that it took for the student to complete the specified subtask. The Time Agent will compare the time-difference with the allowed duration of that subtask. If the student has exceeded the time-limit, the agent will send a message to the Examination Agent. Otherwise, the agent will take no action what so ever.

The Error Agent checks if the student makes errors while carrying out the subtasks. Information from an error logger is used to complete this task. Each log from the error logger contains a subtask number and a list with conditions. Each time the student takes an action the new conditions are logged. Once per second, the Error Agent reads the new logs from the error logger. The subtask number is used to get the postconditions of the subtask. The logged conditions are compared with these postconditions. If a logged condition is a postcondition of the subtask, then the action of the student was correct. But if a logged condition is not a postcondition of the subtask, then the Error Agent deduces that an error was made. When the agent detects an error, there are two possibilities. If a condition is wrong, it can be the case that the opposite of the condition had to be true, or that neither the condition nor the opposite of the condition is a postcondition of the subtask. In both cases, the Error Agent sends a message to the Examination Agent. When the opposite of the condition had to be true, the message contains the subtask number, the opposite of the condition that was wrong, and an indication that the condition was wrong. When neither the condition nor the opposite of the condition is a postcondition of the subtask, the message contains the subtask number, the condition itself and an indication that the subtask was wrong. These indications are used by the Explanation Agent to decide what kind of explanation should be given: an explanation about the condition or an explanation about the subtask.

The Task Observer Agent is responsible for keeping an eye on the order in which the several subtasks are performed. This means that the Task Observer Agent will check whether the order in which the subtasks are performed is correct and, in addition, whether the student doesn't mix up a number of subtasks. An example of the latter is when a student first starts subtask one and then starts subtask two without finishing the first subtask at all. To be able to do his job correctly, the Task Observer Agent uses data provided by a logger, which is a simple Java-class that logs information whenever asked by the Ines Interaction API (and is thus not an agent). This logger will log on every occasion that the student either starts a subtask or finishes one. This log-information can subsequently be accessed by the Task Observer Agent and can thus be used to generate liable information about the order in which the subtasks are performed. Two different checks on this information are performed by the Task Observer Agent. First, the agent will check whether a subtask that has been started, has also been finished before a new subtask has been started. This means that the agent will make sure that the student does not mix up subtasks. To do this, the agent will check the log-information provided by the ordering logger and will check for pairs of subtasknumbers in this information. This is sufficient, since the log-information is time-dependent. The second check performed by the Task Observer Agent is the order of the subtasks. To do this, the agent uses an internal variable that keeps track of the most recent completed subtask. In addition, the agent will store a set of subtasknumbers that are eligible for execution with regard to this most recent completed subtask. These subtasknumbers are determined by using the planner described in section 6. Everytime the agent notices that a new subtask has been completed, he will check whether this subtasknumber is an element of the list of planned subtasknumbers. If so, the order is correct, otherwise the order is incorrect. In either case, the Task Observer Agent will send an appropriate message to the Examination Agent. After the check, the agent will update the most recent completed subtask and the planned subtasks to go along with it.

The Sterile Agent is the only agent specified within Ines that is specifically designed for teaching nursing tasks. Most tasks do not require an agent that keeps an eye on the sterility of the used objects, but nursing tasks and other medical tasks do. Thus, it is necessary to implement this agent within Ines. For all other tasks not using this agent, the agent can be replaced by another kind of agent. The Sterile Agent has to look if there are objects that became not sterile unintentionally. It uses a sterile logger to do this. The system always adds a log to a list in this sterile logger when an object becomes unsterile. The Sterile Agent reads the logs of the sterile logger once in a particular amount of time. For the new logs, it checks if the object became not sterile unintentionally. When the agent discovers that an object became not sterile unintentionally, it sends a message to the Examination Agent. This message contains the number of the subtask in which the object became not sterile, a description of the object, and the string representing the condition that the object became not sterile.

Reactive agents

In the system, there are also four different reactive agents: the Feedback Agent, the Explanation Agent, the Interaction Observer Agent and the Examination Agent.

The Feedback Agent is able to generate either positive or negative feedback. The process of the generation of both positive and negative feedback is identical, and therefore only one agent exists for both types of feedback. The Feedback Agent receives input information from the Examination Agent, which detects whether a student has performed a subtask (in)correctly. This received information is used to generate appropriate feedback. This means that Ines will give positive feedback in case the student has performed the subtask correctly, and negative feedback otherwise. It is, however, very undesirable that Ines will generate feedback on every occasion. Just imagine having feedback after completion of every subtask, especially when a novice has a try at an exercise. The novice would get depressed of all of the negative feedback that (s)he would receive! It is therefore possible to change the settings of the number of times that Ines will give feedback. The number of times that feedback is generated is dependent on the quality of the student (i.e. how good is the student at the exercise. A good student makes less mistakes and thus it is reasonable to be more strict with negative feedback and less strict with positive feedback), and the preferences of the teacher (i.e. teachers differ in strictness with regard to feedback, in that one teacher will provide feedback more often than another teacher). The strictness of the feedback frequency can be set by using the strictness variable. This variable is then used as a countdown towards the generation of feedback.

It is also not very desirable that the Feedback Agent always presents feedback after exactly three times (or any other number of times). This would make Ines appear very rigid, which usually is not the case with real teachers. If Ines is to resemble a real teacher as much as possible, she should be able to 'play' a little with the feedback frequency. To provide this play area, the Feedback Agent is equipped with a method that adds a small variance in the strictness variable. This means that if the strictness is set to three, the agent will variate this strictness between two and four (e.g. sometimes the Feedback Agent will have a strictness equal to two, whereas at other times the strictness will be either three or four).

The Explanation Agent determines when explanations or demonstrations are given, and which explanations and demonstrations are given. There are different kinds of explanations: explanations and demonstrations from subtasks, explanations from conditions and partial order plans. For the different kind of explanations, different algorithms are used to determine if an explanation should be given and which one. Dependent on the input, the Explanation Agent determines which kind of explanation should be given, and thus which algorithm should be used. The Explanation Agent always receives messages from the Examination Agent when something goes wrong with a subtask. The messages contain the name of the agent who detected the mistake. The actions of the Explanation Agent depend on the agent that detected the mistake. Another type of input for the explanation agent comes if the student clicks on one of the buttons in the explanation panel (the bottom part of figure 2). Dependent on the button selected, the Explanation Agent will generate an explanation of the current subtask or a demonstration of the current subtask, or it will return a list with all explanations (both from subtasks and from conditions) containing the string given by the user. Every time the agent gives an explanation or demonstration, it will also send a message to the Interaction Observer Agent. This message contains a string indicating the kind of feedback that was given, and if possible the explanation itself.

The Interaction Observer Agent is responsible for keeping up which feedback the system has given to the student. Every time the Feedback Agent gives feedback or the Explanation Agent gives an explanation or a demonstration, they send a message to the Interaction Observer Agent. Such a message contains the number of the subtask for which the feedback is given and the type of the feedback (positive feedback, negative feedback, explanation or demonstration). When the Interaction Observer Agent receives such a message, it logs the data in a file and in a list. In this way, the data can be used later to see what the student has done and what he or she should know.

The Examination Agent plays a central role in the complete arsenal of agents (see figure 3). The Examination Agent receives all error messages from the sensor agents and acts upon them. Dependent on the agent that has sent the message and on the contents, a new message is sent by the Examination Agent to one of the other processing agents. In addition to handling the stream of messages between the agents, and thus acting like a traffic controller, the Examination Agent is also responsible for updating the student results during the execution of an exercise. This means that the Examination Agent will retrieve the new results of the student and subsequently add these results to the old results of the student. When the student finishes the exercise, the Examination Agent will derive a grade for the student and will write this to the student file. The last task of the Examination Agent is to control the creation of all other agents and their loggers. When instantiating the Examination Agent, all necessary other agents will be instantiated by the Examination Agent. When quitting the Examination Agent, all created agents will also quit.

5. The implemented exercise: the subcutaneous injection

This section describes the exercise that is implemented to demonstrate how the system works. There are two common techniques used for injections, the subcutaneous injection technique (injecting under the skin) and the intramuscular injection technique (injecting in a muscle). There are more injection techniques available, like the intravenous injection (in a blood vessel) and the very specific injections in the heart or a joint. An extra education on top of the standard nursing education is needed for intravenous injections. This type of injection is therefore not admitted to the nursing curriculum. In addition, only doctors and specialists are allowed and trained to perform specific injections into the heart or a joint, so these procedures are not in the nursing curriculum as well.

Using an injection for the administration of medication has a number of advantages with respect to orally administered medication, in that the medicine usually works faster and never comes into the digestive system. An injection also leads to a better balanced amount of medicine in the blood stream. But there are also a number of disadvantages that can be identified. The procedure for administering an injection is quite a bit more difficult than orally administering medication, and therefore more time-consuming. In addition, an injection is not without hazard in that blood vessels or nerves can be damaged easily. Most people are afraid of having an injection and so it is important to execute the injection as painlessly as possible.

There is chosen to implement the subcutaneous injection, because this exercise is a good example of a nursing task that has to be practiced much before it can be done with real patients. In a virtual environment or with help of simulation, it is possible to show what happens when the injection is not given in the right way. For example, it is possible to show what happens with the patient when there is air in the syringe when the injection is given.

Executing a subcutaneous injection consists of a number of steps. The order of these steps is fixed. The nurse has to check the data of the injection: what kind of liquid should be injected and how much. All materials must be made ready for use: a suction needle should be attached to the syringe, the medicine should be drawn up, and then the suction needle should be replaced by an injection needle. Then, the injection should be given, and after that, everything should be cleared up. These are in short the steps of giving an injection, but all the mentioned steps consist of a number of sub-steps.

For this task, an exercise file and an interface are made. The exercise file contains data about all the subtasks, for example their pre- and postconditions and explanations. An example of such a precondition is that the injection needle should be sterile before the injection is given. An example of a postcondition is that the syringe is empty after giving the injection. The implemented interface can be found in figure 2. The student has to click on the description of a subtask on the right side of the interface that (s)he wants to execute. Then, a new window appears in the middle part of the interface. In this window, the student has to execute the chosen subtask, or a movie is played with a demonstration of the subtask.

6. Planning in Ines

In Ines, two kinds of planning are used. The first determines only all subtasks that may be performed next, and is used to determine if the student does the subtasks in a right order. The second is partial order planning, which is used to explain the right order of the subtasks to the student when (s)he makes too many errors. A partial order planner is a planner that can represent plans in which some steps are ordered (before or after) with respect to each other and other steps are unordered [9]. The partial order planning algorithm that is used in Ines is a deterministic implementation of the nondeterministic algorithm described in [9], section 11.6.

The order of the subtasks for the exercise that is used for the prototype, the subcutaneous injection, is fixed. For that reason, the choice could be made to tell exactly to the system in which order the subtasks can be performed. But in the future, the intention is to add new exercises, and to program as little as possible for this in Java. For the new exercises, it is quite possible that the order of the subtasks is not fixed. To prevent that all possible orders have to be programmed in the system (because the number of possible orders increases very fast if there is a number of choices in the order), another choice has been made: for both kinds of planning, the preconditions and postconditions of the subtasks are used. To make it easy to put these conditions in the exercise file, and to write as little Java-code as possible, strings are used for these conditions in the interface and in the exercise file. When a condition is added to the system, it is put into a special class for conditions, which is in fact only a string, but in this way it is easier to use other kinds of conditions in the future, like propositions and predicates.

7. Testing and evaluation

Ines has been tested in two different ways. The first one is by performing unit testing on several classes contained by Ines. This type of test is intended to test the functioning of individual classes, e.g. testing whether the class "timeAgent" is doing what is expected. In addition, Ines has been tested as a whole. This means that an exercise and user interface have been designed for Ines (for the subcutaneous injection) and that the complete system has been tested. The quality of the user interface is not optimal and is not usable for teaching students a subcutaneous injection as if it were real. At most, the order of the subtasks of the exercise is taught. This, however, is sufficient to test Ines with respect to some functions, for example what happens if the student makes an error during a subtask and what happens if the student does the subtasks in a wrong order.

One problematic situation came to light. When a student merely guesses the order in which the subtasks should be executed (and therefore choses the wrong subtask most of the times), but executes the subtasks itself correctly, Ines will present the student with positive and negative feedback or an explanation at the same moment. The reason for this, is that the Feedback and Explanation Agents both receive messages from the Error Agent as well as the Task Observer Agent. The Error Agent communicates the correct execution of the subtask, whereas the Task Observer Agent communicates the wrong order of the subtasks. Both the Feedback and the Explanation Agent respond to both messages, causing the confusing output from Ines. This problem is solved in the following way: the Error Agent does not only check if the subtask is performed in the right way with help of the postconditions of the subtask, but if the subtask is performed correctly, it will also check if the new conditions also hold in the environment conditions. The environment conditions are only updated when the order of the subtasks is correct. Thus, when the order of the subtasks is wrong, the Error Agent will not send a message to the Examination Agent that a subtask is performed correctly.

In all other tested cases, the system gave the expected explanations and feedback that was to the point.

The most important requirement of the system is that it should be flexible, thus maintainable and adaptable to other situations. It should be possible to add new exercises or new agents without any large changes of the system itself. For the exercises, this goal is achieved. Adding new instructional methods is also possible, but not in a fast and handy way. New agents can be added, but they have to be integrated with the other agents, in the sense that the new agent must be able to send messages to the existing agents, and eventually to receive messages from the other agents. To reach this, the existing agents should also be changed a bit. The new agents have to use the agent platform from the Parlevink group.

Ines distinguishes herself from most other ITSs in that is has become a generic learning system. Although implemented specifically for nursing tasks, Ines is capable of teaching other tasks as well, because the user interfaces and the data about the tasks are completely separated from Ines. It is not necessary to make any changes to the instruction- and student models of Ines when other exercises are added.

8. Future work

A next step in the Ines project is to make a more advanced user interface, for example a 3D virtual environment using haptic feedback devices. As said in section 5, in a virtual environment or with help of simulations, students can learn what happens when they make errors, without doing damage, for example to real persons. In this way, virtual environments and simulations offer possibilities for explorative learning. In the already implemented user interface, movies are used for most subtasks, and in this way, the student can only start and stop subtasks and sometimes click on a button. In the new user interface, the student must be able to take objects and to perform actions with them. With such an interface, Ines can be tested by students, and they can give feedback on the working of Ines and tips for improvement and extensions. When Ines is tested in this way and found to be working, new exercises can be added to the system and students can learn them.

Ines is extendable in many ways. A number of extensions we are working on are:

- Change Ines so that students can also be examined. This mode differs from the training mode in that the student is not able to ask any questions and that Ines will not give any feedback or hints while the student is executing the assignment;
- Make Ines able to offer more or less guidance to the student depending on his/her performance;
- Make Ines able to offer feedback about the whole exercise when the student has finished the whole exercise. Now, feedback is only given at the moment that the student does something right or wrong;
- Make a virtual representation of the tutor, that can be seen on the screen. This representation can be made so that it can give demonstrations, and facial expressions can be used to show the students if they are doing well or not.

Presently, the teacher has to use the student XML-file to look at the results of the students and to add new students to the system. A separate program should be written to make it easier to check the results. It should be possible to check which exercises the student has performed and how. It can also be used to look how many students have executed a particular exercise and to calculate the average results. The teacher must be able to print al the results and to add new students to the XML-file.

Because the idea was to make an Intelligent Tutoring System for nursing students, the following idea rose: connect Ines with a mechanical limb that has sensors to provide Ines with input. In this way, the student is able to train for example the subcutaneous injection on a life-like body part, whereas Ines will evaluate the input received from the limb's sensors. This input will then be used by Ines to guide the student through the training process.

References

[1] A. Broersen and A. Nijholt. Developing a virtual piano playing environment. *In IEEE International conference on Advanced Learning Technologies (ICALT 2002)*, pages 278–282, 2002.

[2] M. Evers and A. Nijholt. Jacob - an animated instruction agent for virtual reality. *In Advances in Multimodal Interfaces - ICMI 2000, Proc. Third International Conference on Multimodal Interfaces*, pages 526–533, 2000.

[3] W. Johnson. Pedagogical agents. *In Global Education on the Net 1, Proceedings of ICCE'98, the Sixth International Conference on Computers in Education*, pages 13–22, 1998.

[4] J.L. Los Arcos, W. Muller, O. Fuente, L. Orue, E. Arroyo, I. Leaznibarrutia, and J. Santander. Lahystotrain - integration of virtual environments and its to surgery training. *In Intelligent Tutoring Systems*, pages 43–52, 2000.

[5] A. Nijholt and J. Hulstijn. Multimodal interactions with agents in virtual worlds. *In Future directions for Intelligent Information Systems and Information Science, Studies in Fuzziness and Soft Computing*, pages 148–173, 2000.

[6] A.C. Ornstein and T.J. Lasley. *Strategies for effective teaching*. McGraw-Hill Higher Education, 2000.

[7] J. Rickel and W.L. Johnson. Steve: A pedagogical agent for virtual reality. *In Proceedings of the Second International Conference on Autonomous Agents*, pages 332–333, 1998.

[8] J. Rickel and W.L. Johnson. Animated agents for procedural training in virtual reality: Perception, cognition and motor control. *In Applied Artificial Intelligence*, 13:343–382, 1999.

[9] S. Russell and P. Norvig. *Artificial Intelligence, a modern approach*. Prentice Hall, Inc., 1995.

[10] E. Shaw, R. Ganeshan, W.L. Johnson, and D. Millar. Building a case for agent-assisted learning as a catalyst for curriculum reform in medical education. *In Proceedings of the Int. Conference on Artificial Intelligence in Education*, pages 509–516, 1999.

[11] M. Shaw and D. Garlan. *Software Architecture, perspectives on an emerging discipline*. Prentice Hall, 1996.

Department of Computer Science, University of Twente, Enschede, The Netherlands
E-mail address: {anijholt,infrieks,heylen}@cs.utwente.nl

Carrel: Secure Deployment of an Agent–Based Health Care Application

David Cabanillas et al.

Abstract. The use of Multi-Agent Systems (MAS) in health-care domains is increasing. Such Agent-mediated Medical Systems are designed to manage complex tasks and have the potential to adapt gracefully to unexpected events. However, in this kind of system issues of privacy, security and trust are particularly sensitive and real deployment of Agent technologies in such domains must meet high standards in each of these areas. This paper outlines a existing prototype Agent–Based application in the Organ and Tissue transplant domain and outlines some of the challenges in the area of security which have been identified in moving it from prototype to real usage.

Key words: Agent Mediated Institutions, Transplants, Security

1. Introduction

Organ and tissue transplantation are widely-used therapies against life-threatening diseases. But there are two issues that make transplantation management a very complex issue:

1. *scarcity* of donors, so it is important to try to maximize the number of successful transplants
2. *donor/recipient matching*, because of the diversity and multiplicity of genetic factors involved in the response to the transplant.

In this paper we first describe *Carrel* – an Agent–Based architecture for the tasks involved in managing the vast amount of data to be processed in carrying out:

- recipient selection (e.g., from patient waiting lists and patient records),
- organ/tissue allocation (based on organ and tissue records),
- ensuring adherence to legislation,
- following approved protocols and
- preparing delivery plans (e.g., using train and airline schedules).

As far as we know, the *Carrel* system that we describe in the following sections is the first agent-mediated electronic institution applied to the transplant allocation problem that joins the strengths of *agents* with the advantages of formal specifications. The application has raised significant interest amongst the relevant healthcare organisations as a demonstrator. However this brings us to the next stage in such an application's life: moving toward real deployment and use. In general such a move requires changes in many areas including:

- System robustness,
- Precise implementation of all relevant rules, laws and best practices,
- Extensive work on user interfaces,
- Integration with local, national and international dedicated IT infrastructures,
- Compliance with all relevant privacy requirements,
- Building of user trust,
- Developing strong system security.

While the authors are involved in developments in several of this areas this paper focuses on the last and describes threats and countermeasures identified for the *Carrel* application which would need to considered before real deployments could be possible. The first half of the paper therefore describes the *Carrel* system and the second describes identified security issues and counter measures. A more detailed threat assessment including a serious of tests verifying each of the vulnerabilities can be found in [2].

2. The *Carrel* system

There are very few references in the literature about the use of agents in the transplant domain. In [19] Valls *et al.* describe an agent that uses multi-criteria decision techniques in the selection of the best receiver in a transplant, providing the Hospital Transplant Co-ordinator with a result according to the weights the user assigned to each criteria. Moreno *et al.* present in [12] a hierarchical multi-agent system where the agent on the root node plans transport routes between hospitals using the information obtained from the other agents in the hierarchy, removing routes that will exceed the maximum available time for transportation and avoiding potential fatal delays due to mistakes in coordination of different means of transport. In [11] Moreno *et al.* propose a multi-agent system architecture to coordinate hospital teams for organ transplants. Coordination is achieved through agents that keep track of the personnel schedules and the availability of the facilities (both described as time-tables divided into slots of thirty minutes). Finally, Aldea *et al.* present in [1] an alternative design for a multi-agent architecture for the Spanish organ allocation process. It identifies the agents needed to solve the problem and organizes them in four levels (*Hospital Level*, *Regional Level*, *Zonal Level* and *National Level*). However, no formalism is used in the development of the architecture.

The aim of the *Carrel* system is to assist specialists in the decision-making during the allocation and distribution of *pieces* for transplants, in a manner that is acceptable according to the legislative requirements and other procedures governing the process. To achieve this, the agents composing the *Carrel* system have to be given with the appropriate domain-specific knowledge (kinds of *pieces*, attributes to describe them, etc.) so they can act rationally, and also with the rules they should follow, such as which actions can be done when, what information can be accessed or given out, etc..

In this kind of medical application the use of rules in order to guide the agents' behaviour is mandatory, as any mistake can lead to an unsuccessful transplant and potentially the death of a patient, as well as the waste of a piece which might have better benefited someone else. A further complication is that, as above mentioned, all the agent actions must respect legislation on the distribution and use of *pieces* for transplantation. This need for regulation is one of the reasons why we have modelled the *Carrel* Multi-Agent System as an Electronic Institution [4].

Electronic institutions work with explicit representations of norms [20, 6, 8, 3, 5]. Expressing all the regulations and protocols in the form of computable norms—instead of hard-coding them so they are scattered throughout the logic of a program—not only admits a readily verification, both informal and formal, of adherence but also it gives the system the added flexibility of behaviour that it can be adapted in the light of regulatory changes (an event that is not uncommon).

With all these considerations in mind we propose to use Agent Mediated Electronic Institution and regular multi-agent systems to automate part of the allocation process, finding suitable *pieces* for transplant and giving support to the decision making steps in that process. The over-arching goal is to improve the process of selection and procurement. A key principle of our solution is to deploy software agents to create, negotiate and coordinate plans for the extraction, transfer and implantation of *pieces*.

2.1. The inter-hospital level

At the inter-hospital level we have created the *Carrel Institution* [20], an agent platform which hosts a group of agents (an *agency*) responsible for the allocation of organs and tissues. In this agency different entities (the agents) play different roles that are determined by their goals, rights and duties.

In the case of tissues, the allocation process comprises:

1. The tissue banks keeping the institution updated about tissue availability
2. The agency receiving requests from the hospitals for tissues. For each request (brought by an agent representing the hospital) the institution tries to allocate the *best* tissue available from all the tissue banks that are known.

In the case of organs, the process comprises:

1. Each hospital informing the institution about patients that have been added to or removed from the waiting list of that hospital, or patients either to be added to or removed from the national-wide Maximum Urgency Level[1] Waiting List.
2. When a donor appears, the hospital informs the institution of all the organs suitable for donation in the form of *offers* sent to the organ allocation organization, which then assigns the organs.

Figure 1 depicts all the entities that interact with the *Carrel* system, where TB denotes a tissue bank and *UCTx* denotes a transplant coordination unit. This other system designed to model and automate some of the tasks performed by a Transplant Coordination Unit (*UCTx*) inside a Hospital. It is capable of dealing with *Carrel* in order to meet its own goals, acting as the representative of the hospital in the negotiation. There are:

---

[1] In Spain the Maximum Urgency Level is called Urgency-0

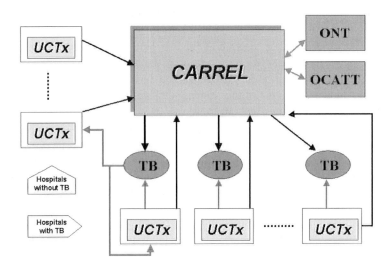

FIGURE 1. The *Carrel* System environment: the *Carrel* Institution and the *UCTx*

- the hospitals that create the piece requests,
- the Tissue Banks, and
- the national organ transplantation organizations, that own the agent platform and act as observers—the figure shows the organizations in Spain: the Organización Nacional de Transplantes[2] (ONT) [14] and the Organització CATalana de Trasplantaments[3] (OCATT).

We make it a requirement in our model that all hospitals, even the ones that own a tissue bank, will make their requests through *Carrel* in order to ensure an acceptable distribution of *pieces* and to ease the tracking of all *pieces* from extraction to implant, in the same manner as ONT and OCATT require for organs. The role of the *Carrel* Institution can be summarized in terms of following tasks:

1. to make sure that all the agents which enter into institution behave properly (that is, that they follow the behavioral norms).
2. to be up to date about all the available *pieces* in the Tissue Banks, and all the recipients that are registered in the waiting lists.
3. to check that all hospitals and tissue banks fulfill all the requirements needed to interact with *Carrel*.
4. to take care of the fulfillment of the commitments undertaken inside the *Carrel* system.
5. to coordinate the piece delivery from one facility to another.
6. to register all incidents relating to a particular piece.

---

[2]National Transplant organization
[3]Catalan Transplant organization

A hospital becomes a member of the *Carrel* institution in order to make use of the services provided. In doing so, they accept to respect the norms that rule the interaction inside *Carrel*. Some of these norms are:

1. All organ offers and tissue requests should be done through the *Carrel* institution.
2. Hospitals must accept the outcomes of the negotiation (assignation) process.
3. Hospitals receiving an organ or tissue from *Carrel* must update the institution with any relevant event related to these organs and tissues.

A hospital is represented in *Carrel* by the Transplant Coordination Unit (*UCTx: Unidad de Coordinación de Transplantes*). This agency serves as interface between the surgeons and *Carrel*. When a surgeon needs a piece she/he makes her/his request through the *UCTx* system, which analyses the information entered by the surgeon, adds the information about the recipient and, finally, creates a *Finder Agent*, that is, the agent that goes to *Carrel* looking for a suitable piece.

The information required by the *Finder Agent* to look for a piece in *Carrel* is held in an electronic *Sealed Envelope*. The information contained in the envelope is summarized in Table 1. The *Selection Function* is the part of the information contained in the *Sealed Envelope* that allows the *Finder Agent* to perform a negotiation. It is composed of a set of rules, each one a constraint on the piece to be selected. Some of these rules may originate from the policy of the whole transplant unit of the hospital, but the others are introduced by the surgeon, who can set the constraints associated with a given recipient. Table 2 lists the kind of predicates a *Selection Function* can include.

2.2. The intra-hospital level

The functioning of the Transplant Coordination Unit (UCT) may also benefit from the use of agents to help coordinate all the people in the hospital related to a particular case. Hence, our modeling of the UCT represents not only the surgeons, but also:

- the human transplant coordinator, who is the overall coordinator and who must coordinate all the tasks to be done and who must also be informed of any transplant related event
- any member of the hospital staff who plays a role at any step of the transplant process, from the moment when the piece arrives to the hospital until the piece has been implanted in the recipient.

2.3. Security considerations

Transplant information is considered high-risk data as it includes sensitive information about people (donors and recipients). Therefore, the *UCTx* and *Carrel* systems have to observe the local, national and European Union legislation on transplants (see the reports of the ONT in [15] and the recommendations of the Transplant Experts Committee in [10]). It also should follow the European directives and the Spanish Law on personal data protection [9] [7] [17]. In particular, both have to ensure confidentiality, privacy and integrity of patient and donor data. This is a long-standing issue in health care that acquires new facets with the use of Electronic Medical Records (EMR). One of the benefits of using electronic records is that it assures access for authorized and authenticated users as well as tracking access as demanded by law. It is important for patient and donor trust that

Urgency level	that works as electronic postage stamp and sets the urgency level of the request (in Spain: normal, urgency-1 or urgency-0)
Hospital identification	a certificate issued by the Certification Authority associated with the *Carrel* institution, to allow the institution to authenticate the sender of each request and ensure that only *Finder Agents* with requests from authorized hospitals can enter and negotiate inside *Carrel*.
Piece information	type, parameters, etc.
recipient data	age, sex, laboratory analysis, etc.
selection function	see Table 2

TABLE 1. The envelope contents

piece	predicates that describe the constraints the selected piece has to satisfy, such as the age of the donor or the dimensions of the piece itself.
origin	predicates that can set constraints about the tissue bank(s) preferred by the surgeon or the hospital
cost	predicates about the cost of the piece, such as price. Note: the cost is just that of extraction and preservation. Settlement is managed via a clearing house.

TABLE 2. The selection function predicates

it can be demonstrated that the information about them may not be used for any purpose beyond that for which it was collected. Our work to make *Carrel* and by extension other similar MAS is reported in 4.

3. Description of the Carrel institution

In the *Carrel* System, the interaction among the agents and the institution is structured using the following scenes:

Reception Room:: is the scene where all the external agents should identify themselves in order to be assigned the roles they are authorized to play. If these agents are carrying either a request for one or more tissues or an offer of one or more organs, then this information is checked to make sure that it is well-formed.

Consultation Room:: is the scene where the institution is updated about any event or incident related to a piece. Agents coming from tissue banks should update the institution about tissue availability, while agents coming from hospitals should update the institution about the waiting lists and also inform it about the reception of all *pieces* (organs or tissues) they have received, the transplant operation and the condition of recipients.

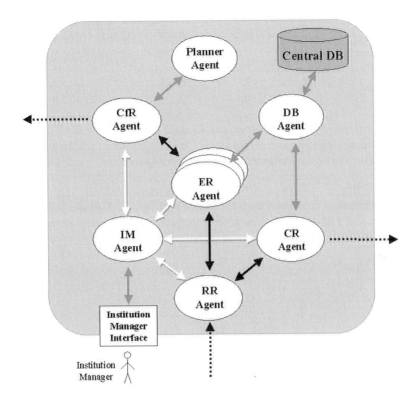

FIGURE 2. The *Carrel* Institution Agency

Exchange Room:: is the scene where assignation of *pieces* takes place. In fact, there are specific exchange rooms for tissue requests (*Tissue Exchange Room*) and for organ offers (*Organ Exchange Room*).

Confirmation Room:: is the scene where the provisional assignments made at the exchange rooms are confirmed, whereafter a delivery plan is constructed, or cancelled, because a new request of higher priority has arrived.

A more extensive description of this platform could be found in [4].

4. Security and the *Carrel* application

In this section we will point out the aspects related to the security in medical scenarios with agents. Medical applications demand security guarantees due to the importance of the information, critical service and dangerous outcomes managed in this area.

Concretely we explain how to improve the security Multi–Agent Systems in medical application. We have focused our efforts in classification of threats to MAS and proposed safeguard cases based on the JADE multi–agent platform in a real scenario.

Our work is framed in Agent Platforms used in open environments as Agentcities. [4] Agentcities is a worldwide initiative to help realize an open network of platforms hosting diverse agent based services and therefore provides a stepping stone toward future more realistic deployments. Our plans to deploy *Carrel* within Agentcities were therefore a significant motivation to begin considering security issues for the application. In the network any could send any message to any part of the *Carrel* application, spy on message traffic or directly attack the Agent Platform deployments the application is based upon.

4.1. Background

This section describes the *Carrel* application and highlights the areas of the system that might be attacked. Figure 3 shows the most obvious locations at which the security in the application needed to be reviewed.

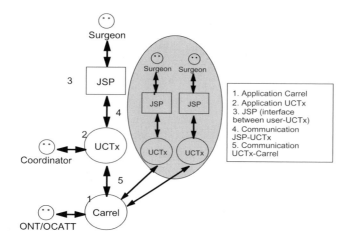

FIGURE 3. Important areas for security assessment

Of those five points, only 1, 2 and 5 are addressed here since items 3 and 4 are not directly related to the agent application itself and can be easily solved using standard techniques. The current implementation of the system uses the open source Jade 2.1 [13], an Oracle database[5] and Java Server Pages (JSP)[6] over Apache Tomcat 4.1.12[7]. In the current prototype one machine hosts the agent *Carrel* application elements (and the database) and another hosts *UCTx* . The final system however is planned for deployment across the

---

[4]http://www.agentcities.org/
[5]http://www.oracle.com
[6]http://java.sun.com/products/jsp/
[7]http://jakarta.apache.org/tomcat/

public Internet with JSP interfaces and *UCTx* in different client hospitals and the *Carrel* system hosted by the Organització CATalana de Trasplantaments.

4.2. Implementation

Having identified potential threat areas we can deal with each in turn to identify the threats actually present. This was done first with an analysis and subsequently a test to check that a particular threat was actually valid (details of the tests are not given here - see [2]). Now, we have a short description and notion about the architecture of *UCTx* (point 2 in figure 4) we can describe the security issues more fully is the *front–end* local application where different users of the system (that is surgeons and coordinator) access the system through a simple password based login. *UCTx* acts as the interface between the user and the agent platform, the two more important tasks are:

1. Local actions such planning equipment use with the appropriate surgeon or consulting/managing the information associated with the hospital.
2. Consultations and petitions of *pieces* (such as organs, tissues and bones) over *Carrel*.

Carrel (point 1 in Figure 3) can be characterized as the *back–end* local application and offers services for the correct management of *pieces* at the Tissue Banks and Hospitals that are members of the system. The principal task *Carrel* carries out is the assignment of the best piece to the recipient that shows the best match with the available *pieces*.

Architectures for these two application elements are depicted in figure 4 (*UCTx*) and in figure 2 (*Carrel*). In addition to the agents shown in these diagram each deployed platform also hosts the standard FIPA[8] infrastructure agents - the Agent Management System (AMS - providing white pages and remote management services) and the the Directory Facilitator (DF - providing yellow page services).

The communication among points 1, 2 and, 5 in figure 3 is made by means of public networks using FIPA standard transport mechanisms (generally HTTP carrying XML encoded messages). We have different *UCTx* platforms (one for each hospital) that communicate with an unique *Carrel* (in the future probably we will have a different *Carrel*, one for each administration / country). This is an important risk because the information could be intercepted (and therefore read by unauthorized people or manipulated). For example, a message from a hospital may contain private information about a patient and *pieces* (illness, diagnosis and so on). The system must insure that the confidentiality of the information between these two points. Also this is a possible attack point for manipulating messages changing them and thereby impeding the correct operation of the application.

The application's behavior in a normal request transaction can be summarized as follows:

- Start the application *Carrel* and one or more *UCTx* in different hospitals
- The surgeon uses a web form (entering name and password) to connect to his/her hospital's local *UCTx* service
- This data is validated by *UCTx*
- The surgeon can then make a petition (request)

---

[8]http://www.fipa.org

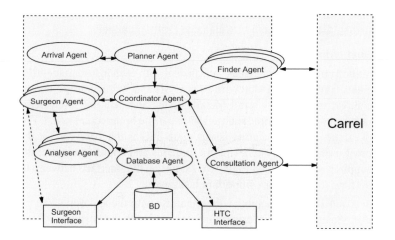

FIGURE 4. Architecture *UCTx*

- The *UCTx* associated to the surgeon sends the petition to *Carrel*
- *Carrel* confirms the authentication and starts the petition
- Finally, *Carrel* sends the result of the petition to the *UCTx* and this responds to the surgeon

In this short list we can see different issues, such as:

1. The agent interaction sequence:
    - Inside each platform: A number of management actions are taken which correspond to those defined in the FIPA Agent standard - such as registering new Agents in the AMS and registering services in the DF so they can later be found and used in the application.[9] Figure 5 shows the sequence and the agents related to a simple DF registration.
    - Between platforms: This sequence (unlike the previous sequence) is specific to our application. In this case the communication is between two different platforms *UCTx–Carrel*; this is shown in figure 6.
2. The hierarchy of users is (roles of the different users):
    In *UCTx*:
    - Coordinator: One unique coordinator for each *UCTx* . She/he creates the surgeon–users. This assignment is decided by hospital's members. She / He is assumed trusted by the *UCTx* owners.
    - Surgeon: They work with *UCTx* and they could make petitions or/and consultations at the system *Carrel*.
    In *Carrel*:
    - Super–user: She/He manages the *Carrel* application and database.
    - Membership: The hospitals that have access to *Carrel*.

---

[9] Services are the actions that our agents offer to others agents.

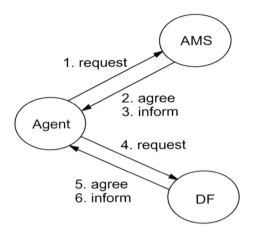

FIGURE 5. Start an agent

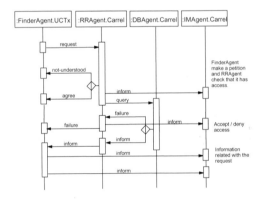

FIGURE 6. Communication between *UCTx* and *Carrel*

3. Distributed applications and distributed information: On one hand, hospitals have a Jade–platform to manage the information associated (patients, users and so on). On the other hand, *Carrel* should guarantee a fair and equitable distribution of *pieces* available in TBs. The institution should ensure that it provides sufficient security for the information it handles.

4.3. Threats

In this section, the aim is to show the different threats that might exist to the correct running of the application. Each of the following subsections describes possible threats, following [16] and [18]:

Attacks on AP			
#	Actions	#	Communication
1	Create / kill η agents. By default agent creation and destruction inside a platform is not controlled. For example, the AMS can send a kill–agent action to DF.	1	Flooding: Adding / creating useless data entries for agents (to overload the system). For example, making the number of petitions increase enormously and finally crashing the application.
2	Register/ Deregister η services in DF. Anybody is able to register and deregister services. For example, an agent can register services that in fact it does not implement.	2	Exceeding the allowed size for messages: The platforms generally have one major subsystem for communication with other agents. This subsystem has a buffer to save the messages receives. If the size of a message is greater than the capacity of the buffer this can create an overflow situation.

TABLE 3. Attacks on AP

Attacks on the Agent Platform

The Agent Platform hosts the essential services required for the applications to run, discover one another and represents the computing resources (runtime) environment needed to execute its code. The two major forms of attack Agent Platform are Actions and Communication attacks as described in Table 3.

Attacks on application information

The problems related with the unauthorized disclosure of information (Eavesdropping) and unauthorized modification of information (Data resend) are described in Table 4.

Identity theft / Impersonation

If we have an identification system and different roles for different identifications then the application may be designed to match permitted (or obliged) actions to each role / individual agent. Attacks in this area can therefore be based on hijacking an identity and accessing forbidden systems as if the attacking agent were somebody else.

Application level threats

Application threats are those which exploit weaknesses in the application layer directly i.e. in the protocols, messages, states or functioning of the agent application. These problems are often related with rules, norms and policies of operation (e.g. surgeons violating best practice in using available data or resources). These are not dealt with in this article.

Information			
#	Eavesdropping	#	Data resend
1	Disclosure: To obtain data that is not intended for a particular receiver (the malicious agent). For example, an entity that eavesdrops on the interaction between agents could extract information on the goals, plans, capabilities etc. of others agents.	1	Copy and Replay: To obtain a message that is used in the application and resend this several times (or just once at opportune moments). For example, repeated simulations of petitions of a certain type to flood the system.
		2	Alteration: To modify the content of a message. For example, manipulating petition details to cause allocation failures.
		3	Spoofing and Masquerading: Assuming the identity of another agent and using this to access information or functions normally not permitted to the intruder. For example, an agent registers as a DF and therefore receives information from other registering agents.

TABLE 4. Attacks over the information

4.4. Existing security safeguards

Next, we describe two existing security mechanisms which could be used to address some of the problems identified and tested in the *Carrel* application.

Jade–S

The first proposal is named Jade Secure Agent Platform (Jade–S [21]). This system is an add-on for security and multi-user support. It includes features such as:

- User / agent authentication and authorization: To be able to users own or perform actions on a component of the platform.
- Secure communication: To use Secure Socket Layer (SSL) protocol providing privacy and integrity for all intra–platform connections.

In the table 5, we summarize the different threats the Jade–S does and does not solve.

X–Security

The second system is named X–Security [10] and is a project developed by Czech Technical University in Prague. The system provided basic identity management and encryption mechanisms for Agent message content:

---

[10] http://agents.felk.cvut.cz/security/main/index.php

#	Solve	Does not solve
		Jade–S
	Agent Platform: Action	
1	√ It is not possible to send a kill–action if you do not have permissions to execute a kill–action. (Restricting arbitrary access to this but also reducing remote management possibilities.)	
2	√ Jade-S refuses AMS and DF registrations from unauthorized users (again this also restricts remote access).	
	Agent Platform: Communication	
1		√ If the number of messages is greater than the dimension of buffer then messages are lost (leading to possible denial of service attacks).
2		√ If the dimension of a single message is greater than the space in the queue of messages then the platform receiver generally crashes (also a denial of service threat).
	Eavesdropping	
1	√ Jade-S uses SSL in order to realize a secure communication between containers although (to date) this doesn't work correctly between platforms.	
	Data resend	
1		√ If one user / agent catch a message in the system this could be resend the same message and it could provoke errors in our application.
	Identity theft	
1	√ Each component in the platform belongs an authenticated user. Authorizations and delegation are supported to allow or deny actions.	

TABLE 5. Threats addressed by Jade–S

- Security Certification Authority (SCA) - stand-alone, application independent agent which allows certificate registration / deregistration and provides other agents in community with these certificates. The Agent is not part of the AP

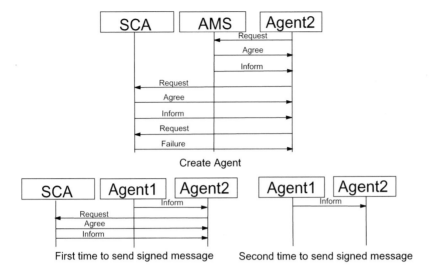

FIGURE 7. Communication in X–Security

(like AMS or DF) and can in principle also be run on remote platforms (and hence its trust services could be provided by a third party).

- Security module - this module has to be included in any agent that needs to use communication security. Using this module agents are able to encrypt and decrypt message content before including it in Agent messages.

In the X–Security table, we summarize the different threats X–Security addresses and which it does not.

In this short summary therefore, the tools now available do cover some of the basic security problems identified. However to date these systems do not yet work together effectively and must be integrated (subject of current work on a more secure version of *Carrel*).

5. Discussion

The threats listed were all verified both on stand alone deployments of *Carrel* and in (in some cases) in the Agentcities network. So for example it was shown that with the correct message it was possible to remotely terminate any Agent on a Agentcities platform using current JADE versions (which implies that if *Carrel* were running in the Agentcities network outsiders could terminate critical agents within *Carrel* at will.[11] As indicated however Jade-S in principle solves this problem through access controls. A similar parallel

---

[11] More details of the threats and tests can be found in [2].

X–Security		
#	Solve	Does not solve
Agent Platform: Action		
1		√ The use of AMS is not limited, anyone could send a kill-agent message.
2		Anyone could register in the DF.√.
Agent Platform: Communication		
1		√ The channel of communication is protected but the message queue is not.
2		
Eavesdropping		
1	√ Messages between platforms are signed and encrypted.	
Data resend		
1	Before delivering a message X–Security checks for correct certificates in the queue of incoming ACL messages.	√ However, only the content of a message is encrypted and it is possible to see other important information (such as sender, type of message and so on).
Identity theft		
1	√ The SCA generates a certificate for the agent. This data is saved in the private space of the agent.	

TABLE 6. Threats addressed by X–Security

can be found in the problems of identity theft which can be countered X-Security's SCA. Both of these examples illustrate the clear tradeoff between:

- Functionality (in particular remotely accessible functionality),
- Safety/Security.

Jade-S for example is very restrictive requiring explicit manual authorization of management actions. Despite being more secure this fact could also significantly complicate a large scale deployment of *Carrel* in which many different *UCTx* end points were present (since these may have dynamically changing hosted agents). Clearly the X–Security SCA solution also in effect moves the trust/identity problem from individual agents to a form of authority. This would require a *Carrel* deployment to identify a trusted authority to host the SCA and other X–Security services in use.

Finally the current tools studied here do not yet cover all identified attacks and in our current prototype are currently being combined with a number of other strategies:

- Role based access to key services / functions,
- Message Filtering,
- Community trust / reputation mechanisms,
- Monitoring Agents.

The fact that *Carrel* uses an experimental agent platform is one reason for some of the security issues encountered and had we used (for example) industry grade J2EE platforms some of these problems may not have occurred. However it is important to note that the majority of the problems are not due to software bugs or something similar - they are generated by the requirements of the system itself (they are structural) and an Agent–Based paradigm is an important way to identify such security issues which may be hidden in (for example) low level implementations of proprietary protocols.

6. Conclusions

Organ transplantation is the best available established technique for the treatment of end stage failure for most essential organs (liver, heart, lung, kidney). With the objective of increasing the potential success of transplantations we introduced a multi-agent mediated institution *Carrel* meant to facilitate the interaction amongst Hospitals and Tissue Banks to improve the quality of the organ and tissue assignation. As we consider how a successful demonstrator could be developed into a real operational system one of the key challenges is to ensure that the system can be operated in a secure manner despite the fact that:

- It needs to operate in a relatively open environment (to link transplant centers in different locations) – possibly even the public Internet,
- The interactions involved are highly sensitive – both in terms of data involved and in the patient care risk incurred if there are failures.

In this paper we have presented some preliminary work on identifying security issues in the deployment of *Carrel* which we are now working on solving using a combination of existing tools and our own additional strategies. We hope also that the analysis will be more generally useful for other Agent systems in the medical domain and elsewhere.

7. Acknowledgements

The authors would like to acknowledge the Agentcities.NET IST-2000-28384 as well as useful discussions in the Agentcities Healthcare and Security Working Groups. In particular we thank Milan Rollo for interesting and fruitful discussion on the application of X–Security to our problem. The views in this paper are not necessarily those of Agentcities.NET.

References

[1] A. Aldea, B. López, A. Moreno, D. Riaño, and A. Valls. A multi-agent system for organ transplant co-ordination. In Barahona Quaglini and Andreassen, editors, *Proceedings of the 8th. European Conference on Artificial Intelligence in Medicine, Portugal, 2001.*, Lecture Notes in Artificial Intelligence 2101: Artificial Intelligence in Medicine, pages 413–416, 2001.

[2] D. Cabanillas, S. Willmott, and U. Cortés. Threats and security safeguards in a multi-agent system medical applications. Technical Report LSI-02-76-R, Software Departament. Technical University of Catalonia. Barcelona Spain, 2002.

[3] R. Conte and C. Castelfranchi. Are incentives good enough to achieve(info)social order? In C. Dellarocas and R. Conte, editors, *Workshop on Norms and Institutions in Multi-Agent Systems*, pages 26–40. ACM-AAAI, ACM Press, 2000.

[4] U. Cortés, A. López-Navidad, J. Vázquez-Salceda, A. Vázquez, D. Busquets, M. Nicolás, S. Lopes, F. Vázquez, and F. Caballero. Carrel: An agent mediated institution for the exchange of human tissues among hospitals for transplantation. In *3er Congrés Català d'Intel.ligencia Artificial*, pages 15–22. ACIA, 2000.

[5] C. Dellarocas and M. Klein. Contractual agent societies: Negotiated shared context and social control in open multi-agent systems. In C. Dellarocas and R. Conte, editors, *Workshop on Norms and Institutions in Multi-Agent Systems*, pages 41–52, 2000.

[6] F. Dignum. Abstract norms and electronic institutions. In G. Lindemann, D. Moldt, M. Paolucci, and B. Yu, editors, *Proceedings of the International Workshop on Regulated Agent-Based Social Systems: Theories and Applications (RASTA '02), Bologna*, volume 318 of *Mitteilung*, pages 93–104, Hamburg, 12 July 2002. Fachbereich Informatik, Universität Hamburg.

[7] Directive 95/46/CE of the European Parliament and of the Council of 24 october 1995 on the protection of individuals with regard to the processing of personal data and of the free movement of such data, October 1995.

[8] N. R. Jennings and Y. Lespérance, editors. *Intelligent Agents VI, Agent Theories, Architectures, and Languages (ATAL), 6th International Workshop, ATAL '99, Orlando, Florida, USA, July 15-17, 1999, Proceedings*, volume 1757 of *Lecture Notes in Computer Science*. Springer, 2000.

[9] Ley Orgánica 15/1999 de protección de datos de carácter personal. Boletín Oficial del Estado 292, 14 de diciembre 1999.

[10] R. Matesanz. Meeting the organ shortage: Current status and strategies for improvement of organ donation. *Newsletter Transplant*, 4(1):5–17, 1999.

[11] A. Moreno, A. Valls, and J. Bocio. Management of hospital teams for organ transplants using multi-agent systems. In Barahona Quaglini and Andreassen (Eds.), editors, *Proceedings of the 8th. European Conference on Artificial Intelligence in Medicine, Portugal, 2001.*, Lecture Notes in Artificial Intelligence 2101: Artificial Intelligence in Medicine, pages 374–383, 2001.

[12] A. Moreno, A. Valls, and A. Ribes. Finding efficient organ transport routes using multi-agent systems. In *IEEE 3rd International Workshop on Enterprise Networking and Computing in Health Care Industry (Healtcom), L'Aquilla, Italy.*, 2001.

[13] Proceedings of the 4th International Conference, Exhibition on the Practical Application of Intelligent Agents, and Multi-Agents, editors. *JADE - A FIPA-Compliant Agent Framework.*, 1999.

[14] Organización Nacional de Transplantes. http://www.msc.es/ont.

[15] Organización Nacional de Transplantes, editor. *Informes y Documentos de Consenso promovidos por la Organización Nacional de Transplantes y la Comisión de Transplantes del Consejo Interterritorial del Sistema Nacional de Salud*. Editorial Complutense S. A., 1st edition, 2000.

[16] A. Poggi, G. Rimassa, and M. Tomaiuolo. Multi-user and security support for multi-agent systems. In Andrea Omicini and Mirko Viroli, editors, *WOA 2001 – Dagli oggetti agli agenti:*

tendenze evolutive dei sistemi software, Modena, Italy, 4–5 September 2001. Pitagora Editrice Bologna.

[17] Real Decreto 994/1999, de 11 de junio, por el que se aprueba el reglamento de medidas de seguridad de los ficheros automatizados que contengan datos de carácter personal. Boletín Oficial del Estado 151, 26 de febrero 2000.

[18] M. Calisti S. Poslad. Towards improved trust and security in fipa agent platforms. *AA2000*, June 2000.

[19] A. Valls, A. Moreno, and D. Sánchez. A multi–criteria decision aid agent applied to the selection of the best receiver in a transplant. In *4th. International Conference on Enterprise Information Systems, Ciudad Real, Spain.*, 2002.

[20] J. Vázquez-Salceda. *The role of Norms and Electronic Institutions in Multi-Agent Systems applied to complex domains. The HARMONIA framework.* PhD thesis, Technical University of Catalonia, 2003.

[21] G. Vitaglione. Jade tutorial–security administrator guide. http://sharon.cselt.it/projects/jade/doc/tutorials/SecurityAdminGuide.pdf, September 2002.

David Cabanillas, Javier Vàzquez-Salceda, Steven Willmott, Ulises Cortés.
Software Department. Technical University of Catalonia.
c/ Jordi Girona 1-3. E08034 Barcelona, Spain.
Phone: +34 93 4017016 Fax: +34 93 4017014.
E-mail address: {dconrado, jvazquez, steve, ia}@lsi.upc.es

Dammien Bouissou.
Tissues Bank. Hospital de la Santa Creu i Sant Pau
c/ St. Antoni M. Claret, 167. E08025 Barcelona, Spain.br Phone +34 93 2919335 Fax +34 93 2919410.
E-mail address: dbouissou@hsp.santpau.es

Assisting the Spanish Organ Transplant Coordination Process with Multi-Agent Systems

Aïda Valls and Antonio Moreno

Abstract. This paper presents a multi-agent support system for the different stages of an organ transplant process. With the automatisation of certain tasks in this complex coordination process, we can decrease the time spent before the organ reaches the medical centre of the receiver. This is very important because organs degrade very quickly and they cannot be frozen. The paper explains how we can improve the: searching of possible receivers, the selection of the most appropriate candidate, the transport of the organ and the scheduling of the surgical operation. The design of this prototype has been done according to the Spanish Model of transplant co-ordination.

1   Introduction

The organ transplant coordination process is quite complex because it involves many different organisations, persons, norms and laws. The *Spanish Model* [1] is one of the coordination models with better success worldwide. It proposes to have a transplant coordinator in each hospital and a hierarchy of higher-level coordinators to assure a rapid and fair distribution of the organs [2]. In spite of the success of this model, the number of successful transplants is still far from the ideal one [3].

At the moment, this coordination process is done by hand by the different transplant coordinators (e.g. they get in touch using the phone and data is sent by fax). In contrast, other areas of health care provision are now using the new technologies; for example, the storing of patient's records in databases, the update of the doctor's timetable from a local computer or from Internet, or the use of some applications to automatically capture data from different electronic devices. For this reason, we propose the use of computers and Internet to improve the organ transplant coordination process. This automation could reduce the time needed to find a receiver for an organ, which is crucial in this application because organs degrade very quickly (e.g. a donated heart stays usable for no more than 6 hours outside the body, livers last up to 24 hours).

The main activities of the organ transplant process are [2]: detection of the potential organ donors, clinical examination of the organ donor, brain-death confirmation, maintenance and handling of the organ donor, legal brain-death confirmation, securing the family consent and the legal authorisation, arrangement of the organisational factors, organisation of the organ extraction and transplant, and clinical examination of the evolution of the receiver. Many different entities must collaborate to perform these activities. It is important to note that each entity maintains its own data. On one hand, hospitals know the patient medical records, the surgeons' schedule and the operating theatres availability. On the other hand, the intermediate transplant coordinators and organisations take care of the searching of possible receivers, the equitable distribution of the organs, the fulfilment of the norms and laws in each country or region, and the collection of data to evaluate the whole process (e.g. the *Organització Catalana de Transplantaments* (OCATT) in Catalonia, the *Organización Nacional de Trasplantes* (ONT) in Spain, the *United Network for Organ Sharing* (UNOS) in the USA, *the Eurotransplant International Foundation* for some countries in the EU, etc.). Finally, other entities are involved in this process, such as the surgeons, anaesthetists, nurses, the people that carry the organ from the donor's hospital to the receiver's hospital, etc.

To be able to work with such a distributed process in which many entities must keep their own identity (e.g. their own rights, norms, private information), we propose the development of a multi-agent system.

1.1   Agents for transplant coordination

Recently there have been different proposals to use intelligent agents to deal with the transplant coordination process in Europe. We must distinguish those systems that deal with the problem of transplants of tissues, like *Carrel* [4], from the ones dealing with transplants of organs, like [5]. The difference relies on the fact that tissues can be frozen and stored for a long time, so each time a patient requires a tissue, the most appropriate must be found in the hospitals' tissue banks. This process does not have the critical time constraints that we find in an organ transplant.

Multi-agent systems offer a distributed platform in which individual entities can be modelled with individual agents that guarantee the rights of the entity. This is interesting for the transplant problem because different hospitals, people and organisations participate in the coordination process. Agents' communication and negotiation abilities are also appropriate to improve this process. Moreover, Internet provides a fast means of communication to obtain the information as soon as possible. Different decision support tools can be embedded into the agents in order to facilitate the tasks of the different participants in the process. Thus, the main benefits are:

- The communication of the data can be done very quickly.
- Information can be presented to the user in a more understandable way (data can be analysed, filtered, ranked according to different criteria, etc.).

These two points are very important if we want to increase the success of organ transplants. For this reason, the Research Group on Artificial Intelligence of Universitat Rovira i Virgili (URV) is developing a Multi-Agent System (MAS) that will support the communication and negotiation layers of the transplant coordination system that we have described in the above lines. This MAS [6] is designed both to support the main activities of the transplant process, and also to be compatible with the current Spanish organisational structure.

The use of a Multi-Agent approach makes the system easy to be adapted to structural changes in the organisational protocol and to be extended to a European framework.

1.2   Organisation of the paper

In this paper we will describe the multi-agent system that we have designed. The system can be divided into 5 different parts that work together following the Spanish Coordination model, which is explained in section 2. Section 3 is devoted to give some general details about the design of the application. Section 4 describes how the agents perform the search of the patients. A multi-agent system internal to the hospital analyses the list of possible receivers; section 5 explains how they check some compatibility rules and obtain a ranking of the patients. Section 6 shows the agents that organise the transport of the organ. The final step is explained in section 7, which consists of a set of agents that arrange all the transplant operation equipment. Finally, section 8 makes an overview of the prototype that we have built and opens some research lines.

2   The Spanish Model

The process starts when an organ is available to be transplanted. Then, the most appropriate receiver for this organ must be found and this search must be done in a very brief period of time (in hours). As it has been said, different organisations co-ordinate all the stages of the donation and transplant process according to the local, regional, national, and international norms and laws. In Spain, all the entities involved must follow the so-called *Spanish model*.

The Spanish model establishes a hierarchy of different levels in the coordination process, in which we can have transplant coordinators that are responsible of the activities that are done at different levels. In Spain this hierarchy has four levels: national, zonal, regional and hospital.

Figure 1 shows the dependencies among the coordinators at the different levels. When an organ can be donated, this hierarchy is followed from the bottom to the top, in order to find an appropriate receiver as near as possible to the hospital that holds the organ. This is done to minimise the travel time and the economic cost.

The process to find an appropriate receiver starts with the communication with other hospitals in the same city; if no potential receivers are found, the search proceeds with the next level. Then the regional co-ordinator is in charge of trying to find a receiver in the same region. If no appropriate patient is found in the current region, we have to look at other regions of the same zone. Finally, we can search in other national zones, if necessary.

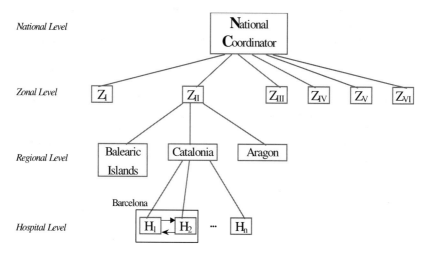

Fig. 1. Hierarchical dependencies among coordinators in Spain

The ONT has divided the territory of Spain into six zones (Figure 2). Each of these zones includes some of the nineteen Spanish autonomous regions. In order to achieve a fair distribution of the organs through the whole country, the zonal and national coordinators maintain a round-robin list. If they receive a petition, they start the search of possible receivers within the region (resp. zone) that is in the first place of the list. When a region R receives an organ from another region, the corresponding zonal coordinator moves R to the end of the list.

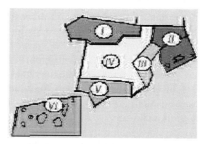

Fig. 2. Spanish division in 6 zones

3   The Transplant Multi-Agent System

The Spanish model establishes the hierarchy for searching possible receivers. However, this is not the only step that must be done before the transplant operation starts. The steps of the transplant coordination process can be summarised as follows:

- Step1: *Searching*: consists of obtaining a list of possible receivers.
- Step2: *Matchmaking*: possible receivers must be compared to the donor and organ characteristics. The compatible receivers are ranked from the best to the worst.
- Step3: *Transport*: the organ must be carried from the donor's hospital to the receiver's one.
- Step4: *Operation team*: while the organ is travelling, the receiver's hospital prepares the operation set (the surgical team and the operation theatre) in order to be able to start the transplant operation as soon as the organ arrives.
- Step5: *Transplant operation*: the last step consists in performing the surgical operation.

The multi-agent system that we propose covers all these steps excepting the last one, which is related to the surgical operation. In addition, the system includes a *Historical Agent* (HA); this agent stores historical data about the transplants in Spain. Information about a transplant is sent to this agent in order to keep track of the patient. The agent will perform different analysis and statistics for the governmental organisations, like ONT and OCATT in Catalonia.

In the next sections we will explain these four systems that have been integrated into a unique prototype.

3.1 Transplants Ontology

An ontology for managing the transplant vocabulary has been defined. We can find concepts related to personal data, medical data, places and time. An example of the objects in the ontology is:

- Address: street, number, city, zip-code, province, country
- Hospital: name, address
- Organ: identifier, type (heart, lung, …), size, …
- Patient: identifier, name, surname, birth-date, sex, height, weight, date-of-inclusion-in-waiting-list,   list-of-organs-needed,   blood-type, antigens, size of needed organs, …

This transplant ontology includes a set of actions related to different processes. For example:

- New-patient (patient, organ): includes a person in the hospital transplant waiting list.
- Find-compatible-patients (organ, patient): with the data about an organ and a donor, we want to obtain an ordered list of possible receivers.

- Assign-organ (id-organ, id-patient): once the hospital's transplant coordinator has decided who is the receiver of the organ, we must use this action to register this in our databases.
- Organ-rejection (id-organ, id-patient): this action is used to require the modification of the state of the patient when he/she has suffered an organ rejection.

This is an initial version of a transplant ontology. More medical information should be added in collaboration with transplant experts.

3.2 Application Interface

This prototype has been implemented using JADE [7]. JADE is a collection of Java libraries that ease the implementation of FIPA-compliant[1] multi-agent systems. As the system is programmed in Java, it can be used in any platform that supports Java.

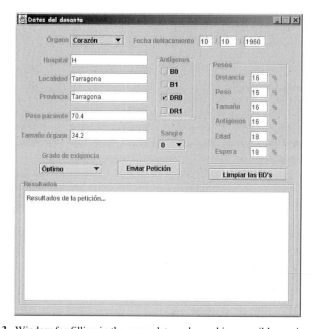

Fig. 3. Window for filling in the organ data and searching possible receivers.

---

[1] FIPA (*Foundation for Intelligent Physical Agents*) is a non-profit association that provides internationally agreed specifications for developing agent-based applications.

The interfaces of the system are in Spanish. Figure 3 shows the window in which the user can fill in the information about an organ. In the right hand-side we can give different weights to the attributes. For example, if the organ is not in good conditions, we can give more weight to the "distance" criterion in order to find compatible patients as near as possible. The display in the lower part of the window will show us the list of compatible patients ranked according to the criteria.

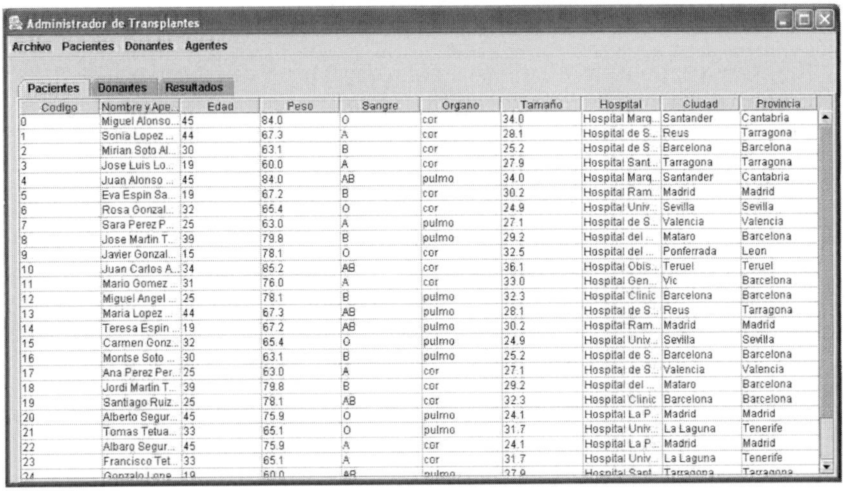

Codigo	Nombre y Ape.	Edad	Peso	Sangre	Organo	Tamaño	Hospital	Ciudad	Provincia
0	Miguel Alonso...	45	84.0	O	cor	34.0	Hospital Marq...	Santander	Cantabria
1	Sonia Lopez ...	44	67.3	A	cor	28.1	Hospital de S...	Reus	Tarragona
2	Mirian Soto Al...	30	63.1	B	cor	25.2	Hospital de S...	Barcelona	Barcelona
3	Jose Luis Lo...	19	60.0	A	cor	27.9	Hospital Sant...	Tarragona	Tarragona
4	Juan Alonso ...	45	84.0	AB	pulmo	34.0	Hospital Marq...	Santander	Cantabria
5	Eva Espin Sa...	19	67.2	B	cor	30.2	Hospital Ram...	Madrid	Madrid
6	Rosa Gonzal...	32	65.4	O	cor	24.9	Hospital Univ...	Sevilla	Sevilla
7	Sara Perez P...	25	63.0	A	pulmo	27.1	Hospital de S...	Valencia	Valencia
8	Jose Martin T...	39	79.8	B	pulmo	29.2	Hospital del ...	Mataro	Barcelona
9	Javier Gonzal...	15	78.1	O	cor	32.5	Hospital del ...	Ponferrada	Leon
10	Juan Carlos A...	34	85.2	AB	cor	36.1	Hospital Obis...	Teruel	Teruel
11	Mario Gomez ...	31	76.0	A	cor	33.0	Hospital Gen...	Vic	Barcelona
12	Miguel Angel ...	25	78.1	B	pulmo	32.3	Hospital Clinic	Barcelona	Barcelona
13	Maria Lopez ...	44	67.3	AB	pulmo	28.1	Hospital de S...	Reus	Tarragona
14	Teresa Espin ...	19	67.2	AB	pulmo	30.2	Hospital Ram...	Madrid	Madrid
15	Carmen Gonz...	32	65.4	O	pulmo	24.9	Hospital Univ...	Sevilla	Sevilla
16	Montse Soto ...	30	63.1	B	pulmo	25.2	Hospital de S...	Barcelona	Barcelona
17	Ana Perez Per...	25	63.0	A	cor	27.1	Hospital de S...	Valencia	Valencia
18	Jordi Martin T...	39	79.8	B	cor	29.2	Hospital del ...	Mataro	Barcelona
19	Santiago Ruiz...	25	78.1	AB	cor	32.3	Hospital Clinic	Barcelona	Barcelona
20	Alberto Segur...	45	75.9	O	pulmo	24.1	Hospital La P...	Madrid	Madrid
21	Tomas Tetua...	33	65.1	O	pulmo	31.7	Hospital Univ...	La Laguna	Tenerife
22	Albaro Segur...	45	75.9	A	cor	24.1	Hospital La P...	Madrid	Madrid
23	Francisco Tet...	33	65.1	A	cor	31.7	Hospital Univ...	La Laguna	Tenerife
24	Gonzalo Lope...	19	60.0	AB	pulmo	27.9	Hospital Sant...	Tarragona	Tarragona

Fig. 4. Window to monitor the list of patients waiting for an organ transplant.

To test the prototype some additional windows have been implemented. Figure 4 shows a list of all the patients in waiting lists in Spain. With this information the user can check if the system works well.

4   The Searching Process

The multi-agent system that we have designed and implemented follows the guidelines of the Spanish model. The system includes an agent for each of the transplants coordinators, in order to help them in the searching process. So, we have an agent that is in charge of the national petitions, six agents in charge of zonal petitions, 19 agents for regional petitions and one agent for each hospital transplant coordinator (HTC). Each of these agents will be executed in a different computer. Moreover, we have added an *Urgency 0 Agent* (UA). This agent maintains a centralised database of patients that need an urgent transplant. Before starting the hierarchical search explained in section 2, the hospital transplant coordinator must contact with UA.

If there is a compatible person with this high degree of emergency, the organ will be given to him/her. UA maintains all the information about the patients in this critical stage. Any hospital that detects a person that needs an urgent transplant, notifies it to UA immediately. After doing the transplant, information about the state of the patient is also communicated to UA (e.g. a rejection of the organ, the death of the patient, the recovery of the patient).

In figure 5 you can see the architecture of the multi-agent system developed for performing the search of possible receivers. Notice that the organisation is the same than the one proposed by the Spanish model (figure 2).

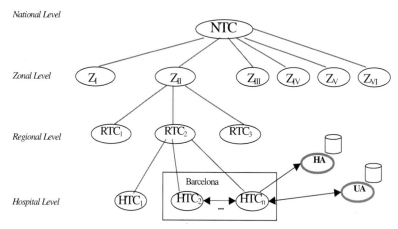

Fig. 5. Organ Transplant Multi-agent System Architecture.

Now we will explain the communication between the agents. Let us suppose that a liver is available in hospital n in Barcelona. The corresponding hospital transplant co-ordinator agent, HTC_n, will immediately send a query to find out if there is any possible receiver in state of urgency 0 (with a message to UA). If there is not any urgent compatible receiver, HTC_n will make a query at the local database of its own hospital, to see whether there is any patient that can use the organ. In case a suitable receiver is found, the rest of the steps become very simple because there is no need to transport the organ and there is "plenty of" time to arrange everything. However, usually the hierarchical search process must start. First, the other HTCs of Barcelona are contacted, and they can provide their lists of possible receivers for the liver. Then, a matchmaking process is done in order to see if there is an appropriate receiver for the organ. If not, the agent HTC_n will continue the search process following the hierarchy of coordinators. RTC_2 will request to the other HTCs of the same region their lists of potential receivers of the organ; if none of them is good enough, we must continue in the upper levels of the hierarchy.

The zonal agent (Z_{II}) and the national transplant coordinator agent (NTC) maintain a round-robin list as explained in section 2. So, the process is exactly the same than the one that is now done manually. Z_{II} will send a *call for proposals* to the first region in the list. Proposals are given to HTC_n. If no sufficiently good patient is found, Z_{II} repeats the process with the agents in the second region, and so on. Each time that HTC_n receives a list (from a regional, zonal or national agent) an internal matchmaking process is done in order to determine if there are any appropriate candidates for this organ transplant. Finally, when a suitable receiver is found, HTC sends the data about the donor and the receiver to the historical agent, HA.

5   The Matchmaking Process

Although this part of the transplant coordination process has been introduced as a second step, it is actually done during the search process. Each time a list of possible receivers is obtained, the donor's hospital analyses the candidates in order to find a person compatible with the characteristics of the organ. Compatibility is determined by looking to some attributes whose values must be under some strict constraints. For example, the maximum difference between the donor's and receiver's age is 25 years, for a heart transplant the patient should not be more than 60 years old, for the blood type to be compatible we must look at the ABO Table (Table 1).

Table 1. ABO: table of blood compatibility

Donor	Receiver
O	O, A, B, AB
A	A, AB
B	B, AB
AB	AB

In our multi-agent system [8], these constraints are analysed by the Transplant Specialist agent (TS). At the moment, this agent is in charge of filtering all those patients that do not fulfil the basic compatibility conditions. Nevertheless, in the future, other medical knowledge could be treated by this agent.

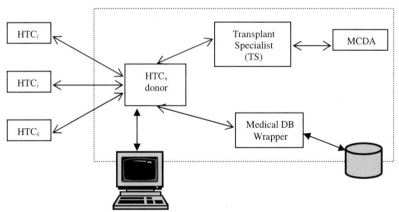

Fig. 6. Intra-Hospital Multi-Agent System Architecture

The second step in the matchmaking process consists of analysing the characteristics of the compatible candidates. Nowadays, this process is done by the human transplant coordinator with the help of medical staff. This is a very important point in the whole process, since the final success of the transplant depends on the degree of compatibility between the donor and the receiver. The more similar they are, the more possible it will be to avoid an organ rejection. To help in this process, we propose the use of Multi-Criteria Decision Aid techniques. For this reason, we have introduced a MCDA agent. The agents that will be executing at the same hospital are inside the dotted box of Figure 6.

Having specialised agents for the processes of filtering and ranking, we achieve a greater flexibility of the system. Each hospital can decide to incorporate a different agent to perform this filtering or ranking according to their own protocols.

TS is in charge of making the filtering and, after that, comparing the attributes of the donor with the ones of the candidates. In the initial prototype TS only takes into consideration 6 attributes of the receivers, which can be expressed with numerical or qualitative values:

- Weight.
- Size of the organ needed.
- Antigens.
- Age.
- Location of the hospital where the transplant should be performed.
- Amount of time that the person has been waiting for the organ.

TS analyses each attribute separately and builds a preference criterion according to the similarity with the donor. The preferences are expressed with linguistic values in predetermined vocabularies that are easy to interpret for the Hospital Transplant Coordinator (see Table 2).

Table 2. Vocabularies of the qualitative preference criteria used in the prototype

	worst value ... *best value*
Weight	inadequate, feasible, good, optimum
Size	inadequate, feasible, good, optimum
Antigens	different, similar, identical
Age	more_thn_20, more_thn_17, more_thn_14, more_thn_11, more_thn_8, more_thn_5, the_same
Distance	country, zone, region, city, hospital
Waiting time	very_short, short, acceptable, long, very_long

Thus, the final criteria are the following:

- Difference between the weights of the donor and the receiver.
- Difference between the size of the donor's organ and the size of the organ needed by the receiver.
- Number of different antigens.
- Difference of age between the donor and the receiver.
- Distance to cover to bring the organ to the receiver.
- Amount of time that the receiver has been waiting for this organ.

For the ranking step, there are many different multi-criteria decision methods that can be used. There are big differences between the basis of different groups of MCDA methods, and it is very difficult to choose one in advance. For this reason, we have decided to incorporate different MCDA agents in the system and include some learning tools in the HTC agent [9]. During the learning stage, each time that the user starts the evaluation of a list of possible receivers, the system returns different rankings. The user must give a mark to each one, and these marks are used to discover which methods are always receiving bad (resp. good) marks or producing similar results under the same conditions. With this information the HTC agent can decide not to send any further requests to the methods with bad results. In the long run, only one method should survive and the user would see a single ranking.

As we have said, we can find many different MCDA techniques; however, we are interested in distinguishing those that work with numerical values and those that work with qualitative ones (i.e. linguistic terms). The qualitative approach is required when conventional numerical scales cannot be applied to a criterion (e.g. mental disposition to accept a transplant). In other cases, it is only used to deal with uncertainty or lack of precision in the data (e.g. great accuracy to express the distance between the donor and the receiver is not needed). Thus, we have implemented three qualitative MCDA methods: 2-tuple [10], linguistic aggregation [11] and clustering [12]. These methods have been selected because they work with words using different approximations: the fuzzy linguistic method uses the well known fuzzy sets theory, the 2-tuple approach uses a notation consisting of a tuple that has a word and a numerical value indicating the deviation of the real value from the usual meaning of the word, and the clustering approach uses a semantics based on negation functions. Moreover, these methods produce a qualitative ranking, that is, at the end the user can see a ranking in which each patient is described with a qualitative preference term (see [12] for a detailed description of the matchmaking and ranking processes).

6   The Transport Process

Once an appropriate receiver has been found, we have to arrange the transport of the organ from the donor's hospital to the receiver's hospital. We have designed and implemented another multi-agent system that works at national level [13]. Although it is certainly unrealistic to assume that organs are transported using standard means of transport, this multi-agent system proves the point that the coordination of the transport process could be made with the help of a multi-agent system.

When a hospital transplant coordinator (e.g. HTC_n) decides that the organ must be sent to another (e.g HTC_r), a petition for transport organisation could be sent to this centralised SMA, which can calculate the best possible route for the organ in order to spend the minimum time in the travel. Then, the estimated arrival time should be notified to HTC_r, which must have everything ready for that time.

In some cases, the transport is simply done by helicopter. However, if the two hospitals are very far, the scheduling of the transport of the organ involves looking up several (spatially distributed) databases with timetables of means of transport, such as trains or planes, and making spatial and temporal reasoning to provide the most efficient route.

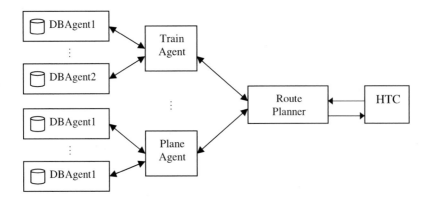

Fig. 7. MAS for scheduling organ transport

In Figure 7 we can see the architecture of the system. There are 3 types of agents:

- •*Database wrappers*: they keep the database of a specific transport company (e.g. an airline)
- •*Transport Specialists*: they are in charge of organising the scheduling of a particular means of transport. (like the train and plane agents). Each of these specialists is aware of all the companies that provide services related to a particular means of transport. When a request is received, it sends the appropriate queries to these databases.
- •*Route planner*: this agent receives a request from a user (in this case from a hospital transplant coordinator) with the information about the origin, the destination and the time deadline. Then, the route planner makes the appropriate requests of information to the transport specialist agents that send back the different timetables. Once all the information has been gathered, this agent performs a planning process in order to obtain the best route from the origin to the destination that assures that the organ will arrive in sufficiently good conditions to be transplanted.

The scheduling process starts with a petition of the HTC. The route planner agent has some geographical knowledge about Spain, which is represented with an undirected labelled multi-graph. The nodes of the graph represent the Spanish province capitals (52 cities). The arcs represent a direct connection between two cities. These arcs are labelled with the means of transport that makes the connection possible and the maximum time needed to make the trip.

The first step consists of discovering the paths that go from the origin to the destination. These paths are computed by making a limited breadth-first search in the multi-graph. Any path that exceeds the time deadline is eliminated from the study. However, the paths discovered are just expressing possible ways of going from one city to another. For instance, imagine that it is 15:00 and we must find a way to go to the destination before 20:00. There is a flight between the origin and the city X (it takes 1 hour) and a train that connects X with the destination (in 35 minutes). Now we need to know the departure times.

The route planner agent sends a query for each connection to the corresponding specialised agent. The answer includes all the timetables of all trains/planes that connect the two cities throughout the day. Then, the route planner agent uses the timetables to see if there is a possible way to link the two cities. In the example, we have found that departure times of the flight to X are 14:30, 16:00 and 18:00. The first one is not useful because it is 15:00 now. Leaving at 16:00 we would arrive at X at 17:00, so the agent must see if there is any train after 17:00. If the departures of the train are every 2 hours from 10:00, we can take the train at 18:00 and arrive to the destination at 18:35. As you can see, if there are different companies and different means of transport connecting two cities, the process is more complex, because all combinations must be analysed.

After the process, different proposals are sent to the user, who can choose the most appropriate depending on economic considerations, confidence on the different means of transport, urgency of the transplant, etc.

7   The Operation Arrangement Process

Each patient that is waiting for a transplant is associated to a specific hospital. As soon as the receiver for an organ transplant is selected, his/her corresponding hospital receives a notification (via the HTC).

While the organ is being transported to the recipient's hospital, everything must be set up there so that the operation may be performed when the organ arrives. In case it is not possible to have an operation theatre and a surgical team ready before the organ expiration time, the system must inform the transplant coordinator, who will choose another patient from the waiting list. Then, the processes of selection and planning of the transport of the organ have to be redone. For this reason, it is crucial to know the availability of the hospital equipment as soon as possible.

The required medical team depends on the type of organ, but they include doctors, nurses, anaesthetists and an equipped operation theatre. In our system [14], each of these persons is represented by an agent. Figure 8 shows the agents needed in this process as well as their interactions. The Hospital Transplant Co-ordinator agent contacts with the Surgery Team Coordinator to see if there is an available room and team to perform the transplant within the time constraints.

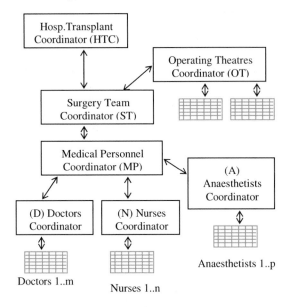

Fig. 8. Agents that perform the operation scheduling.

ST receives the basic data necessary for arranging the operation (type of organ and arrival time), and passes it along to the operating theatres coordinator (OT) and the medical personnel coordinator (MP). When ST receives from these agents the times in which there are free operating theatres and there is enough personnel, it tries to match them to find an appropriate time for the operation. If this matching is successful, OT and MP will receive the confirmation of the selected operating theatre and medical team.

So, on one hand, OT gets in touch with the agents associated to the operating theatres to find out which of them are available in appropriate time intervals. After receiving the different possibilities in which the operation may be performed, it sends them to ST (which tries to match them against the times in which there is enough personnel available). On the other hand, MP sends the request to the agents that co-ordinate the schedules of doctors (D), nurses (N) and anaesthetists (A). This agent knows the configuration of the surgery teams needed for each type of transplant. When it receives the proposals from the agents it tries to form medical teams with the appropriate number of people of each of the three categories. The possible team proposals are sent to ST.

Each doctor, nurse and anaesthetist has an agent that keeps track of the schedule of the person. When the agents D, N and A receive a request, they collect the data of all available staff members that are prepared to do a particular type of transplant (f.i. if we have to transplant a kidney, only the kidney specialists will be queried).

When ST has analysed the list of proposals, it can see if there is more than one possible interval in which there is both an available medical team and a free operating theatre (e.g. from 03:30 to 06:30 or from 8:00 to 11:00). In order to decide which is the best possibility, the system follows this criterion: it is interesting that the time intervals in which operating theatres (or staff members) are available are as long as possible, since that will leave the possibility of assigning more operations in the future. To achieve that goal, ST sends the possible intervals to the operating theatres coordinator, OT, which forwards them to the agents that control the schedule of each operating theatre. Each of these agents replies to OT with a *score* for each possibility. This score reflects how well the interval "fits" in the empty spaces in the operating theatre's schedule, and it is computed as follows. If the operating theatre is not free in the given interval, the score is 0. If the given interval fits perfectly in a free space in the operating theatre's schedule (i.e. there are not free slots just before and after the interval), the score is 3, because no unusable intervals are generated. If there are empty slots right before and after the interval, the score is 1. If there is an empty slot in one side of the interval but the other side is not free, the score is 2. These marks are then used by ST to make the final decision.

8   Conclusions and Future Work

To develop this prototype we have divided the complex coordination process into four different multi-agent systems that work together. The Hospital Transplant Coordinator agent (HTC) is the one that allows the integration of the four subsystems. This separation is interesting because some of the subproblems are not specific of the transplant framework. For example, the operation team scheduling could be used to arrange any other type of surgical operations, or the transport multi-agent system could be also useful in very different kinds of applications.

Although we have now an initial version of the whole system, there is a lot of work to be done before starting to test it in the hospitals. We will now mention some open lines with respect to some of the different subsytems.

- Matchmaking process: this is a very critical part for the users of the system. People is usually reluctant to follow the recommendations of computer systems because they cannot control how the result is obtained. The multicriteria decision aid community is concerned with this problem, and many methods try to give explanations to the user in order to let him/her know some information about the ranking process. In addition, it is interesting to give to the user a trustworthiness value attached to the ranking list. Some methods, like ClusDM ([8], [12]), are able to calculate a degree of confidence on the result. So, the user can know if the ranking is reliable enough.
- In the matchmaking process it would also be very important to add decision rules that depend on the type of organ (e.g. antigen compatibility is very

important in kidney transplants, but not in liver transplants). At the moment the relative importance of attributes can be expressed with the weights attached to them in the matchmaking and ranking process. A more detailed medical description of the donors and receivers should also be made before a real use of the system.

- Transport process: at the moment, we have assumed that it is always possible to find a combination to go from the origin to the destination using the normal trains and flights. However, sometimes this is not a realistic assumption. We should also consider the possibility of having to use some helicopters to do part of the transport, or use private flights. So, the companies should be able to propose alternative departure times apart from the regular ones.

- Operation arrangement process: The way of assigning operating theatres and people to the transplant operations, which tries to keep the empty spaces in their schedules as large as possible, does not take into account that the work should be evenly distributed between all the members of the staff. In addition, it would also be interesting to include the preferences of the staff with respect to their colleagues, because in these difficult operations the coordination among the medical team is very important (sometimes, doctors feel more comfortable with some particular nurses or anaesthetists).

Apart from the improvements that can be done in some of the parts of the process, we must develop the Historical Agent. As it has been said, this agent will be used by the organisations in charge of the transplants in each country. For this reason, we must study their requirements and their norms for working with this type of medical data.

Finally, another interesting research line is the development of a complete transplant ontology. Several medical ontologies exist, but some of them are private and others are too general or too specific. These ontologies would be used to extend the one we have started to develop for this prototype.

References

[1]   Matesanz, R., Miranda, B.: Coordinación y Trasplantes: El modelo español. Editorial Aula Médica, ISBN 84-7885-060-0 (1995)
[2]   López-Navidad, A., Domingo, P., Viedma, M.A.: Professional characteristics of the transplant coordinator. Transplantation Proceedings, 29 Elsevier Science Inc. (1997) 1607-1613.
[3]   López-Navidad, A., Kulisevsky, J., Caballero, F.: El donante de órganos y tejidos. Evaluación y manejo. Springer-Verlag Ibérica (1997).
[4]   Vázquez-Salceda, J., Padget, J.A., Cortés, U., López-Navidad, A., Caballero, F.: Formalizing an electronic institution for the distribution of human tissues, AI in Medicine special issue on Software Agents in Health Care, Eds: A.Moreno, C.Garbay (2003) in press.

[5] Calisti, M., Funk, P., Brunschwig, P.: Software Support for Organ Transplant Management. Proceedings of the Medical Informatics Europe (2003).

[6] Aldea, A., López, B., Moreno, A., Riaño, D., Valls, A.: A multi-agent system for organ transplant coordination, accepted in the Eighth European Conference on Artificial Intelligence in Medicine (2001)

[7] Bellifemine, F., Poggi, A., Rimassa, G.: JADE - A FIPA compliant agent framework, Proceedings of Practical Applications of Intelligent Agents and Multi-Agents, PAAM (1999) 97-108

[8] Valls, A., Moreno, A., Sánchez, D.: A multi-criteria decision aid agent applied to the selection of the best receiver in a transplant, 4th. International Conference on Enterprise Information Systems, Ciudad Real, Spain (2002) 431-438

[9] Valls, A., Moreno, A., Alonso, H., Sánchez, D.: A multi-agent system to support the assignement of transplantable organs, Student Session at the joint European Agent Systems Summer School (EASSS) and the Advanced Course on Artificial Intelligence (ACAI), Prague, Czech Republic (2001) 200-207

[10] Herrera, F, Martínez, L.: A 2-tuple fuzzy linguistic representation model for computing with words, IEEE Transactions on Fuzzy Systems, 8:6 (2000)

[11] Herrera, F., Herrera-Viedma, E., Martínez, L.: A fusion approach for managing multi-granularity linguistic term sets in decision making, Fuzzy Sets & Systems,114 (2000) 43-58

[12] Valls, A., ClusDM: A multicriteria decision making method for heterogeneous data sets, Ph.D.Thesis, Universitat Politècnia de Catalunya, Barcelona, Spain, ISBN: 84-688-1348-6 (2002)

[13] Moreno, A., Valls, A., Ribes, A.: Finding efficient organ transport routes using Multi-Agent Systems, IEEE 3rd International Workshop on Enterprise Networking and Computing in Health Care Industry (Healthcom), Italy (2001)

[14] Moreno, A., Valls, A., Bocio, J.: Management of hospital teams for organ transplants using Multi-Agent Systems, Lecture Notes in Artificial Intelligence 2101: Artificial Intelligence in Medicine. Quaglini, Barahona and Andreassen (eds.), Springer-Verlag (Papers of the 8th. European Conference on Artificial Intelligence in Medicine) (2001) 374-383

Acknowledgements

Several computer science students have collaborated in the implementation of this system: Jaime Bocio, David Sánchez, Héctor Alonso, Alberto Ribes and Cristóbal Ledesma. The ideas presented in this paper come from the collaborative work of the members of the AI research group of Universitat Rovira i Virgili. Many thanks to all of them.

Banzai: Research Group on Artificial Intelligence. Computer Science & Mathematics Dept.. Universitat Rovira i Virgili. Campus Sescelades, Avda. Països Catalans, 26. 43007 Tarragona, Spain

E-mail address: {avalls, amoreno}@etse.urv.es

A Multi-Agent System for Organ Transplant Management

Monique Calisti, Petra Funk, Sven Biellman, Thomas Bugnon

Abstract. This paper describes the *Organ Transplant Management* (OTM) system, an agent-based platform to be deployed by medical practitioners as a smart software support for data management and decision making. The twofold goal is to identify the main challenges and benefits that the OTM paradigm brings along in order to validate and/or eventually modify and refine our choices. This also hopes to provide the readers with a concrete feedback on the feasibility and utility of deploying software agents in today's medical environments.

1. Introduction

During the last few years, there have been significant improvements in the area of organ transplant. Transplants are no longer the last-option kind of therapies, and recent important successes are contributing to increase the number of transplants all over Europe. However, despite significant advances in the surgery process itself, the coordination of the preliminary activities involved in an organ transplant operation is still a very challenging, complex, and not yet well understood process [18] (see also concrete examples in [4, 8, 21]). The way distinct OTM tasks are currently performed still lacks from a comprehensive computational support and it is to a great part not or poorly coordinated. Medical experts have to match available organs to long lists of potential recipients with very weak local computerized support in processing large amount of data. Coordination is mainly achieved by telephone calls, pagers and/or other highly human-dependent means to track down suitable recipients, and contact physicians at both the extraction and insertion sites. Furthermore, the storage and the transport of organs involve a set of activities under the direct control of external and distinct organizations, which need to interact in a rapid way (available organs cannot be preserved for long time).

In this context, several recent initiatives are trying to address the need for more flexible and powerful support for medical practitioners involved in the OTM process by working at different key levels (i.e., legal procedures, hospital infrastructures, coordination centers organization, software support, etc.). The main goal of the work presented in this paper is the definition and implementation of a software agent-based approach,

Key words and phrases. organ transplant, agents, medical knowledge representation, eHealth, ontology.

namely the OTM system, as a comprehensive solution offering computational support for two crucial sets of tasks which medical teams involved in the OTM process have to face:

- *Information gathering and data management tasks*: both, potential recipients (i.e., patients waiting for a transplant) and donors need to be characterized by a certain amount of data that has to be collected, stored, processed and dynamically maintained by the transplant centers and/or specific institution/s involved in the OTM process. This is a very challenging issue, as no common comprehensive standard framework is available nowadays to uniquely represent, store, process and visualize medical data, in particular in the OTM context. The critical point is not only to agree upon a given formalism for data representation (e.g., XML, RDF, DAML+OIL, etc.), but rather to provide a semantic grounding for knowledge representation that can be easily understood by humans and effectively manipulated by software entities at the same time.

- *Decision making processes*: when organs become available, the responsible medical teams in the involved transplant centers have to process a significant amount of information (organ and corresponding waiting patients descriptions) to verify whether there is a compatible recipient on the corresponding waiting lists. This decision has to be taken under very strong time constraints by considering a large set of interrelated match making criteria, including several deterministic medical factors (about the 80% of the total amount of data to be checked) plus a number of aspects (soft constraints) that are more difficult to quantify and estimate, but that can heavily influence the final selection of a specific patient. The additional issue here is that different "degrees of compatibility" can be determined in relation to those soft constraints. Therefore, the final answer could rather be a list ranked according to the compatibility rates.

This paper describes the OTM system aiming at identifying the main challenges and benefits that our agent-based approach brings along to validate and/or eventually modify our choices. This hopes to stimulate discussion and provide feedback on the feasibility and utility of deploying software agents in today's medical environments. The remaining of the paper is organized as follows. Section 2 focuses on the description of the OTM system. Section 3 reports on the knowledge modelling and OTM ontology definition work. The experience achieved in building the agent-based OTM demonstrator leads to the discussion of the main issues encountered so far as well as the expected benefits out of the deployment of software agents (see Section 4), before concluding the paper with an overview of ongoing work (Section 5).

2. The Organ Transplant Management System

The OTM system [1] is a modular software agent-based platform, including adaptive and user friendly graphical interfaces to facilitate the access for nurses, physicians, surgeons, etc. (who are not necessarily IT experts) to both the data and the mechanisms required for effective coordination of the main OTM tasks. Agent technology is one of the most

promising approaches for designing and implementing autonomous, intelligent and social software assistants capable of supporting human decision making [9]. As mentioned
earlier, the fundamental idea in the OTM context is to provide computational help for
decisions that have to be taken by considering a substantial number of medical factors as
well as legal rules and requirements under very strong time pressure.

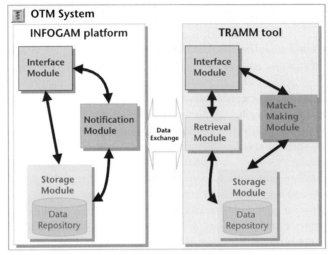

FIGURE 1. An overview of the OTM system architecture.

In this perspective, we propose a pro-active, modular and flexible approach consisting of two main sub-systems: the *Information GAthering Module* (INFOGAM) and
the *TRAnsplant Match Making* (TRAMM) tool (see Figure 1). Various agents populating
these two sub-systems interact and coordinate on behalf of medical practitioners, transplant coordinators and patients in order to improve the OTM process. The development
tools that have been deployed to implement the OTM system are:

- *Jade* v. 3.0b1, a software development framework to develop multi-agent systems
  and applications conforming to FIPA standards for intelligent agents. (http://sharon.cselt.it/projects/jade/).
- The Sun Java Development Kit v. 1.4 (http://www.javasoft.com).
- *Protege* v. 1.8, an ontology editor used to create the OTM ontology in combination with the UMLS tab and the Bean Generator plug-in.
  (http://protege.stanford.edu/)

Before a more detailed description of the various software components, the definitions of some recurrent terms are given for clarity's sake.

Definition 2.1. Donor: a person who donates organs for organ transplantation.

Definition 2.2. Hard constraint: a compatibility condition on the selection of a patient
for a given available organ that must be satisfied.

Definition 2.3. Patient: a person who receives medical attention, care, or treatment. A
patient can be a recipient as well as a potential donor.

Definition 2.4. Recipient: a patient who is waiting for an organ transplant. A recipient is registered in one or more waiting lists (for different organs) in the OTM system within a given transplant center.

Definition 2.5. Soft constraint: a compatibility condition on the selection of a patient for a given available organ that can be satisfied.

Definition 2.6. User: a person accessing the OTM system. Various user types (e.g., patients[1], nurses, doctors, surgeons, etc.) have different access rights.

2.1. The Information Gathering Module

The INFOGAM platform consists of three main parts. The *Storage Module*, SM, contains one or possibly more databases in which all the relevant OTM data (user profiles, Electronic Health Records (EHR), etc.) is stored and the agents responsible for the various data management operations, including the database access control. The *Interfacing Module*, IM, consists of all the required components enabling interactions with human users, i.e., enabling human-agent interaction to be carried on in a flexible and user-friendly way. The third component, i.e., the *Notification Module*, NM, allows the system to pro-actively notify users. The category of notifications we actually implemented in the system includes reminders, alerts and suggestions (1) to patients having to take some medical tests, (2) to selected recipients for quickly contact the hospital, in case they are not there, (3) to nurses for recalling patient's medication and/or special treatments, or for alerting about shortage in resources, (4) to physicians whenever organs become available, etc. Reactive (mainly as consequence of events monitoring and user commands) and pro-active (mainly as output of goal-driven agents reasoning) notifications represent a key aspect of the capabilities of software agents and thereby of the services supplied by the OTM system. While *reactivity* mainly guarantees to face expected categories of events (such as shortage of blood of a certain type, lack surgical material, etc.), *pro-activity* is intended in this context as the capability of goal-driven deductions/actions whenever unexpected situations occur (e.g., suggesting specific medical crossed patients tests involving more than one medical team), taking the initiative of performing given actions in a way to prevent undesired events to take place (for instance, suggesting to order additional medical material not as a consequence of a shortage in the current resources, but because of a forecasted greater need whenever the number of registered patients in the hospital increases).

    The Storage Module. The database contained in this module is maintained by the DataBase Connectivity Agent (DBCA). Any entity in the system having to store information requests the DBCA to perform this service. This centralized approach has been chosen mainly for consistency, modularity and security reasons. By having a unique access point, authorized operations and data consistency can be more easily controlled. On the other hand, this requires to set up appropriate mechanisms to ensure failure recovery (in our case, the back up of the DBCA in case of crashes) and scalability (in the OTM system, the DBCA can delegate part of its tasks to authorized agents). There are four other types of agents in the SM, all heavily interacting with the DBCA. Each of these agents

---

[1] Patients are users of the system in the sense that they might directly enter and keep up to date their personal data (address, phone number, etc.) and they might also have access for visualizing their own medical status.

is responsible for manipulating a specific part of the knowledge base: the User DataBase Agent (UDBA), the Patient DataBase Agent (PDBA), the Waiting List Agent (WLA) and the Notification DataBase Agent (NDBA). The UDBA manages the user information, i.e. the identity, the access rights, contact information, etc. The PDBA maintains the patients EHRs: it creates, modifies, fetches EHRs, etc. The UDBA and PDBA interact mainly with the Interfacing Module. The WLA maintains the waiting lists, i.e. adds new patients, update their conditions, notifies the medical staff about missing information, etc. The WLA interacts with all the other INFOGAM modules and most important with the TRAMM tool. The NDBA stores the end users notification preferences and mainly interacts with all other agents in the NM. All the SM agents can refer to a specific user or patient using his/her unique identifier, which enables an efficient separation of the different sets of data. Note that the UDBA is also acting as Key Distribution Center (KDC) for security purposes. Each user has indeed restricted access to the data stored in the OTM platform. Therefore, the system needs to know which user is requesting data and/or willing to perform any action before allowing any access/execution. The proposed solution is to make use of a Kerberos-like approach[2] and has been designed and implemented according to [10], [11]. This is a username/password based mechanism in which the authentication credentials are needed only once for the whole session and they are not stored, cached nor sent into the network. The protocol is based on *tickets*. To have access to a service, an OTM agent needs the proper ticket. An agent asks the ticket granting service (TGS) for tickets. Each ticket can be used only once. To avoid having to specify the password each time a service has to be accessed, the agent first gets a special *ticket granting ticket* (TGT) from a unique TGS in the system called Authentication Server (AS). Such TGT is valid during a whole session and usually expires after eight hours. Once an agent obtained the TGT it will use it in order to request from the TGS the proper ticket for specific services. Most of the time, the AS and the TGS are the same server called then the Key Distribution Center. As stated above, in the OTM system the UDBA acts as KDC.

The Interface Module. This module provides the medical staff with a broad range of specific interfaces to access the platform. This highly user-centered approach aims to facilitate the personalization of tools, services and actions to be performed, but also to appropriately customize the access control to the OTM system. The embedded Graphical User Interface Agent (GUIA) takes care of contacting the specialized interface agent (SIA) with the proper features corresponding to a given user with specific access rights. Personalized graphical interfaces are then instantiated for patients (PIA), medical practitioners (MIA), nurses (NIA), administrators (AIA) and laboratories (LIA). This choice of separating the common features, such as authentication (performed by the GUIA), from the role specific features by means of different specialized agents has been done for modularity and security reasons. Since there exists a large range of (more or less) standard forms, reports and letters related to organ transplantation that need to be filled in, printed and/or modified, we also created specific devoted software entities: the Input/Output Agents (IOAs). An IOA can provide an empty form to be filled in by a user,

---

[2]More details on access control and security within the OTM system are addressed by the authors in a separate paper to appear.

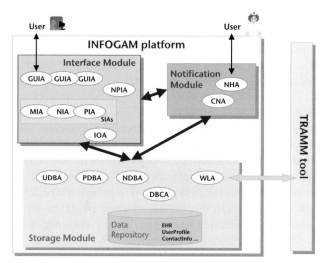

FIGURE 2. An overview of the INFOGAM architecture.

save a form in the database or print it, and fill in (when authorized/required) forms by itself with data directly retrieved from the database. Finally, the Notification Preferences Interface Agent (NPIA) provides an interface accessible to all OTM users so that they can set their notification preferences. A notification preference specifies by which means the final end users can be notified (e.g., telephone call, SMS, e-mail, etc.), depending on the type and priority of the notification[3]. The NPIA asks then the NDBA to store the stated preferences.

  The Notification Module. Proactive OTM agents have the capability of reporting events, notifying (e.g., a deadline is crossed and requires somebody's attention), taking the initiative of performing specific actions and thereby informing end users, asking questions or suggesting/requesting to perform specific actions, e.g. data can be missing. To do so, the Notification Module embeds two main agents: the Central Notification Agent (CNA) and the Notification Handler Agent (NHA). When an agent has to notify a given user U about a specific event E, it sends the proper request, specifying a given priority level L, to the CNA. The latter checks the notification preferences of user U (first interacting with the NDBA to recover the notification priority profile) by adopting the following procedure: (1) if user U has set a notification preference for event E, make use of the specified notification means M for E; (2) if no preference is pre-defined for event E, make use of the specified notification means M for the given priority level L; (3) if no means is pre-selected for L, make use of the means for the lowest priority level L' higher than level L the user U has set. We force users to select at least one priority means to be deployed for notification. When the notification means M is selected, the CNA contacts the suitable

---

[3]Besides pre-defined notifications, OTM agents can pro-actively decide to notify end-users depending on their goal-driven behavior.

NHA. Each NHA is devoted to perform a specific type of notification (SMS, pager, e-mail, phone call, etc). At the moment, OTM agents are able to send text messages via SMS, e-mail and graphical displays (i.e., text and alert icons in the GUIs).

2.2. The Transplant Match Making Tool

The TRAMM tool architecture has been articulated over 4 main modules, by following design requirements dictated by current practice in the hospitals we are collaborating with, but also for guaranteeing a more easily manageable separation of concerns, access rights and responsibilities of the various agents. Although, some of the embedded agents perform similar duties and present analogous characteristics to the corresponding agents in the INFOGAM modules (like enabling access to the system -interface management- or enabling database management), the corresponding actions into the system are centered on supporting the match making process and act on different sets of data.

The Interface Module. This module, by means of the Graphical User Interface Agent (GUIA), manages the various graphical interfaces required to access the TRAMM platform. This includes: (1) the login interface used to identify and authenticate a user by means of the user name and password; (2) the match making interface needed to enter donor and organ specific data, display the ranked matching list and possibly indicate (communicate back to the system) the final decision of medical experts; and (3) the administrator interface deployed to create, modify and delete user profiles. Once a user has been identified and authorized to access the platform, it is possible to have access to all the different functions offered by the TRAMM system. The Match Making Interface Agent (MMIA) collects data about a donor and the donated organ(s), as they are entered by responsible nurses and/or physicians, and display the result of the match making process, i.e. the organ specific ranked matching list. The Administrator Interface Agent (AIA) agent provides the administrator of the TRAMM tool with an appropriate interface to manage the user profiles, e.g. creating/deleting user profiles, modifying user roles, etc. Finally, the Input Output Agent (IOA) takes care of input and output actions like printing forms, mapping forms to objects and vice-versa, saving/retrieving forms in/from the database, and receiving data from Swisstransplant (national coordination center).

The Interchange Module. This modules coordinates the flow of data and information exchanged between the INFOGAM and the TRAMM sub-systems. By means of the embedded Data Management Agent (DMA) all information needed by the TRAMM agents (i.e., waiting lists information, patients characterization, etc.) and maintained by INFOGAM software entities is retrieved. This data flow is then appropriately processed and forwarded so that information can be communicated to the interface module (whenever visualization of information to medical practitioners is needed/required), and to the match making module (for recipient selection out of selected waiting lists). On the other hand, whenever decisions are taken (a recipient is selected) and waiting lists need to be updated the DMA notifies the WLA in the INFOGAM platform.

The Storage Module. Analogously to what happens in the INFOGAM platform, this module is responsible for the data management part. In this case, however, the information managed concerns (1) donors (e.g. create, insert, update, view donor data records); (2) available organs (e.g. storage/retrieval of organ specific characteristics); (3) TRAMM

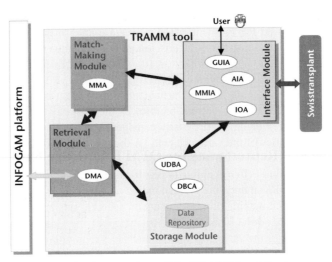

FIGURE 3. An overview of the TRAMM architecture.

users data (e.g. storage/retrieval of user names, passwords, access rights to the TRAMM services); and (4) final transplant decision (e.g. keeping track of selected recipients for given organ/s, reasons, motivations, match making results, etc.). The DBCA agent is responsible for managing the TRAMM database and retrieve/store/update information according to the various OTM agents and users requests. The UDBA is responsible to create, modify, update, delete and retrieve user information by processing requests from agents in the TRAMM Interface Module and by identifying and authenticating users that access the TRAMM services.

The Match Making Module. The Match Making Module (MMM) provides mechanisms for the selection of appropriate recipient candidates whenever organs become available. This includes facilities for the Match Making Agent (MMA) to be able to perform (1) the selection of organ specific match making policies to be used; (2) the retrieval of organ specific match making rules, including hard and soft constraints to be applied; (3) the selection of a set of compatible candidates from a waiting list according to organ specific hard constraints; (4) the computation of a score for each selected potential compatible recipient according to organ specific soft constraints. The MMA compiles a ranked matching list of potential recipients (when available), by taking into account statistics data about former and similar decisions on the computation of the matching score. The MMA provides this list together with an explanation of the computed scores, listing possible positive factors and risk factors. The organ specific matching rules can be retrieved from the SM database by interacting with the DBCA and as a future extension directly from XML based file repository directly managed by the National transplant coordinator. With regard to the match making process, although we have looked at some solid work done in the same problem area [24], we have currently implemented a constraint satisfaction based approach [7] combined with case-based reasoning techniques [12]. The set of hard constraints (between 4 and 10 depending on the organ type[4]) is used in order to select which patients' descriptions to recover from the waiting lists (search space pre-pruning). Based upon the pre-selected list of patients satisfying hard constraints, the MMA runs then consistency techniques [5] on the set of soft constraints for final scoring and ranking of the patients. Upon request of surgeons, case based reasoning methods can also be used in order to correlate current cases to previous choices recorded by the system (if any).

3. Modelling and Representing the OTM Knowledge Base

For multi-agent systems, re-usable and sharable conceptualizations of domain-dependent contexts are vital communication enablers as they provide common definitions of terms including the relations holding among them, which thereby allows the elaboration of co-ordinated plans and solutions. It is beyond the scope of this paper to report on extensive works for formalizing and defining compact, standard and reusable ontologies in multi-agent systems. The aim here is to report on the experience gained when building the OTM ontology, in order to discuss the main concrete issues that need to be faced when building structured knowledge basis for software agents in the organ transplant area.

3.1. Requirements

The OTM ontology has to include all concepts required to support the various agents when performing the OTM *application tasks* for information management (i.e., creation, maintenance, update, deletion of health state descriptions of patients, electronic health records, waiting list management etc.) and multi-criteria matchmaking (specific laboratory values analysis and interpretation, organ specific rules and factors etc.). This requires (1) a set of notions that describe the possible agents' actions, (2) a set of concepts, including medical, personal (i.e., user related), and logistic terms (e.g., organ descriptions, transplant indications) that define the corresponding actions' domains and objects, and (3) a way to express how actions and concepts (or terms) relates to each other in the given OTM context (i.e., a set of predicates for describing the state of the world in terms for instance of actions' results, objects' values, etc.). When referring to medical concepts (e.g., organ description), the re-use and integration of existing medical ontologies and/or vocabularies[5] becomes essential. This is very important because well-structured and organized medical know-how, when available, can be more appropriately outsourced, understood and used by agent developers (or IT people in general), and more easily maintained and deployed by medical practitioners. For this reason, when building the OTM ontology, we carefully considered the re-use of existing pre-defined medical concepts (when available).

---

[4]The current OTM prototype enables the management of liver and kidney transplants. The main reason is that given the collaboration with two specific Swiss hospitals, we have been able to recover more detailed information for those two types of organs.

[5]By vocabularies we means collection of medical terms, where relations among them have not been directly included.

3.2. Relevant Medical Knowledge Sources

Some of the existing medical vocabularies address specialized tasks, while others are intended to cover broader knowledge providing the medical foundation of various electronic health care applications. Among the most well known structured medical knowledge bases, GALEN [16], SNOMED [19], and UMLS [23] have been more extensively described [15] as possible candidates for usage in agent-oriented applications.

In our framework, after having analyzed and discussed several optional choices, we decided to build the OTM ontology by making use of the *Unified Medical Language Systems* (UMLS). The main reason resides in the meta-description level of medical concepts that is provided. The creators and maintainers of the UMLS (the American National Library of Medicine), NLM [14], collect and distribute electronic medical knowledge sources provided by medical experts, organizations and companies. The NLM has built a relational database connecting over 60 vocabularies and medical ontologies by means of a conceptual unification. The main goal is to make the various existing medical *Knowledge Sources* (KS) accessible and usable through a common meta-level interface. UMLS users can choose distinct KS for specific purposes/applications by simply expressing which KS-dependent definition is associated to a given meta-level UMLS concept. The advantage of having a standard high-level interface is that when adding, updating or changing the various KS included by UMLS one can simply adapt its knowledge base by appropriately updating the mappings between UMLS concepts and KS definitions. UMLS creates for each concept (i.e., medical term) a unique identifier (CUI). This is used to associate the UMLS meta-level definition (if any) of the given concept to all the various instances in the different KS, in which a concrete definition of the specific concept (or any of its synonyms) is given. For instance, the term *organ* is a UMLS concept used in 4 distinct KS. By means of its UMLS CUI, i.e., C0178784, it can be uniquely identified. It is then possible to associate to this same concept different meanings (or different concrete definitions) by referring to one of the 4 different KS. If any of the knowledge sources is changing, it is still possible to use the same concept (and thereby the same ontology structure) either by referring the new definition or by switching to another KS (i.e., changing the association from the CUI to the selected KS). Of course, when changing concrete KS definitions, the corresponding objects in the OTM ontology might need to be updated, but eventually the relationships among various concepts do not need to be modified. Finally, by referring to meta-level descriptions, it is possible to adapt the OTM ontology to different KS (adopted for instance in distinct hospitals) by simply changing the mapping between UMLS concept identifiers and specific definitions in selected KS.

3.3. Building the OTM Ontology

The currently defined and used OTM knowledge base consists of approximately 75 concepts plus the relationships holding among these. This includes:

- A sophisticated and complete electronic health record, partially based on [22], including all necessary related medical concepts;
- Users identity and authentication related concepts for access control to the OTM system;

- Matchmaking factors and organ specific rules for recipient selection.

While for the OTM specific functionality, such as access control and recipient selection criteria, we defined the required objects, predicates and actions from the scratch, we referred (when possible) to UMLS for most of the medical concepts. There are two alternative ways of making use of UMLS definitions:

- *Direct Connection*: the UMLS knowledge sources can be directly accessed through the Internet by means of a JAVA API or plug-ins for tools such as Protégé-2000 [17]. However, while this remote access to the overall UMLS databases infrastructure can be quite useful for agent developers, it is quite slow for agents access given the huge amount of data to be processes.
- *Compliancy*: UMLS can be used as a reference knowledge base for the creation and formalization of the required domain-related concepts. This means to make sure that the medical concepts deployed in the OTM ontology (e.g., organ descriptions, transplant indication descriptors etc.), including definitions, relations and hierarchies are compliant to UMLS.

In the OTM context, we adopted this latter approach, because while it is still possible to easily adapt the OTM knowledge base by changing the mapping from meta-level concepts to specific knowledge base definitions (few values have to be changed in the OTM ontology specification), it is much faster and efficient for agents to directly access the required medical concepts in a local knowledge base.

4. Discussion

After several discussions with OTM experts, extensive studies of other works, research projects [2], [3], and existing systems offered in the market (see [1] for various references), we realized that even though some tools are available the majority of transplant centers have to face a serious fragmentation in the way such support is provided. There is no comprehensive approach, as far as we know, providing a compact computational solution integrating patients' data management tasks, match making and decision support procedures, which includes *proactive monitoring and goal-driven notification about patients conditions*. The OTM software agents are monitoring, interpreting and reacting to events in the environment they sense (such as changes in a patient's conditions, shortage of a specific type of blood for a given surgery operation), autonomously reasoning and pro-actively notifying the medical responsible interacting with the system (see Section 2). The main idea is to provide help in tracking events and managing data (i.e., faster and personalized access to stored information, user friendly visualization, etc.), in order to enable smart computational support for interpreting and explaining why data changed in a certain way and what such changes can mean in relation to dynamic health care patients conditions. In this perspective, autonomous software entities acting on behalf of patients and/or medical practitioners can:

- *Speed-up and automate many tedious and simple tasks currently performed by humans*. The resources saved by relying upon software instruments could be re-used for more demanding and delicate tasks;

- *Reduce the complexity of various tasks* such as multi-criteria match-making, dynamic coordination under stringent constraints by implementing smart techniques that can support the human decision making and optimize several processes;
- *Offer added value services*, such as the integration of some activities performed during the OTM with other medical services and vice versa, or the personalization and custom-tailoring of some tasks for which there is currently no way of differentiating the way patients are monitored and cured.

For the formalization of the medical knowledge, as anticipated above, we referred, when possible, to existing standard UMLS concepts and definitions. Besides, finding the correct balance between application driven knowledge, medical concepts and the integration efforts required to make this combination usable within an agent environment, we faced several challenging issues:

- Most of the existing medical ontologies and vocabularies are very complex, difficult to understand for not medical experts, and have not been necessarily designed to be used within an agent-based environment.
- Given the huge amount of available medical knowledge bases, it is important to carefully analyze the usefulness and usability of these in the context of the OTM application, and thereby select the most appropriate one.
- The integration of an existing medical ontology/terminology into an agent-based context, especially in compliance with the communication stack given by the FIPA [6] standards or in relation to the deployment of a specific agent platform, such as JADE [20] in our case, possibly requires changes or adaptation in the way the knowledge is formally represented and thereby encoded.

The closest and most comprehensive approach we have been looking at has been developed by the GruSMA group [13] and it is tailored to the Spanish transplant framework and rules. In our case, the overall OTM data modelling and system functionalities have been defined in relation to the Swiss context.

5. Conclusion and Future Work

In the health care scene, while the automation of some activities and the deployment of auxiliary software tools have partly enabled to address pressing requirements for more effective information management and decision-making, there is still a strong need for addressing the complexity of integrating new solutions within existing hospitals' infrastructures (i.e., pervasive health care). This requires taking into account users' needs and various existing constraints (medical, legal, etc.) in a more flexible, dynamic and personalized way, in particular in the OTM context. We strongly believe in the potential of our agent-based approach to be used as a distributed software support tool that would enable a better taking care of the individuality of the patients, saving precious resources and would finally facilitate the tasks of physicians and coordinators.

The currently available OTM prototype requires various refinements and extensive validation and testing on the field. Both the INFOGAM and TRAMM modules have been implemented and preliminarily validated. Agents deploying the OTM ontology work on a set of simulated organ transplant cases. At the moment, we are working at different levels:

- Improving the various graphical interfaces in order to facilitate the deployment of the system.
- Working in close collaboration with some medical experts to better define and model the OTM ontology, the soft constraints and the various deployed match making rules and policies.
- Increasing security for system access and data exchange.
- Refining the cased-based reasoning part based upon the feedback from medical experts.

For the future, the aim is to validate the OTM approach on real clinical cases, besides covering the matchmaking process of other organ types.

References

[1] M. Calisti, P. Funk, and P. Brunschwig. Software support for organ transplant management. In *Proceedings of Medical Informatics Europe 2003*, 2003.

[2] U. Cortés, A. López-Navidad, J. Vázquez-Salceda, D. Busquets, M. Nicolás, S. López, A. Vázquez, F. Vázquez, and F. Caballero. UCTx: a multi-agent approach to model a transplant coordination unit. In *In Proceedings of the 3rd. Congrés Català d'Intelligència Artificial. CCIA 2000*, October 2000.

[3] U. Cortés, A. López-Navidad, J. Vázquez-Salceda, A. Vázquez, D. Busquets, M. Nicolás, S. Lopes, F. Vázquez, and F. Caballero. Carrel: An agent mediated institution for the exchange of human tissues among hospitals for transplantation. Technical Report LSI-00-33-R, Software Department. UPC, http:/www-lsi.upc.es/dept/techreps/ps/R00-33.ps.gz, 2000.

[4] M. R. Costanzo. Selection and treatment of candidates for heart transplantation. Seminar report on thorax cardiovascular surgery, American Heart Association, Inc, 1995. http://www.americanheart.org/presenter.jhtml?identifier=1298.

[5] Rina Dechter. Constraint networks. In Stuart C. Shapiro, editor, *Encyclopedia of Artificial Intelligence*, pages 276–285. Wiley, 1992. Volume 1, second edition.

[6] Fipa. http://www.fipa.org.

[7] Eugene C. Freuder and Richard J. Wallace. Suggestion strategies for constraint-based matchmaker agents. In *Principles and Practice of Constraint Programming*, pages 192–204, 1998.

[8] S. Goddard and D. H. Adams. New approaches to immunosuppression in liver transplantation. *Journal Gastroenterol Hepatol*, 17(2):116–126, February 2001.

[9] N. R. Jennings. Building complex software systems. *Communications of the ACM*, 44(4):35–41, June 2001.

[10] Kerberos 5 release 1.2. http://web.mit.edu/kerberos/www/krb5-1.2/index.html.

[11] The moron's guide to kerberos. http://www.isi.edu/ brian/security/kerberos.html.

[12] David Leake. Case Based Reasoning in context: The present and future. Technical report, 1996.

[13] A. Moreno, A. Valls, and J. Bocio. A multi-agent system to schedule organ transplant operations. *Inteligencia Artificial (Revista Iberoamericana de Inteligencia Artificial), Special issue on Development of Multi-Agent Systems*, (13):36–44, 2001.

[14] National library of medicine. http://www.nlm.nih.gov/.

[15] J. L. Nealon and A. Moreno. The application of agent technology to health care. In *AAMAS02 Workshop on the Application of Agent Technology to Health Care*, 2002.

[16] openGALEN. http://www.opengalen.org.

[17] Protégé-2000. http://protege.stanford.edu.

[18] Meeting the organ shortage: Current status and strategies for improvement of organ donation. Newsletter Transplant, 4(1):5–17, 1999.

[19] SNOMED. http://www.snomed.org.

[20] Jade Open Source Development Team. Java Agent Development Environment. Technical report, Open Source Project, 2001.

[21] U. Thalheimer and F. Capra. Liver transplantation: making the best out of what we have. *Digital Distributed Science*, 47(5):945–953, May 2002.

[22] A. S. Tonnesen. Contents of the Electronic Patient Record (EPR). http://www.google.ch/search?q=cache:ZOOtMRRlFk4C:www.uth.tmc.edu/atonnese/cprdata.html, 1996.

[23] UMLS. http://www.nlm.nih.gov./research/umls.

[24] A. Valls, A. Moreno, and D. Sànchez. A multi-criteria decision aid agent applied to the selection of the best receiver in a transplant. In *4th. International Conference on Enterprise Information Systems (ICEIS)*, pages 431–438.

Acknowledgment

We are very grateful to Prof. C. Lovis from the Informatics Department of the University Hospital of Geneva for his precious support. Many thanks also to the Swisstransplant team for the valuable input and to the rest of the Whitestein team, in particular to Patrick Brunschwig.

Gotthardstrasse 50, CH-8002, Zurich, Switzerland
E-mail address: mca@whitestein.com